PROLOGUE TO PROFESSIONALISM

a History of Nursing

M. Louise Fitzpatrick, Ed.D.,RN, FAAN

Dean and Professor
College of Nursing
Villanova University
Villanova, PA

▶ 10851

Robert J. Brady Co.

A Prentice-Hall Publishing and
Communications Company

Bowie, MD 20715

Executive Editor: Richard A. Weimer
Production Editor/Text Designer: Michael J. Rogers
Cover Design: Don Sellers
Index: Leah Kramer
Composition: York Graphic Services, York, PA
Printing: Fairfield Graphics, Fairfield, PA

Prologue to Professionalism

Library of Congress Cataloging in Publication Data
Main entry under title:

Prologue to Professionalism.

    Includes index.
    1. Nursing—United   States—History. I. Fitzpatrick,
M. Louise.
RT4. P76   1983   610.73′0973   83-2526
ISBN 0-89303-773-7 (pbk.)

Prentice-Hall International, Inc., London
Prentice-Hall Canada, Inc., Scarborough, Ontario
Prentice-Hall of Australia, Pty., Ltd., Sydney
Prentice-Hall of India Private Limited, New Delhi
Prentice-Hall of Japan, Inc., Tokyo
Prentice-Hall of Southeast Asia Pte. Ltd., Singapore
Whitehall Books, Limited, Petone, New Zealand
Editora Prentice-Hall Do Brasil LTDA., Rio de Janeiro

Printed in the United States of America

83 84 85 86 87 88 89 90 91 92 93   1 2 3 4 5 6 7 8 9 10

Contributors

SUSAN BACORN BASTABLE, Ed.D., RN
Consultant in Nursing and Nursing Education
Westerley, Rhode Island

NETTIE S. BIRNBACH, Ed.D., RN
Assistant Professor
Molloy College
Rockville Centre, New York

M. LOUISE FITZPATRICK, Ed.D., RN, FAAN
Dean and Professor, College of Nursing
Villanova University
Villanova, Pennsylvania

BARBARA R. HELLER, Ed.D., RN, FAAN
Associate Professor, School of Nursing
University of Maryland
Baltimore, Maryland

ELEANOR KROHN HERRMANN, Ed.D., RN
Associate Professor, School of Nursing
Yale University
New Haven, Connecticut

WANDA C. HIESTAND, Ed.D., RN
Associate Professor, Lienhard School of Nursing
Pace University
Pleasantville, New York

NANCY L. NOEL, Ed.D., RN
Assistant Professor of Nursing History, School of Nursing
Curator, Nursing Archives, Mugar Memorial Library
Boston University
Boston, Massachusetts

JANIE BROWN NOWAK, Ed.D., RN
Associate Professor, College of Nursing
Villanova University
Villanova, Pennsylvania

ROBERT V. PIEMONTE, Ed.D., RN
Division Director—House, Board, and Cabinet Affairs
American Nurses' Association, Inc.
Kansas City, Missouri

ELIZABETH A. SHIELDS, Ed.D., RN
Assistant Director of Nursing
The Mt. Sinai Hospital
New York, New York

Contents

Contents

Preface

American nursing has reached its maturity. No longer a fledgling profession, it has evolved into a well-developed field with an identifiable body of knowledge. It has a growing and impressive research orientation, a sophisticated practice, and a complex educational system. Progress in nursing has not eliminated the questions, controversies, and dilemmas that face the profession. Instead, it has created new forms of issues that are recurring themes in the field.

A paradox that exists among contemporary nurses is their heightened awareness of current trends, yet their relative lack of knowledge and understanding about the historical antecedents of these events. Nurses and students of nursing need to be informed about their collective past so that they will be better prepared to interpret the present and predict the future course of events, which they must determine.

This book is intended to provide a focused, historical backdrop for understanding the state of the profession today, as reflected by some of its most important concerns: nursing education, the role of professional organizations, the development of practice, and credentialing. Attention has been given to selected leaders and innovators in nursing, whose ideas and careers influenced the course of American nursing. They represent a much larger cadre of pioneers in the field. Topics that have been included are germane to the development of the profession and necessary for an informed view of contemporary issues. The book is not a comprehensive survey of nursing history, but it will augment a wide variety of nursing courses in all types of educational programs. Most of all, it is hoped that this contribution will assist nurses in understanding and appreciating their collective past and professional identity.

Sincere appreciation is extended to all who contributed to this effort. The authors developed a strong belief in the value and importance of nursing history at the Department of Nursing Education, Teachers College, Columbia University, where we all received our graduate preparation and where I had the privilege of guiding historical research as a faculty member. Appropriately, *Prologue to Professionalism* is an expression of the knowledge and expertise in historical inquiry gained there.

M.L.F.
Villanova, Pennsylvania

1

Nursing Practice—Home, Hospital, and Battlefield

Nursing care of the bedridden sick and wounded is as old as human society. Even in prehistoric times, wounds from the hunt, burns from open fires, and infection surely presented the need for treatment and care. Ideas about what constituted good care, both curative and nurturant, gradually became part of the store of human knowledge and culture. Throughout history, the scope and nature of nursing has been based on what people believed about each other and on whatever the current society deemed to be knowledge about health and disease.

Nursing Care in the Home

Prehistoric Health Care

Our prehistoric ancestors were amazingly knowledgeable. Primitive man lanced abscesses, amputated limbs, and stopped bleeding with hot stones. Skulls dating from the Neolithic Age show that trephining was practiced. Innoculation against smallpox has been practiced since antiquity, both in tribal cultures as well as in highly developed pre-Christian societies in Central Asia, India, and Africa. Surely such treatments required a period of nursing care during recovery. Innoculation and trephining make sense to us today in terms of modern science, but their practice in prehistory is a matter for speculation about belief in the supernatural and religious ritual.

Understanding the "whys" of health practice and care of the sick demand some appreciation of how people regard themselves as a logical part of the whole universe of nature as well as understanding (to the extent possible) the social and spiritual beliefs at each point in history. For example, many primitive cultures viewed the whole of nature as being alive as men were alive. It seemed logical that thunder, water, wind, plants, earth, and fire also had volition, in-

1

tent, and a mysterious spiritual side in much the same way that human beings have a spiritual nature. If the spirit of man lived in a world of spirits and could be released to appear in dreams or visions, then so too could the spirits of thunder, water, wind, plants, earth, and fire be released in some way. These animistic beliefs about the nature of the world and man's place in the scheme of things provided the logic for all considered actions.

Although today we tend to recognize as explanations of natural events only scientific "facts," some of our most ordinary experiences continue to defy these kinds of explanations. We have all experienced particularly realistic and frightening dreams. To this day, dreaming is not clearly explained by science. Is it any wonder that those who provided interpretation of dreams and visions became the mystical and spiritual leaders? Priests, magicians, witches, and medicine men emerged as important people in early history because of their social role in regard to mystical events.

Sickness can easily be viewed as a mysterious event. Fever and chills, convulsions, paralysis, delirium, and coma are still frightening. Sickness does change the person's usual behavior and responses—even relatively minor illness. Imagine how easily these symptoms can be explained as divine punishment or possession of the human body by evil spirits!

If one believes that evil spirits are the cause of sickness, then it follows that the evil spirit must be driven out. The person's body must become an uncomfortable place to inhabit. Hence, horrifying masks, noises, bad smells, sweating, cold baths, squeezing, pummelling, special potions, and starving have all been practiced to varying degrees as curative care in order to persuade the evil spirits to go elsewhere. With this logic, such therapies plus magical gestures and incantations became associated with religious ritual, blending with what we would now call medical practice and nursing care of the ill. This reasoning has been the foundation for therapeutic measures through thousands of years in many diverse cultures.

Nursing in Antiquity

Nurse is an acient word derived from the Middle English nurice, Old French norrice, and the Latin nutricius or nourishing. It is associated with cherishing, fostering, tender caring, conservation of energy, and giving curative care. Nursing care as we understand it today was not differentiated during early history. It was, in fact, often integrated as part of the practice of medicine men, priests, wise women, and midwives. For example, ritualistic application of ointments and hot or cold packs, massage, purifying baths, taking medicinal herbal preparations, and special diets for religious reasons can be viewed as religious practice, medical practice, or nursing practice from today's perspective. The treatment might well show positive results even though the rationale for giving the treatment might be rooted in belief of witches or demons instead of germs.

Care of the sick at home probably fell primarily to the women or those who managed nurturant functions for the social group. It was common practice in many ancient societies for the sick to be placed in the street so that people passing by could discuss symptoms or offer recipes for remedies and advice based on experience. It was probably a household duty to carry out appropriate advice and care for the comfort of those in need of it. We can speculate that in this manner, knowledge eventually became systematized and preserved.

Some of the most ancient writings are concerned with remedies for curing disease, although nursing itself is seldom mentioned. Health practices are often associated with a religious philosophy. One of the oldest examples is the *Ayur-Veda*. This book is said to have been given by the Indian god Brahma to provide guidance for the practice of medicine and surgery as well as for prevention of disease through good health practices. The *Ayur-Veda* has eight parts, dealing with major and minor surgery and bandaging; diseases of the head and nervous system; medical diseases; demoniacal possession; poisons and their antidotes; genitourinary problems; and pharmaceutical drugs (28).

The *Charaka-Samhita*, an ancient Indian treatise that reflects the accumulated health and medical knowledge of thousands of years B.C., is organized into lessons for healthful living, some of which are still valid. It bears the name of a physician, Charaka, who lived in 3500 B.C. and is believed to be the reincarnation of the thousand-headed serpent-god who retained all medical knowledge and wisdom in the sciences. It is in the *Charaka-Samhita* that nurses are mentioned as a special group of caregivers, although they were seldom women. Lesson IX describes the virtues of four essential agents in the curing process (28):

Physician. Thorough mastery of the scriptures, large experience, cleverness, and purity (of body and mind) are the principal qualities of the physician.

Nurse. Knowledge of the manner in which drugs should be prepared or compounded for administration, cleverness, devotedness to the patient waited upon, and purity (both of mind and body) are the four qualifications of the attending nurse.

Patient. Memory, obedience to direction, fearlessness, and communicativeness (with respect to all that is experienced internally and done by him during the intervals between visits) are qualities of the patient.

The fourth aspect describes virtues of the drugs used as therapy, which are to be adaptable to a variety of illnesses and have chemical stability.

The highly developed pre-Christian societies of Ceylon, Egypt, Babylon, and Assyria contributed substantially to systematized knowledge about human health in another way, and other kinds of elite groups had access to the information. The practice of embalming the dead promoted knowledge of human anatomy and recognition of disease processes. Surgery was a well-advanced art in antiquity.

Hundreds of papyri from the medical libraries of ancient Egypt have survived the ages. These texts are a mix of superstitions, ineffectual magical remedies, and remedies that have been shown to have some therapeutic value. The Ebers Papyrus records over 700 remedies for a variety of sicknesses in use between 4688 and 1552 B.C. (20, 28). The Kahun Medical Papyrus (Petri Papyrus), found in 1889, offers contraceptive advice and prescriptions that had been used since before 1850 B.C. (17).

It was in ancient Greece, the cradle of Western culture, that a logic more familiar to us as "scientific" eventually took root with the work of Hippocrates (460–370 B.C.), "father of medicine." Ancient Greece was dotted with temples maintained by the even more ancient cult of Aesculapius, worshipers of the snake. The cult of Aesculapius established temples that were actually sanitorium-like health spas, where people congregated for healing and care during sickness. These date from 1134 B.C. By the time of Hippocrates, these institutions were nearly 700 years old and had developed a close association with medical education and health care of the time. It was at Cos, the site of a major temple of Aesculapius, that Hippocrates was born. Aesculapius was deified in myth as the god of healing (20, 28). To this day the ancient Greek influence is present in the Hippocratic oath taken by medical students, the caduceus as the symbol of medicine, and the language that has integrated the names of the mythical daughters of Aesculapius—Panacea, restorer of health, and Hygiea, goddess of health.

Although the civilizations of Greece maintained hospital-like temples, not everyone could benefit. Nursing may or may not have been a part of the function of temple priestesses. In Greece, the incurable were not admitted to these places. In Epidaurus, those about to die and women about to deliver a child were carried outside the gates of these sacred precincts and left to fate. Birth and death were believed to pollute the sacred environment. This practice meant that a great deal of nursing care was given at home by those who had no formal role and only empirical knowledge, i.e., knowledge rooted in trial and error experience.

Throughout history, formal systematized knowledge has not been available to all people. For the most part, it was available to only elite "holy" men. Because of the blurred boundaries between religious ritual and medical therapy, much of the knowledge of "cures" was held to be sacred and for the secret use of priests only. The written word is not the only way knowledge is preserved and transmitted over time. Folk ways are perhaps even more important in developing the knowledge base by which people make their health care decisions. Those who found themselves a part of the non-elite social groups also gave birth, got sick, and needed therapy and nursing care. To the extent that knowledge about the health needs of women and children was developed, it surely came from women themselves. From time immemorial midwives and wise women performed health services for women and children, but as modern civilization emerged, the contribution of women was held in low esteem, often ignored, and probably much of it lost.

Home Nursing During the Middle Ages

During the Middle Ages nurses gave care in hospitals, war camps, and some religious charitable home nursing systems. These nurses may well have been very knowledgeable about nursing care; however, most people had no access to them. Consequently, nursing at home was given by untrained women who knew only the folk ways of a given culture. How to care for the sick was learned from having the personal experience, by observing what seemed to work, and by doing. Of course some effective measures were discovered, but most "cures" could only be called magical and ineffective in reality.

Some cultures fostered outstandingly good veterinary and medical skills, particularly among the early Nordic and Germanic groups, and women filled this care-giving role. Roman historians reported that Germanic women were experts at splinting, bandaging, and taking care of their wounded men on the battlefield. These women were honored as community leaders and decision-makers. The midwives among them were in the forefront of developing knowledge about midwifery and apprenticeship for midwifery in the 1500s. So important was the role of the midwife, that some were licensed by the Catholic Church as early as 1303 to prevent heretical practices.

For example, the dried umbilical cord and placental matter were used in devil worship ceremonies and witchcraft. Apart from such religious concern, midwifery came under municipal regulations as early as 1452 in some Germanic towns to protect the well-being of mother and infant and the family integrity. The oaths taken by these early midwives stressed honesty and integrity of the midwife. Although how she was to be prepared for this role is not explicitly stated, some form of learning is implied.

Learned health caregivers of any kind were scarce. For most Europeans who lived during the Middle Ages and the American colonial period, health care was based on superstition and magic intermingled with practical folk knowledge of dubious effectiveness. Members of the health care establishment who had an occupational identity (physicians, apothecaries, surgeons, and midwives) made little real difference for their patients in terms of comfort, cure, longevity, or prevention of disease. No group could show clearly superior results in practice.

American Home Nursing: Colonial Period to the Civil War

Colonial families lived without hospitals, medical schools, or religiously inspired nursing orders. For those who could read, health care was self-care according to a how-to-do-it textbook. A great favorite in the American colonies was Jane Sharp's *The Midwives Book*, published in 1671. Advice quoted here reflects the mix of superstition and knowledge developed out of practical life experience (19):

> Some children grow lean, and pine away, and the cause is not known; if it be from Witchcraft, good prayers to God are the best remedy; yet some hang Amber, and Coral about the child neck, as a Sovereign Amulet. But leanness may proceed from a dry distemper of the whole body, then it is bath it in a decoction of Mallows, Marshmallows, Branc-Ursine, Sheeps heads and anoint with oil of sweet Almonds,—the Child may be lean from want of milk, or bad milk from the nurse . . . sometimes worms in the body draw away the nourishment.

Sometimes home surgery was required to cure childhood ailments. For the "tongue-tyed" cutting the ligament ". . . . that is too short" is necessary. Unfortunate boys with urinary problems or possessed of a penis that pointed downward rather than straight were subjected to further cutting of a "ligament" or to insertion of a rod to ". . . remove the impending stone from the bladder" (19).

During this period and until the Civil War, nursing as an occupation had no clear identity. In an 1851 census of nurses conducted by Florence Nightingale, nurses were categorized by the labels "Nurse (not Domestic Servant) and Nurse (Domestic Servant)." Incidentally, their ages ranged from five years through eighty five and upward (27)! Even though this was a survey conducted in Britain, attitudes toward nurses were very similar and unsavory. Hired nurses in both countries had no training, were often very old or alcoholic, untidy, filthy, and in general viewed with distaste. As a rule, middle-class American women did not practice nursing in the homes of others for pay. There was no place where education could take place. The few existing hospitals were feared as indecent dangerous pesthouses. It was a sad truth that they were in fact a last refuge for the hopeless and homeless.

How such prejudice against the nurse was overcome and nursing service made available in a community is recounted by Linda Richards (1841–1930), America's first trained nurse through the use of a "born nurse." The "born nurse" was known for her qualities of love of ministering, keen observations, and sympathetic nature. Only personal illness prevented her from responding to the need for nursing care. Richards herself was known as a born nurse during her teens, before she entered the New England Hospital for Women and Children in Roxbury, Massachusetts as the first pupil. Richards reports (33) that the born nurse received ". . .no compensation . . . save that of an approving conscience and the honor of bearing the title of 'born nurse.' If she were a mother with a family of her own, some one was called in to take her place in her own home, while she cheerfully hurried away to care for the sick one."

Modern American Nursing in the Home

Modern American nursing dates from 1873, when three "Nightingale schools" were founded. For the first time, systematic learning could prepare women in large numbers for nursing as a non-servant occupation. Nursing became suitable work for women who needed a way to be self-supporting. (Keep in mind that the germ theory of disease, general use of anesthesia, modern surgery, control of communicable disease, and antibiotic miracle drugs are much more recent in history than is modern nursing.) American Nightingale schools were at least ten years old when the germ theory ushered in the "goldern age of bacteriology." While Nightingale believed in cleanliness and good ventilation, she scoffed at the idea that germs caused disease (27, 29). However, the principles of scrupulous cleanliness, sanitary environment for the sick, good personal hygiene,

and sound nutrition along with training in observation and management of the medical regimen meant that nursing care made more
differences in terms of survival, comfort, and full recovery than did
any other single factor. Hence trained nurses were in great demand.

As scientific knowledge of bacteriology and surgery developed,
nursing care expanded in scope and became more sophisticated. In
the new scientific age, nursing soon moved beyond the capacity of
the well-intentioned untrained who might manage quite well with
ventilation and hygienic cleanliness as guideposts for practice. Good
nursing practice increasingly demanded knowledge of the latest scientific information and technical skill. It is important to remember
that before the 1920s, hospitals were avoided. Those who could stay
out of a hospital did so. The sick were kept at home if at all possible.
Even though nurses were trained in hospitals, after graduation—and
sometimes before—nursing care was given in the home. Hospitals
were staffed for the most part by student nurses.

What this meant for home nursing is illustrated by the following
excerpt from the *American Journal of Nursing* from 1903, which
provides guidance for a family member until a nurse could be obtained (15):

> *Emergencies may arise in every home that call for surgical aid,
> and when—as frequently happens—to save life an operation
> has to be performed with the utmost speed, it is of the first
> importance to have some rules for the preparation required
> that may be put into practice without delay.*

This article, written by a nurse, goes on to discuss how to select the
room with the best light for surgery and how to prepare the room
itself by scrubbing and appropriate placement of necessities for
major surgery: "one strong kitchen table, four small tables, three
common chairs, three large china basins and pitcher, two slop-jars
or foot tubs, five gallons of boiled water. . ." and other homely items
pressed into service. In such circumstances, it becomes clear why a
trained nurse was so valued.

As medical knowledge and practice changed dramatically during
the 1920s and public support for human welfare and health care
emerged during the 1930s, hospitals replaced the home as the center
of medical care. The increasingly sophisticated technologies of medicine and surgery required complicated equipment. How to manage
Wagonstein suction, take blood pressure, give oxygen, and monitor
blood transfusions transformed the nature of nursing care. Knowledge generated during World War II about surgery and rehabilitation
therapy revolutionized therapeutic practices even further and
greatly reduced prolonged immobility.

Today, home care of the sick, depending on the nature of the disability, might be provided by a visiting professional nurse, a practical nurse, a nurse's aid, or a family member. Nursing care during acute illness is provided in a hospital. Increasingly, convalescent care centers staffed by professional nurses prepare patients and their families for self-care at home. As we have seen, the need for nursing care would seem to be a basic social need in all societies. The specific practices and the reasons for it are rooted in cultural values, beliefs about each other, and the knowledge base of a particular time in history.

Public Health Nursing

Public health nursing, the older term for community health nursing, also has its origins in antiquity. It springs from the early Christian practice of visiting nurses and evolved together with concern for the health of the public through a community system of services for protection of the environment as well as of families and individuals. If one were to ask for a definition of public health nursing, the expert would point to its unique blending of nursing practice with public health practice as an "... area of human services directed toward developing and enhancing the health capabilities of people—either singly, as individuals, or collectively, as groups and communities" (10). Hence, there are two major strands to the historical overview of public health nursing, visiting nursing and the public health movement. These two joined forces about the turn of the twentieth century to produce the modern profession of public health nursing.

The Public Health in Antiquity

Concern for the health of the public or the community as an entity is ancient. Nearly all primitive tribes observed social customs that effectively prevented fouling the family or tribal quarters and maintained a relatively hygienic environment. A kind of common sense, usually coupled with superstition or religious proscriptions, often fostered desirable sanitary practices. For example, many American Indian tribes have the custom of using the downstream side of a stream for excretory purposes. Some groups bury excreta. Burning or burial of the dead is another social rule that effectively protects the environment.

As the civilizations of antiquity developed technological capacities, sewer systems and clean water delivery to urban centers became basic features. The Minoan (3000–1500 B.C.) and the Cretan

(3000–1000 B.C.) civilizations have left archeological evidence of advanced water drainage systems including flushing. Egyptians of about 1000 B.C. constructed earth closets and public drainage pipes.

The ancient Greeks, Egyptians, Jews, and Brahmins have left written records of concern for personal hygiene, diet, and even exercise on the part of the Greeks. Concern about disease and its communicability as well as a great body of literature on therapeutic practice and pharmaceutical formulas testifies to a great concern for good health throughout this early period of history.

It was the Jews, in about 1500 B.C., who articulated in Leviticus what is perhaps the world's first written hygienic code. Personal cleanliness and hygiene, maternity, and community responsibility for environmental sanitation and prevention of the spread of communicable diseases are specifically addressed.

Roman civilization subsequently developed other aspects of public health practice still central to community health: the periodic census as a way to monitor the population for its characteristics; supervision of weights and measures, public bars, and houses of prostitution; provision of sanitary services, street cleaning, and baths; regulation of building construction; prevention of public nuisances, unsafe structures, and foul smells; and provision of good cheap grain for all the population and a safe public water supply through construction of aqueducts still useable in modern times (13).

In these pre-Christian societies resides the nucleus of modern public health philosophy and its comprehensive concern for the community as a whole and the individuals within it, bringing together health and well-being for the ". . .common attainment of the highest level of physical, mental and social well-being and longevity consistent with available knowledge and resources at a given time and place. It holds this goal as its contribution to the most effective total development and life of the individual and his society" (13).

Visiting Nursing in Early Christianity

The altruistic impetus inspired by ancient religious writings of the Jews and Buddhists, which lay down as religious duties the provision of halls for the destitute sick, together with food, bedding, and medicine, was followed by sincere early Christians. The Jews also required neighborly sharing of fire, decent burial of the unclaimed dead, and visiting the sick in order to cheer them up and relieve their suffering—even if the sick person was not of their faith (27).

This view of visiting nursing as a religious expression was continued in early Christianity by deaconesses.

Deaconesses of the early church were laywomen of good social standing appointed by bishops to assist in the good works of the church. Phoebe is often cited as the first deaconess and visiting nurse. Fabiola, Paula, and Marcella were Roman matrons of the fourth and fifth centuries who ministered to the sick poor at home. Deaconesses sought out the needy, provided home nursing care, and often brought the sick into their own homes or the home of the bishop for care. These *diakonia*, as rooms in private homes were called, soon developed into an expanding system attached to churches, serving as centers for the dispensation of charity to the sick poor and needy.

Public Health Under Medieval Christianity

This view of community responsibility for health and well-being failed to serve as a guiding principle during the Middle Ages and the early stages of the Industrial Revolution. With Christianity came changed attitudes toward the human body. It was believed that worldly matters and physical comfort were at variance with the attainment of heaven after death. "Mortification of the flesh" came to be admired religious behavior. It was considered immoral to see even one's own body. People believed frequent bathing was decadent. Filthy garments and deplorable hygienic and sanitary practices became widespread, this factor probably promoted the rapid spread of destructive pandemics such as cholera and the bubonic plague (the Black Death) as trade routes developed, urban centers grew, and large migrations occurred.

On the other hand, the doctrines of Christianity fostered the idea that each individual soul was worthy and important. Eventually, philosophers of the Renaissance articulated a more modern view, which supported the search for scientific truth and recognized human dignity as guiding social concepts.

Visiting Nursing in Medieval Christianity

Religiously inspired nursing orders developed throughout Europe as a result of the Crusades. Increasing numbers of hospitals as places for care of the sick depended on women who gave nursing care as a religious work. Together with the strictly religious nursing orders, there developed a more secularized system of visiting nursing. For example, members of the Third Order of St. Francis (who were both male and female) did not give up social life or take vows of chastity. Rather, they devotedly gave service to improve their home communities. A major part of their dedication was expressed in nursing in hospitals and in homes.

In the early 1600s, St. Vincent de Paul together with Louise de Marilac persuaded upper class Parisian women to devote time and finances to provide nursing care for the sick and alms for the needy. Organized as the Sisters of Charity, this new order cared for the sick poor with the idea that the homes of the sick and the public streets would serve as monastary and cloister. They worked out of a central motherhouse, often serving some time in remote rural areas as visiting nurses (8). As the Daughters of Charity, this nursing order has provided nursing care down through the centuries in many parts of the world, also assisting Florence Nightingale in the Crimea.

Public Health Measures and the Industrial Revolution

Throughout recorded history, leprosy, syphilis, smallpox, anthrax, measles, yellow fever, typhoid, diphtheria, scarlet fever, typhus, and tuberculosis have taken turns in producing human misery and death. Not until relatively recently have contagious diseases been brought under scientific control. Hence, the earliest public health measures were those designed to stop contagion. Isolation and quarantine were among the earliest efforts directed toward community protection against contagion. For example, isolation of the victims of leprosy was often achieved by declaring the leper civilly dead and banishing him (or her) from human society. The leper was often required to wear identifying clothing and ring a bell to warn of his presence. In spite of the efforts of nursing orders, who attempted to provide care for lepers, a rapid death from starvation and exposure was usually assured. This nevertheless had the effect of removing leprosy from western Europe as a public health menace.

After the fearful ravages of the bubonic plague in the fourteenth century, which killed approximately 60 million people, quarantine procedures were more widely instituted. These were most often enforced at ports where travelers from suspect places were required to live disease free for certain periods of time before entry to a city was permitted.

Although public health reform was a concern in many European countries, the public health movement in England was most influential on that in the United States. With the Industrial Revolution in England in the mid-eighteenth century came a ground swell of social and health reform growing out of concern for the plight of exploited and abused children, conditions in prisons, and the grossly unsanitary urban and industrial areas. Conditions were similar in the United States. In early nineteenth century America, epidemics of smallpox, cholera, yellow fever, and typhoid repeatedly terrorized the people of small villages and large towns alike, as their streets displayed the "dirt and filth of human aggregation." In 1850 Massachusetts, the tuberculosis death rate was over 300 per 100,000 population and the infant mortality was about 200 per 1000 live births. Smallpox, scarlet fever, and typhoid were leading causes of death (13). Such epidemics and poor sanitary conditions intensified concern of the government as the new United States experienced rapid industrial expansion and great migrations from Europe. During these epidemics, there was no occupational group of nurses except for a few religious sisterhoods to care for the sick, which they did with consistent distinction.

When the evils of unregulated urban life became overwhelming enough to affect both the poor and the rich, public concern led to governmental controls, enhanced by scientific knowledge from bacteriology. Authority to quarantine American ports was legislated in 1878, with physicians of the Marine Hospital Service of the United States (which had been established in 1789) authorized to carry out medical inspection of all immigrants in 1890. In 1901, the Hygienic Laboratory was established and the newest scientific discoveries emanating from the germ theory meant that public health officials and scientists could monitor and study infectious diseases (13).

After this point, progress was rapid in public health knowledge and reform activity. What remained to be implemented was individual health education and programs for prevention at the personal level.

Role of Modern Nursing

After the value of nursing care had been demonstrated in the Crimean War, Florence Nightingale established a system of education for nursing in England in 1860 and then turned much of her attention to sanitary reform in the British Army and statistical studies of population health and disease. In 1873, after the Civil War gave a similar demonstration in America, professional nursing became established in the United States. This new women's profession fostered a rapid expansion of hospitals, as medical-surgical knowledge emerged apace with discoveries of modern science.

Within twenty years, the American nursing profession had organized and developed interests that went beyond organization of the housekeeping and staffing of hospitals. As British nurses became closely associated with the public health movement and social reform, their influence was felt in America. Promotion of good health, prevention of disease, and focus on the well-being of the family as a nursing concern came together in a new philosophy of district nursing and would greatly affect the basic premises of American professional nursing practice, going beyond care of the sick at home.

Visiting Nursing in the Modern Age

Protestant nursing sisterhoods were very important in the development of district nursing in England and were a forerunner of modern public health nursing. Elizabeth Gurney Fry, a member of the Society of Friends, after years of charitable nursing service in the homes of the poor, founded a society for visiting nursing. Initially called the Protestant Sisters of Charity, it later became known as the Nursing Sisters. In 1836, Pastor Theodor Fliedner and his two wives, Frederike Munster and Caroline Berteau, established a training program for deaconesses in Kaiserswerth, Germany. Florence Nightingale spent time and prepared for nursing in this institution. As described by Pastor Fliedner himself, Kaiserswerth addresses four branches of work as a ". . .free religious association, not dependent on state or church authorities." Nursing consisted of hospital, private, and parish or district nursing, i.e., visiting nursing. There was a program of relief for the poor, one for the care of children, and "work among unfortunate women . . . prisoners and Magdalens" (27).

In 1859 Mr. William Rathbone, a Quaker member of Parliament from Liverpool, became interested in the sick poor, whose deplorable home conditions prevented good nursing care. After establishing a home nursing program, it became clear that qualified nurses did not exist in sufficient numbers. In consultation with Florence Nightingale, the Liverpool Training School and Home for Nurses was established to prepare nurses for home care and health teaching.

Divided into districts along parish lines but under secular control, the poor population was served by a trained nurse and a lady visitor in each district. Lady visitors were trained nurses who supervised health care and combined health teaching with charitable work. By 1874, this successful demonstration of the effectiveness of district nursing in Liverpool, Birmingham, and Manchester had stimulated the establishment in London of the Metropolitan and National Nursing Association (8).

So successful was district nursing in England that Queen Victoria, in the 1887 celebration of her fiftieth year as reigning monarch, created the Queen's Jubilee Institute. The Institute was intended to aid local groups in establishing nonsectarian district nursing agencies by providing standard guidelines and support. Canadian women in 1897, using this model, established the Victorian Order of Nurses under a central administration. Thus, district nursing became a national institution in Britain and Canada, providing services based on local community units in response to local needs.

The American public health movement was enhanced by a fervent spirit of philanthropic social reform in which professionals and lay volunteers joined their efforts to improve the quality of life for the poor immigrant populations in nearly all its aspects, from work and housing to personal hygiene and clean milk for infants as well as education on the prevention of communicable disease. Although visiting nursing care and charity had been sporadically offered in a few places, a systematic service was first provided by the Women's Branch of the New York City Mission in 1877. The Ethical Culture Society of New York City established another nursing service based in the public dispensaries under the supervision of physicians and without religious proselytizing. During the 1880s, visiting nurse services were organized in Boston, Chicago, and Philadelphia by public-spirited citizens.

Modern Public Health Nursing

Lillian D. Wald (1867–1940) is the recognized founder of what we now call public health or community nursing. Merging the tradition of visiting nursing with the social values of the settlement movement and district nursing, Lillian Wald and Mary Brewster in 1883 went to live among the immigrants of the lower east side of Manhattan as nurses and citizens. Lillian Wald soon became the foremost leader in the American public health movement.

Called the Henry Street (Nurses) Settlement, this agency became a vital center for pioneers of a new kind of nursing practice, which actively blended an emphasis on bedside care of the sick at home and family-focused health teaching, with participation in promoting community health. With community health in mind, dealing with health-related social, cultural, economic, and political factors became an important aspect of the public health nurse's role. One outcome was to expand the scope of nursing to concern with the total well-being and development of the client in the family and community settings.

The comprehensive scope of the new public health nursing practice might best be illustrated by describing how country places and convalescent homes acquired by the Henry Street Settlement were used to provide nursing care quite apart from that which was hospital affiliated or prescribed by physicians.

The fate of children at the turn of the century was especially poignant and affecting to Wald and early public health nurses. Desperately poor immigrant families lived in crowded squalor within a maze of garbage-strewn streets. Victims of periodic economic depressions, periodic epidemics, and low-quality care during pregnancy and childbirth, children were among those most greatly afflicted. Often, mothering the family was left to a child of nine or ten years. Many children worked long hours for low wages and assumed family burdens far beyond their years.

Almost immediately the welfare of children became a major cause for those at Henry Street. In the course of time, Wald's genius sparked the beginning of school nursing and movement to establish a federal children's bureau. In association with other great reformers, Henry Street helped to create parks and playgrounds, special education programs in the public schools, vocational education for youth, and protective legislation for children. In fact, the first community project of Henry Street was to build a backyard playground. Awareness of the simple right of children to play in safe, wholesome places led not only to much social reform but also to direct concrete services for those unfortunate children who otherwise could not even dream of a vacation in the country.

A country vacation for children was provided in places like Riverholm in rural Rockland County, New York (16). Life at Riverhold was intended to add to personal growth through "ministration and education." Life at Riverholm was lived family style in a home-life atmosphere. The house was simple but attractively furnished, and there were a few treasured objects that the children learned to respect. The intimacy of life shared with the nurses and other staff allowed for the development of a relationship in which guidance could be provided at critical moments as a natural part of life.

Wholesome recreation and fun was a major aim. The positive effects of living in the midst of nature's beauty with good food, clean air, space for play with people who valued fun, and consideration for others probably reshaped many lives. Wald believed that "good manners were minor morals." Many children were first introduced to the basis for good nutrition, good housekeeping, good table manners, and orderly living at places like Riverholm by Henry Street nurses.

Eventually, Riverholm became a summer home for babies and

small children. However, these basic tenets of care were equally suitable. In 1920, three Henry Street nurses provided care for a grand total of eighty-one children between the ages of ten months and eight years. Most were under six years and stayed for three weeks. One twenty-one month-old girl stayed for seventeen weeks. During the summer of 1920, the nurses coped with diphtheria, which the local physician failed to diagnose. In consequence, Schick tests were given to all children before they were accepted the following year. Surely, the gift of fun, beauty, and participation in a socially desired way of life for its time was an inspired way of countering the grim lives led by so many children (16, 42, 44).

On a tract of land immediately next door to Riverholm was a convalescent home built especially for Henry Street nurses as a gift. Called "The Rest," those patients whom Henry Street nurses judged to be most desperately in need of a period of convalescence in the country air were admitted without orders from or consultation with any physician (42, 44).

Although Wald focused on care of the sick, it was a fundamental principle underlying all the nursing care rendered that the best way to prevent illness and maintain well-being is to teach people how to care for themselves. Teaching good personal hygiene, child care, and nutrition was so successfully implemented by Henry Street nurses that Wald's view of the comprehensive nature of nursing practice excited other nurses, social reformers, and philanthropists and stimulated a rapid growth of similar nursing associations. By 1909, there were 566 public health nursing associations in Buffalo, Rochester, Cleveland, Wilmington, Baltimore, and Detroit. These associations usually provided hourly nursing care of the sick in their homes based on what the family could afford, even if only a few pennies. Some of these expanded into contractual arrangements with the Metropolitan Life Insurance Company for nursing home care during illness or for maternity care.

The public health nurse might visit eight to twelve patients per day. She might report a case of communicable disease to the health department, bathe a dying patient, dress an ulcer or surgical wound, teach infant care to a new mother, or visit a pregnant women to monitor her health and well-being and help the family prepare for a home birth. Prior to the 1940s, childbirth quite often took place at home with public health nursing assistance.

Throughout the 1920s and thereafter, as governmental programs for maternal and child health expanded into rural areas, the public health nurse provided invaluable service in both actual care giving and teaching of families, local midwives, and home aides. She was the backbone and indispensible tool for public health service in a multitude of programs for all age groups and in all classes of people.

By 1913, public health nursing had become so well established that the *Visiting Nurse Quarterly* (later called *Public Health Nursing*) and the *American Journal of Nursing* were regularly publishing articles directed to this nursing group. A university course for graduate nurses in public health nursing had been initiated at Teachers College, Columbia University, and the National Organization for Public Health Nursing was formed (8). Until its dissolution in 1952, public health nursing through this organization was involved in virtually all community health planning efforts with state and national governments and community groups.

Characteristically, the public health nurse is able to operate with a great deal of autonomy and creativity within a wide arena of public life. Long an advocate for improved care for the underserved and inarticulate, public health nursing continues to express the early views so clearly stated by Lillian D. Wald, who saw nursing as primary health care in which the family is the unit of care and where the significance of having a well community is recognized (42, 43).

Today public health nurses are to be found in nearly all programs in which the family is the unit of care, usually outside the hospital walls. Community health nursing continues to be committed to nursing the entire population and concerned with the broad scope of health from crisis care to promotion of "wholesome healthiness."

Nursing Care in the Hospital

For much of the nineteenth century, hospitalization for an illness was an unusual occurrence. Instead, sick individuals were cared for at home by family and friends, with occasional visits from a physician, who usually arrived by a horse and buggy. Individuals who became hospital patients were most often sick indigents or aged persons who did not have the good fortune of having someone else to attend to their needs. Such adversity was coupled with another problem: hospitals were disorganized, unsanitary places that frequently proved to be a further menace to regaining health.

Illness, in general, commonly was attributed to one of two causes: nature, including changes and fluctuations of seasons, atmospheric moisture, and electricity; or man's behavior, such as intemperance in eating and drinking and excessive self-exposure to environmental dangers. Specific problems were identified by either the body region affected or the obvious signs that were present. Thus, patients were described as having such conditions as fever, heartburn, boils, biliousness, and female disorders. Because of the amorphic nature of the causes for the problems, and the lack of knowledge about specific remedies for them, the treatments given were often of a general and systemic nature. For example, bleeding, purging, and the administration of large quantities of alcohol and opiates were common prescriptions. Surgery, often in the form of amputations, was perhaps the most specific type of intervention. However, since septic infections were virtually endemic, surgery was almost tantamount to signing a death certificate in advance.

During the late quarter of the nineteenth century, the period that corresponds to the origins of "modern nursing" in the United States, hospitals were just beginning to gain some favorable attention from the public. The change in attitudes evolved as scientific advances were made and gradually incorporated into medical treatment. Notable among them were the greater understanding of anatomy and cellular pathology, the recognition that germs were a cause of disease, the discovery of the principles of asepsis and anesthesia, and the development of the science of bacteriology. Further extending the physician's diagnostic and treatment abilities as the invention of physical devices such as the ophthalmoscope, stethoscope, hypodermic syringe, and x-rays.

Even more important, however, was the reformation of hospitals that occurred as a result of the trained nurses. Through the systematic use of basic housekeeping skills and principles of antisepsis, the nurses transformed the often squalid and foul-smelling hospitals into clean and efficient places where both the elements of nature and the benefits of advancing scientific understanding could work in the patient's behalf.

However, even at the turn of the century, most people preferred not to go to a hospital for care. Those who did enter voluntarily generally went because it was thought that their prognosis was so grim that continual nursing care was the only factor that might alter the outcome. In that respect it might be said that the hospitals of the period were the earliest counterparts of our present critical care units. The individuals who were admitted then were also usually seriously ill. They required constant surveillance, keen medical and nursing attention, special equipment, and the most advanced forms of treatment then known. While the illnesses themselves, the treatments used, and the underlying rationale for managing the health problems were often different from those recognized and accepted today, there is little reason to believe that the care given was any less zealous or that the tenacity and devotion of those early caregivers was any less fervent than that encountered now. The then life-threatening diseases were as much a challenge as the contemporary ones are.

Nurses of that era, however, are often portrayed as simple ward-housewives, individuals who saw that the hospital was kept meticulously clean and who unquestioningly followed the orders prescribed by the physicians. In light of current equal rights efforts, that typical male/female Victorian-age relationship is now frequently deprecated by the application of such labels as submissive, subservient, or insecure behavior. But those nurses knew that their work with physicians was mutually interdependent—that the execution of the physician's orders, the washing of soiled dressings and poultice cloths, or even scrubbing walls and dirty utensils represented but a portion of their talents. They knew that in many cases the recovery of the patient would "depend more upon the nursing care he received than upon medical skills" (45).

The care of an individual with pneumonia, a common disease occasionally so prevalent in some localities that it assumed the guise of an epidemic, clearly illustrates the nurse's unique responsibilities. The usual treatment for pneumonia was symptomatic: relief of pain, cough, and difficult breathing. A plan of care for an adult with lobar pneumonia as a nurse might have conceived it at the turn of the century is outlined in Table 1-1. In addition to citing the various techniques used, it reflects the fact that the greatest concern was not the lung involvement per se, but the condition of the patient's heart. It was feared that the heart would grow so weak during the illness that it would not tolerate the "crisis," a sudden fall of temperature after which convalescence began, and that the patient would succumb to exhaustion.

Not generally recognized is the fact that many of the hallmarks of present day nursing were also valued by the earlier nurses. Their concern for sound physical assessment skills, clinical judgments, and intervention can be seen in the following passage from Clara S. Weeks' *A Textbook of Nursing* (45), published in 1885. When charged with giving anesthesia,

> *keep your finger on (the patient's) pulse, and your eyes on his face, and at the first warning indications stop giving the vapor. If the dangerous symptoms continue, draw the tongue forward, so that it will not obstruct the trachea, admit fresh air freely, apply friction to the extremities, and resort if necessary to artificial respiration.*

The same source points out the need for nurses to learn all they could "of the previous history of the case" (data base), to classify symptoms as "subjective" or "objective," to "judge and discrimi-

**Table 1-1. Turn-of-the-Century Nursing Care Plan
for an Adult with Lobar Pneumonia.**

Nursing Actions	*Rationale*
1. Preserve sputa for doctor's inspection.	1. To determine if tubercle bacillus is present; to differentiate between consumption and pneumonia.
2. Take temperature (with clinical thermometer) and pulse at regular intervals.	2. To exhibit accurately the cycles of fluctuations; to determine when the crisis sets in; pulse rate of 140–160 indicative of danger to life.
3. Give generous amounts of fluid food. —Chiefly cool sweet milk or equivalent 8 oz q2h —Cool pure water ad lib —Beef tea or bland soups occasionally	3. For nourishment; increases secretions; carries off poisonous wastes. —Most complete form of food; readily digested. —Relieves thirst; increases bowel activity which fever ties up; increases urine and makes it less irritating. —Tea is a stimulant; both give warmth and are somewhat nutritious.
4. Apply linseed poultice or mustard plasters to chest q4h.	4. Warmth and moisture soften tissue and dilate capillaries relieving tension and congestion of inflamed parts, and so relieve pain.
5. Keep in recumbent position or upon affected side at all times.	5. Must give healthy lung every advantage for full expansion and decrease demand on the circulatory and bodily powers.
6. Ventilate room frequently.	6. Bad air depresses vital powers and aggravates existing disease. Draft and cold air become harmful only when fever has receded and recovery has begun.
7. Prepare oxygen inhalations (to be given by doctor for a few minutes q½h–1h or continuously across lips p.r.n.)	7. To provide sufficient oxygen; lungs are not working normally.

Table 1-1. Turn-of-the-Century Nursing Care Plan for an Adult with Lobar Pneumonia (*continued*).

Nursing Actions	Rationale
8. Conserve patient's strength in every possible way. —Absolute bed rest. —Allow no unnecessary talking. —Do not overload stomach.	8. Exertion and pressure must be avoided because the patient's breath is short and there is great danger of failure of the heart.
9. Medications —Whiskey ½oz. or q.s. to strengthen pulse (mix with hot water) —Sodium bromide gr. 8–30 —Quinia gr. 2–3times/day —Tinct. opium Mv–xxv	9. To assist with recuperation —Stimulant; fever produces circulatory weakness as indicated by rapid, weak pulse. —Sedative; quiets nervous system by lessening amount of blood sent to brain; relieves pain, restlessness and anxiety. —Antipyretic; lessens fever. —Narcotic; reduces coughing spasms.
10. During convalescence apply snug-fitting oil-silk jacket lined throughout with flannel.	10. To protect chest from cold. For safety, remove gradually by cutting off an inch from the bottom each day.

References: 31, 34, 45, 46

nate the urgency of special indications" (assess), and to "know-what kind of action is called for" (plan). While the steps were not referred to as components of the new familiar nursing process, it is apparent that the nurses used a similar problem-solving approach when giving nursing care. Additionally, they knew the basic information about the more common diseases and how to perform a vast array of nursing procedures to deal with them, and they were encouraged "to be familiar with underlying principles as well as the details of practice" (45).

Nurses had made an impact on hospital care. By organizing the hospitals, extending their own services, and facilitating those of others with whom they worked, they contributed significantly to the favorable progress of the newly developing hospitals. In other words, rational, systematic, and organized care, in both nursing and medicine, began to replace the empiricism seen earlier in the century.

The Early Twentieth Century

The early 1900s witnessed an expansion and proliferation of hospitals. Their functions had also changed. Instead of being refuges for the destitute, they were increasingly becoming eminent domains of physicians who practiced all but the most general forms of medicine. Social and scientific advances had called for expensive diagnostic and treatment equipment, more commodious accommodations for patients, increased numbers of hospital personnel, and further support services. Amidst the commotion that the growth generated, there were both subtle and overt concerns about such things as who would control the hospitals, the growing expense of hospitalization, and the unavailability of such costly care to a large segment of the population, which was ever growing with the arrival of new immigrants.

During the transformation, the quality of nursing care in hospitals was also affected. The majority of graduate nurses were employed to do private duty in patients' homes. That situation developed because student nurses almost exclusively staffed any hospital that was affiliated with a school of nursing. In addition to providing cheap or free labor, the students worked for up to twelve hours a day, often six and a half days a week, and usually without the direct tutelage of experienced nurses. The nursing care that they gave was simply a mimicry of what more senior students had taught them. Furthermore, out of fear of expulsion from the school, students voiced few objections and, instead, carefully complied with the strict rules and regulations enforced by a nursing supervisor. Under those conditions, it is understandable why nursing care during the period became almost static. The students were novices whose energies were virtually drained by their responsibilities. Even if they had the knowledge or inclination, they had little time, vitality, or authority to design and introduce more modern nursing care. As a result, most of the nursing care given in hospitals followed the previously established procedures, with adjustments only as necessary to handle day-to-day events.

While it appears now that the development of hospital nursing had been neglected, it should be acknowledged that other important relevant concerns had been addressed by the nursing leaders in the interim. Among them were the formation of an effective nursing association, campaigns for nurse registration, the founding of an official journal for nurses, and the utilization of nurses for the growing public health movement. The outbreak of World War I, however, necessarily refocused attention on hospital care. It accentuated the need for trained nurses who would be adept at caring for those who suffered from acute wartime afflictions while other nurses met the needs of the returning wounded soldiers, draftees, and the civilian population.

The unfamiliar results of gas warfare and new military munitions, coupled with the filth of the battlefields and trenches, produced incredible casualties. Bodies were dismembered, mutilated and maimed, and then further insulted by gross infections. Hospital personnel worked valiantly using the newest medications, equipment, and methods to monitor the effects of poisonous and irritant gases and to treat wounds that often defied immediate closure because of overwhelming infection and tissue injury. At the same time, many wards of the military hospitals were filled with soldiers suffering from communicable diseases for which there were no protective measures. However, even if the immediate physical ailments were cured, wounds of moral and spirit often remained. All required more than intuitive and traditional nursing care.

Two very significant responses to the wartime emergency had been the founding of the Vassar Training Camp for Nurses and the Army School of Nursing. While the former clearly demonstrated an effective alternative way of preparing nurses, the latter also demonstrated the irrefutable advantages of maintaining the highest standards for patient care. Unfortunately, however, few hospitals were interested in or capable of emulating the exemplars. Instead, hospital nursing care continued to evolve slowly as nurses assumed some of the simpler skills that were theretofore considered "medical," clarified the knowledge base for common nursing procedures, and learned the nursing responsibilities attached to new medical procedures.

Table 1-2 presents nursing care as it might have been given to a patient with pneumonia in 1925. While it was still believed that pneumonia "must run its course," it can be seen that there were more alternate nursing interventions, more sophisticated rationale for nursing actions, and an emphasis on prevention of secondary complications that could arise from pneumonia. A significant medical advance was the specific antipneumococcus serum treatment for group I pneumonia patients.

**Table 1-2. 1925 Nursing Care Plan
for an Adult with Lobar Pneumonia.**

Nursing Actions	*Rationale*
1. Obtain sputum specimen.	1. To identify organism present and the type or group to which pneumococcus belongs.
—Disinfect all remaining sputum.	—Sputum is a source of infection for others.
2. Take pulse and temperature. —When crisis occurs, cover patient with warm blankets and put hot water bottle at feet.	2. The period of greatest danger is the day or two before crisis, when the heart is burdened by the work of forcing blood through consolidated lung tissue while its working capacity is diminished by fever and toxemia. Sudden rapid irregular pulse (> 130/min) may indicate heart failure.
3. Give diet (during acute stage): —Chiefly milk and its substitutes —Water in abundance —Lemonade, orangeade and imperial drink Give diet (after crisis): —Soft and convalescent foods —Avoid fats and milk sugar	3. Patient is toxic, appetite poor, digestion impaired. Since febrile course is short, no attempt is made to force diet. —Milk is nutritious; fruit juices refreshing. To increase caloric value of diet. —To promote digestion and avoid tympanites.
4. Position patient in recumbent position with one pillow on affected side, if possible. —If semi-recumbent or sitting, support and prevent from sliding down. —Turn patient at half-hour intervals.	4. To limit motion of that side of chest and diminish pain; to spare all causes of strain on the heart. —To prevent hypostatic congestion.
5. Strap chest with adhesive.	5. To rest lungs, prevent friction, and relieve pain and cough due to pleurisy.

Table 1-2. 1925 Nursing Care Plan
for an Adult with Lobar Pneumonia (*continued*).

Nursing Actions	*Rationale*
6. Conserve patient's strength: Make him entirely passive. —Avoid voluntary movements by patient, e.g., turning, reaching, wiping mouth. —Limit or exclude visitors.	6. Every effort means extra strain on the heart; patient needs to muster all his forces to combat disease. —Excitement may induce delirium.
7. Cleanse nose, back of nose, and mouth.	7. Accumulated secretions interfere with breathing, are a source of discomfort, and may result in sores, interference with digestion and secondary infection.
8. Apply turpentine stupes to abdomen, and/or —give cleansing enemata, and/or —insert rectal tube	8. To relieve tympanites, which press the diaphragm up against the heart and lungs and so interferes with their work. There is a greater tendency toward constipation due to toxic effect on intestinal muscle.
9. Apply cold chest compresses and/or —ice bag to chest and/or —ice cap to head and/or —sponge or cold pack	9. To relieve pain and coughing, congestion in lungs, dyspnea and cyanosis; acts as tonic to tumultuous heart; reduces fever and relieves toxemia.
10. Give outdoor fresh open-air treatment. —Expose only face; have patient wear hood. —Keep body and extremities snug and warm. —Protect from winds and drafts. —Place hot water bottle at feet. —Do not restrict movement of chest with blankets.	10. The circulation is interfered with so that body cells are smothering for oxygen and vital centers are poisoned by toxins. Reflex effect of cold stimulates nerve endings in skin and reflexly the vital centers controlling the heart, lungs, blood vessels and other organs. Pulse becomes slower, appetite improves and cyanosis,

**Table 1-2. 1925 Nursing Care Plan
for an Adult with Lobar Pneumonia (*continued*).**

Nursing Actions	*Rationale*
—Move indoors for examinations, bathing, use of bedpan and other treatments.	headache, delirium and sleeplessness are relieved.
11. Apply heat/counterirritants. —poultices/fomentations to chest and/or —steam inhalations and/or —warm sponge bath and/or —mustard paste or dry cupping	11. Sometimes gives more relief and comfort for distressing symptoms than cold treatments do.
12. Report cyanosis, livid, bloated face and full, bounding pulse to M.D.	12. Pulmonary congestion and obstruction may be present and require venesection to take burden from heart and prevent dilatation.
13. Medications: —Codeine or morphine —Bromides, veronal, trional and paraldehyde —Caffeine, camphor, strychnine and adrenaline —Caffeine or atropine	13. To relieve symptoms —to relieve pain, coughing, headache, and delirium —to promote sleep and relieve restlessness —to stimulate heart —to stimulate respiratory system
14. Assist with administration of antipneumococcus serum (100 cc to be given IV q6–12 h until disease is checked). —Warm serum to body temperature. —Observe for unfavorable reactions (sudden flushing of face, restlessness, increased pulse, difficulty breathing, urticaria).	14. Antipneumococcus serum is therapeutic in type I pneumonia and is said to reduce mortality from 25% to 10%. —to prevent otherwise severe chills —can produce serious collapse and fatal outcome

References: 9, 14, 30

The Depression Years

The Great Depression, which followed the 1929 stock market crash and extended well into the 1930s, had both an immediate and a lasting impact on hospital nursing care. The collapse of the national economy created widespread unemployment among all segments of society and virtually devastated the practice field of private duty nursing, the mainstay of employment for graduate nurses. While people continued to need nursing services, the majority turned to either periodic care by visiting nurses or hospital care since private duty nursing was beyond the financial means of most. Furthermore, student nurses continued to occupy most of the available nursing positions in hospitals, which still preferred them to hired graduate nurses because they were cheaper forms of labor. Few other agencies had the economic capacity to hire additional nurses either. Consequently, massive numbers of graduate nurses were left without jobs and had almost no alternative places to seek employment.

Efforts were made by the American Nurses' Association, privately financed groups, and, eventually, government agencies such as the National Recovery Act (NRA) and the Works Progress Administration (WPA) to provide work for the unemployed nurses. Strategies included closing small inferior schools of nursing, thus creating a demand for graduate nurses' services; advocating a "share the work" plan, which would shorten nurses' work days from twelve to eight hours and thereby increase the daily need by one-third; and establishing new government health programs and public-supported hospitals without schools of nursing, which would then hire graduate nurses for their staff. Additionally, chronic illnesses associated with longevity began to replace communicable and childhood diseases as the leading cause of death, while the growth of hospital insurance programs began to make it possible for a larger number of people to afford hospital care. At the same time, technical developments in health care demanded more than unskilled labor. It was the combination of these factors that re-opened the field of hospital staff nursing to graduate nurses. However, that change transformed the vast majority of nurses from private practitioners to hospital employees. Simultaneously, the nurses were forced to relinquish the autonomy commensurate with private duty nursing and instead work according to the dictates of institutions (40).

A further innovation in hospitals that affected nurses and the modality by which nursing care was delivered was the adoption of the Taylor system, more often called scientific management or efficiency engineering. It called for dividing work into the smallest possible tasks, such as giving baths or medications, and then assigning all similar tasks to one nurse, while non-nursing tasks, such as delivering a dietary tray or cleaning a discharged patient's hospital unit, were assigned to semiskilled or unskilled workers. The introduction of ancillary workers, practical nurses, and new specialty occupations such as oxygen therapists, further altered hospital nursing practice. The transition promulgated a fragmented, functional style of nursing care and brought about the demise of the case or one-to-one method of giving care to patients in hospitals. That change, coupled with the loss of autonomy experienced by nurses who returned to hospital work, resulted in a marked loss of control over nursing practice in the hospital setting.

The World War II Era

While the Depression had ultimately created jobs for graduate nurses in hospitals, hospitals continued to sustain shortages of nurses, even before the outbreak of World War II. Many of the nurses who had returned found the hospital conditions untenable. The functional method of care giving was personally unrewarding; efficiency to further the now business-like operation of dispensing medicine seemed to be the primary objective. Nurses did not share the hospitals' prosperity. Instead, they continued to work long hours, received low pay, and were usually denied fringe benefits, such as paid vacations. With the entry of the United States into World War II, the nursing shortage reached critical dimensions. A spectrum of solutions was favored, ranging from training volunteers and holding refresher courses for inactive nurses to proposed legislation to draft nurses and most importantly, the establishment of the Cadet Nurse Corps, which prepared large numbers of women for nursing service (6, 20).

Despite these efforts, the availability of adequate nursing services for civilian as well as military needs continued to be a grave concern. The demands of war on foreign soil had greatly depleted the health resources at home, and the massive defense industry boom required nurses for health education and preventive care. More individuals went to hospitals for care because house calls and home care were seldom feasible. Nurses had to assume many hospital duties that were formerly in the domain of the attending physician. Hospital staffs grew smaller as ancillary personnel, and some nurses, left hospitals to work in the war plants.

However, the irony that caring professions and institutions that offered care, were invigorated by the bloodshed and casualties of military action was apparent again during World War II. Attempts at bold and risky surgery for war injuries were acceptable actions and led to advances in surgical techniques. The collection of blood donations for battle victims became the forerunner of the blood bank system. The early discharge of patients from crowded hospitals confirmed the suspicions about the hazards of immobility and improved patients' likelihood of rapid recovery. Maimed bodies prompted innovative mechanical and rehabilitation developments to restore the lives of patients who otherwise would have been cripples. Scientific investigations that had been progressing step by laborious step for many decades were suddenly accelerated to fulfill wartime demands.

A most spectacular advance was the introduction of sulfonamides and antibiotics, particularly penicillin, which revolutionized the practice of both nursing and medicine and infinitely changed the patterns of hospital care. For example, the use of penicillin so modified the classic picture of pneumonia that the natural evolution of the disease henceforth was seen infrequently. The acute phase was dramatically shortened and the lengthy period of hospitalization previously required for convalescence was markedly decreased. Earlier, discrimination as to the anatomical involvement of the lung had been sufficient, e.g., lobar pneumonia. Now it was obvious that it was more appropriate to classify the pneumonia according to the causative organism, e.g., pneumococcal pneumonia.

With the advent of antibiotic therapy, care for a patient with pneumonia changed from that of giving essential symptomatic relief to that of attacking virulent microscopic organisms. Although many of the time-honored nursing techniques were still carried out, nursing care was no longer viewed as a vital part of the curative process. Instead, it was regarded as supportive action, providing necessary rest for the patient and information for the doctor about the effectiveness of the medication. It was the beginning of nursing's subtle realignment with medicine. Increasingly, nurses' judgments regarding physiological processes were being called on. Nurses had to develop an understanding of disease consistent with that of the medical establishment. The mid-century nursing care plan for an adult with pneumonia (Table 1-3) demonstrates that change. Additionally, it reflects the gradual relaxation of nursing measures that previously were considered obligatory.

Table 1-3. Mid-Century Nursing Care Plan for an Adult with Pneumonia.

Nursing Actions	Rationale
1. Assist with diagnostic tests.	1. To differentiate and confirm diagnosis
—sputum specimen	—to distinguish pneumococci from atypical pneumonia
—chest x-ray	—pneumonia shows characteristic homogeneous shadow spreading out from hilus
—blood count	—leukocytosis of 15,000-30,000 usually present; anemia frequent
—urine specimen	—often contains trace of protein
2. Take T.P.R.	2. Will indicate response to treatment and give early warning of unfavorable reaction; a rise in either after acute stage may be early sign of empyema
3. Give liquid diet (during acute stage).	3. Dehydration may occur rapidly during high fever and contribute to development of shock. Urine specific gravity below 1.020 is indicative of adequate hydration.
—small amounts at frequent intervals	
—urge 3-4 liters/day (water, very weak tea, Vichy, ginger ale)	
—supplement with 1% salty broth	—Serum sodium may be low during acute infection. Supplementary sodium chloride is contraindicated in presence of C.H.F.
Give IV saline if patient unable to take p.o. fluids.	
Give semi-solid diet (as soon as tolerated):	
—cereals	
—additional salt	
—avoid gas-forming foods	—May cause abdominal distention which may further respiratory and circulatory embarrassment.
4. Maintain absolute bedrest.	4. Rest is of primary importance. Nursing care involves all that can be done to put patient at rest, make him comfortable, promote relaxation, spare exertion, protect patient, and encourage morale.
—Group nursing care to provide uninterrupted periods of rest for patient. Use judgment: may omit bath, taking temperature for sake of patient's rest	

Table 1-3. Mid-Century Nursing Care Plan
for an Adult with Pneumonia (*continued*).

Nursing Actions	Rationale
—Guard patient against reaching and turning. —Avoid weight of bed covers. —Exclude or limit visitors. —Feed patient. —Reduce environmental stimuli.	
5. Put patient in position in which he is most comfortable: flat or propped up with pillows. —Lying on affected side usually more comfortable.	5. Comfort is the only criterion for correct position, and can be determined by patient's ease of breathing. —Splints the side and lessens unnecessary coughing.
6. Apply elastic binder around lower costal margin or apply chest binder (pinned from bottom up, tight, with shoulder straps to keep it in place).	6. Is preferable to adhesive strapping because it interferes less with pulmonary ventilation and coughing.
7. Give special nose/mouth care: —Saline or boric acid to cleanse tongue, teeth, buccal membranes —Albolene to dry tongue and nares —Cold cream or petrolatum to dry lips —Calamine lotion to moisten herpes; liquid petrolatum to dry herpes	7. Since mouth breathing is common, care contributes to comfort and has some effect in preventing re-infection and extension of infection.
8. Insert rectal tube for 20″ and/or —give small enema and/or —apply turpentine stupes for 20″ q2h	8. To relieve G.I. tract distention which can embarrass respiratory and cardiac action.
9. Apply counterirritants to chest: —ice bag for 30″–1′ q1h and/or —hot water bottle for 30″–1′ q1h or —mustard plaster	9. By stimulating the cutaneous nerves, pleural pain (caused by stretching of the inflamed parietal pleura) is relieved; respiration improves and cyanosis and anoxemia are diminished.
10. Administer oxygen continuously —via oxygen tent or —via nasal or oropharyngeal catheter	10. To relieve cyanosis and arterial anoxemia caused by increased metabolic rate and diminished diffusion of oxygen from air; oxygen mask unsuitable because of patient's cough and expectoration.

**Table 1-3. Mid-Century Nursing Care Plan
for an Adult with Pneumonia (*continued*).**

Nursing Actions	*Rationale*
11. Medications:	11.
—Morphine sulfate gr. 1/8-1/16 H	—To relieve pain, alleviate cough and produce rest and sleep
—Codeine phosphate gr. ½–1 H (Administer as ordered without hesitation.)	—Codeine is less depressing to respirations and less constipating than M.S., but better pain relief obtained from M.S.
—Peppermint water or Prostigmine methylsufate PRN	—To relieve abdominal distention
—Aqueous penicillin 40,000-80,000 U. q3h IM (Space injection sites widely.)	—Drug of choice in pneumococcal pneumonia; crisis usually occurs in 8-48 h in 85% of cases.
—Administer drug on time; awaken patient if necessary.	—A consistent adequate blood level of the drug must be maintained.
—Observe for untoward signs-e.g., urticaria, skin eruptions.	—Penicillin is generally nontoxic.
12. Take isolation precautions. —Burn sputum. —Boil dishes and linen. —Have room damp dusted daily. —Exclude or limit visitors (if present, must wear gown and mask). —Wear gown and mask when giving direct nursing care. —Instruct patient to use and dispose of tissues properly.	12. Measures are taken to protect patient from superinfection, and nurse, doctor and others from contracting pneumonia via close contact with infected patient, his articles, sputum carried by coughing or drafts of air, or by organisms which have survived in dust.
13. During convalescence: —have patient resume activities gradually —take pulse before activity and 5″ after activity	13. Pneumonia is a prostrating disease and requires gradual resumption of activity which can be gauged by pulse which should return to former rate within 5″ after if activity was not too strenuous.

References: 2, 7

Post World War II

The expected oversupply of nurses for civilian work following World War II had not occurred. Instead of returning to nursing practice, large numbers of nurses elected to devote their time to family responsibilities rather than acquiesce to authoritarian hospital administrations that would not accept nurses' joint planning or decision-making efforts. When that situation was coupled with the need for more skilled nursing personnel, brought about by scientific and technological advances, an acute nursing shortage raged again.

Further complicating the situation was the gradual introduction of a new organization pattern for general hospital care. Resuscitation stations that had been set up on the front lines during World War II had demonstrated the value of special units for patient care. Using that model, hospitals established postanesthesia and recovery rooms to prevent hazardous postoperative complications and secondary medical problems. The Mobile Army Surgical Hospitals (MASH) used during the Korean Conflict to triage and treat battle casualties with expert care by nurses and physicians had had similar success. Subsequently, by the mid 1950s, hospitals were developing intensive care units, soon to be followed by intermediate, self-care, long-term care, and home care units, collectively known as "progressive patient care" (11). That concept eliminated the traditional pattern of segregation of patients by clinical diagnoses, sex, and economic status and instead classified patients according to their degree of illness and their need for medical and nursing care. Additionally, each type of unit called for varying nurse-patient ratios and specialized nursing skills.

At about the same time that hospitals were being reorganized according to patients' needs, the concept of "team nursing" was also being introduced. Its aim was to assemble the many different types of hospital nursing personnel into cohesive teams that would provide a quality of nursing care for groups of patients that was unattainable by the same workers when they were assigned to fragmented tasks and individual procedures (22). Unique features of the concept included direct supervision of all patients and team members by a professional nurse, team conferences for the planning and evaluation of patient care, continuity of care through individualized nursing care plans, and on-site training and in-service education for team members.

However, more than a change in methodological approach to patient care was needed. Continuing surges of new scientific knowledge during the 1950s and 1960s had revolutionized diagnostic and treatment procedures and rapidly generated even more sophisticated technology. A sampling of major advances during the two decades includes the development of the heart-lung machine, open heart surgery, cardiac catheterization, renal dialysis, laser surgery, high-frequency implements for blood coagulation, and new vaccines, pharmaceuticals, and monitoring devices. The expanding field of medical science had made nursing care increasingly more complex and had made demands of increasing gravity on nurses as well. To effectively give care, nurses needed to be able to identify very subtle changes in patients' status, learn new sophisticated treatment techniques, increase their ability to interpret laboratory data, recognize delicate physiological interrelationships, and closely monitor the efficacy of potent and sometimes experimental forms of drug therapy.

While the joint endeavors of team nursing seemed to promote satisfaction among nonprofessional personnel, the concept fell short of reaching the goals of optimal professional nursing care. Although the work was coordinated, the nursing care remained fragmented. Furthermore, the professional nurses' hands-on expertise and ability to make immediate bedside clinical decisions were minimized as teaching, supervisory, and administrative responsibilities increasingly consumed more of their time. Almost as if to counterbalance that loss and to regain a sense of professional worth, becoming a *leader* of nursing care, rather than a *giver* of nursing care, gradually became the recognized measure of a nurse's success.

Paralleling that development was nursing's growing alliance with bedside technology—cardiac monitors, IPPB machines, gastric cooling apparatus, automatic rotating tourniquets, chest tubes, and peritoneal dialysis, to name a few. Although the relationship was most apparent initially in critical care units, it soon permeated almost all other nursing care units in the hospital as well. The nurses' activities were both necessary and valued because they complemented the application of the most modern medical techniques. Despite the favorable aspects of these changes, however, it is now clear that both the scientific advances and the organizational modifications decisively altered the nursing care given in hospitals. Nursing had distanced itself from patients as the changes evolved.

However, one working example in the early 1960s was championing the benefits of direct professional nursing service. At the Loeb Center for Nursing and Rehabilitation at Montefiore Hospital in New York, the transition for patients from an acute care setting to their home was bridged by nursing care given solely by professional nurses. Together, the patient, his family, and the nurse analyzed and solved the problems that hindered the patient from achieving a state of maximum wellness. The presumption at Loeb was that as the patient needed less medical care, he needed "not only more nursing care, but more *professional* nursing care and teaching" (12). A nurse, Lydia Hall, pioneered this idea.

Gradually, acute care hospitals began to recognize the need for adoption of a similar approach. Attempts were made under such titles as comprehensive or total nursing care, and students of nursing were imbued with commensurate ideals. Unfortunately, after graduation, most nurses found that it was impossible to practice nursing in such a fashion: nursing staff were not adequate and most hospitals retained a focus that emphasized medical treatments and efficiency rather than a patient orientation.

Primary Nursing

It was not until 1970 that a model actually emerged in a general hospital that permitted the implementation of those goals. The approach was labeled "primary nursing" (23, 24). Like the Loeb Center nurse, the primary nurse is responsible for the patient's total nursing care, 24 hours a day, 7 days a week, for the entire length of the patient's hospitalization. This is accomplished through direct personal care or, in the absence of the primary nurse, by an associate nurse. Primary nurses are accountable for their practice and work interdependently with other health professionals and social and health agencies. The introduction of primary nursing was an effort on the part of nurses to reclaim direct access to patients (a territory that had been lost as nurses tried to incorporate the large numbers of caregivers who emerged on the hospital scene during the 1940s) and to re-establish the opportunities to exercise sound independent judgment within their professional nursing practice.

The role includes health teaching, consulting with families, and documenting the patient's physical and emotional responses to treatments. The primary nurse is the patient's advocate in the health care system (47).

Primary nursing promotes quality care to patients and their families to meet individualized needs. As a system it holds nursing accountable for its own practice on a daily basis in any setting. It is important that the individual nurse assume responsibility and accountability for comprehensive care for a caseload of patients.

Primary nursing's intent is to provide comprehensive care with continuity. The primary nurse is responsible for obtaining a complete history and physical assessment, determining the plan of care and evaluating care, and recording care on a patient progress note. Many institutions have agreed to have nurses chart on the progress note. The primary nurse is responsible for teaching and discharge planning for the patient and makes referrals to other nursing personnel on ancillary service—personnel who can assist the patient in learning or receiving needed information. The environment must be supportive for creative problem-solving. Clearly there is more to know than one person can acquire and more skills than one nurse can master, thus the resources of clinical specialists are helpful in assisting primary nurses in the hospital setting.

Clinical specialists with masters degree preparation, have become the nurse experts and consultants in hospitals. They are a resource for nurses and patients. The clinical specialist assists in the design and implementation of the professional practice model and is expected to give leadership in practice. The hospital has not always had an environment conducive to the professional practice of nursing: staffing patterns were built around patient care needs, but needed staff have not always been available. Primary nursing is not simply a different staffing pattern, but a philosophy of nursing in action.

Entering the 1980s

The increasing acceptance of primary nursing as the preferred modality for giving nursing care has its roots in the events of the 1960s and 1970s. Basic changes in attitude toward health were emerging in the general public. Ease of access to health care, as well as medical care, became a growing demand. It was further amplified by the greater number of chronic problems in the aging population, as well as by such persistent conditions as drug dependency and the delayed post-traumatic stress syndrome experienced by a large number of Vietnam veterans. Additionally, nursing shortages had forced some hospitals to close their critical care units and thereby restrict the amount of surgery done. Because the problems could not be solved as they had in the past by calling in lesser qualified personnel, hospital administrators began to adopt policies to attract and retain the professional nurses they needed. Simultaneously, the static conformity of females was denounced, and the myths about the traditional roles of women were vehemently challenged by the women's liberation movement. In the meantime, nursing was also changing. Standards of nursing practice designed by nurses were being established. Nurses developed new physical assessment and history-taking skills, and increasing numbers of nurses were obtaining advanced preparation in specialized areas of nursing practice. Furthermore, schools of nursing no longer produced only homogeneous groups of compliant graduates. In general, nurses began to express publicly their role as patients' advocates as well as their demands for better treatment of both patients and themselves. Slowly the public is becoming aware of the actual and potential contributions of nurses. And slowly, the age of holistic treatment for all individuals, nursing care givers and those in need of nursing care, is dawning.

Returning again to the example of care for an individual with pneumonia, but this time as a summation of its treatment during the century, it can be recognized that the most dramatic changes have occurred because of the application of technological and scientific advances by committed professionals. Accuracy, specificity, and refinement have altered the course of a major infectious disease. Ironically, however, pneumonia, which was formerly a disease of young adults, is now a problem that most often occurs in the elderly, the chronically ill, and the immunologically compromised individual. "It is no longer primarily exposure to a virulent organism spreading by 'contagion,' but variations in the host that determines who gets infected" [1]. Furthermore, it now appears that antisepsis, including preventive antibiotics, is reaching its zenith and that asepsis has probably been developed to nearly its greatest capacity. Most exploitable now is probably the last remaining and oldest major avenue of control, preservation of host defenses [19]. This approach will not be a difficult one for nurses, as modern hospital care by nurses was founded on that principle over 100 years ago.

Nursing in the Military

Until the Civil War, medical service in the U.S. Army was as haphazardly organized as it was in the armies of all nations. Fortunate, indeed, was the occasional wounded soldier who fell into the hands of a reasonably competent physician who had a reasonably well-equipped working place.

During the Civil War, close to 10,000 women served in various roles as nurses. Some were compensated while others were volunteers or camp followers. Most of these women had no training in nursing. Most of the physicians, and a surprisingly large number of the soldiers, did not welcome these nurses. They believed that respectable women should not be working in hospitals, caring for wounded men, or doing the many menial tasks involved in nursing. In spite of this prejudice, harrassment, and adverse working conditions, these courageous women managed to provide a measure of comfort to the patients.

By the time of the Spanish American War the U.S. Army Medical Department had 983 members. That number was barely sufficient to care for the 28,000 members of the army, and the numbers of corpsmen could not be increased rapidly enough to supply the medical support for an army that was increasing tenfold because of the war.

Spanish American War

The U.S. Army Medical Department had little prestige in the army at this time. Surgeon General Sternberg was an eminent research scientist not an administrator. The surgeon general had not foreseen the need for nurses during the war, but many nurses volunteered to serve. Dr. Anita Newcome McGee, a practicing physician in Washington, D.C. and vice-president general of the Daughters of the American Revolution (DAR) offered to have the DAR evaluate all nurse applications for contracts with the army. The war started April 25, 1898, and by May 7 the surgeon general had received requests for three "immune" (immune to yellow fever) trained nurses to go to Key West. It was then noted that there was only one "immune" trained nurse available (35).

The DAR reviewed applications of the nurses for personal reputation, health, and professional ability. The candidate was to be a graduate of a two-year school of nursing and have the endorsement of the superintendent of the school. Other volunteer organizations also offered to assist the army in obtaining nurses, among them was the Red Cross Society for Maintenance of Trained Nurses, Auxiliary No. 3 of New York. Each hospital surgeon could also contract for a nurse. The need for nurses arose not from battle casualties but from the casualities of disease.

When it was apparent that nurses were needed because of typhoid, they were contacted by the DAR and agreed to serve on a contract basis for $30.00 a month plus room and meals. Thankfully, the war lasted only until July 17, 1898. By that time the troops in Cuba were nearly exterminated by yellow fever, malaria, dysentery, and food poisoning. The troops were moved from Cuba to Montauk Point in New York in attempts to keep them alive. Other camp sites were in Georgia and Florida.

Troops were moved to southern camps in the United States to acclimatize the men for the tropics. Many of these camp sites did not use proper sanitation techniques. The men frequently used any wooded area around the camp to relieve themselves. As the temperature increased so also did the amount of disease.

When nurses arrived at army hospitals, few could have been prepared for what they found. The hospital corpsmen were from line units and were the dregs of those units. The corpsmen could be taught a few basic items of care, and the nurse would find that they would not be reassigned to the hospital the next day. The corpsmen also were seen using the same bucket for food and for excrement.

Anna Maxwell took a leave of absence from her position as superintendent of the Presbyterian Hospital Training School for Nurses in New York because she believed she could demonstrate that carefully selected, well-trained, disciplined nurses could give material aide to the government in time of war. She was assigned to Sternberg Hospital at Camp Thomas. The hospital consisted of 140 tents and 12 wooden buildings and was designed to accommodate 1000 patients. Miss Maxwell stated that when the patients first arrived, there was one bed pan that had to do for 136 patients in six hours. The first twenty nurses who arrived at the camp were called on not only to give 18-hour service but to furnish basins, sponges, towels, thermometers, and drugs from their own personal supplies until the government supplies arrived (25).

Camp Thomas Chickamanga Park was one of the larger hospital sites, and what happened there happened at many of the other army hospitals. The census grew from 2200 patients on July 25 to 4400 on August 15. Typhoid patients sometimes lay in their own excrement for as long as 24 hours because the hospital lacked staff and supplies to care for the volume of patients.

The wards had long rows of narrow cots occupied by once strong, splendid men who were reduced to hollow-eyed, emaciated individuals muttering in the delirium of fever. It was not uncommon to find encrusted dead flies in the sores of their mouths (26). The hospital tents were on platforms, and during the rain the holes in the tents made it difficult to keep the patients from being drenched. The nurses working under these conditions often worked both day and night. Treatment of the patient with typhoid consisted of several ice baths daily and nourishment every two hours.

During the Spanish American War, 275 died of wounds while 35,000 died of disease (18). Many of the nurses who served were not carefully screened or selected "army nurses"; scandalous behavior was reported in the New York papers and all nurses' reputations suffered because of the report (5). Because the nurses were civilians under contract, there were no provisions for care when they became ill. Many simply returned home. Many of the head nurses suggested to the nurse that it would look better if the reason for discharge was "at own request." There are no records stating the number of nurses who left the army because of illness. The chief nurse did not have to file a report until September of 1898, so there is no accurate record.

It was not until 1926 that nurses who had served under contract during the Spanish American War received military recognition and benefits. More than 1500 female nurses had signed contracts with the army during the last eight months of 1898. Other nurses served as Red Cross nurses and did not sign contracts, and they never received any benefits from the army. It is known that there were 140 cases of typhoid fever and 12 deaths among the contract nurses; others who also may have been ill cannot be documented.

Emergence of the Army and Navy Nurse Corps

Dr. McGee had been a civilian volunteer until August, when the troops were brought back from Cuba. She was then made acting assistant surgeon. Dr. McGee lobbied to have a bill passed making the nurse corps a permanent part of the U.S. Army Medical Department. The Associated Nurses' Alumni also proposed a bill, but it proposed that only members of the Associated Alumni be appointed and that the superintendent of the corps be a nurse. They wanted the bill because they believed that nursing in the army "should not again be deferred until the emergency actually occurs, nor should it be left to patriotism and charity"; it should have the sanction and permanence of law. Neither of these bills passed. A number of surgeons spoke before Congress of the nurses' indispensable care of serious cases of typhoid and how that improved the survival of many of the typhoid patients. It was only after a number of surgeons had spoken before the Congress on behalf of nursing that the army reorganization bill was introduced, including nurses as members of the U.S. Army Medical Department. From 1901 to pre-World War I only 100 to 200 nurses were serving at a few army hospitals in the United States and overseas. The bill that passed in 1901 stated that the U.S. Army nurse's salary was $40.00 per month for duty in the United States and $50.00 per month for duty elsewhere, still unequal to the pay in civilian hospitals. She was to be a graduate of a hospital-trained school, not a two-year training school. Meanwhile, nurses at large civilian hospitals received $50.00 per month if they were head nurses and $40.00 per month if they were an assistant head nurse (38).

The superintendent of the corps was to be a nurse graduate of a two-year program; thus Dr. McGee, who was not a nurse, was forced into retirement. The superintendent of the Army Nurse Corps had little power over the nurses in the corps. She could not change any of the rules governing the nurses and could not either designate or evaluate the chief nurse of a hospital. The chief nurse at an army hospital wrote the efficiency reports of the nurses serving under her, but the chief surgeon of the hospital appended a statement as to whether he agreed with the chief nurse's evaluation. Thus, it was the hospital surgeon who ultimately controlled the nurse's career in the army. The superintendent could not visit or inspect the nurses without the surgeon general's permission. Nurses could not communicate with the superintendent of the Army Nurse Corps unless the hospital surgeon approved of the correspondence. The benefits the nurse received consisted of a vacation with pay and medical treatment when ill, but if that illness became permanent the nurse would be discharged without pay or any other benefits. Meanwhile in England, army nurses had already received relative rank, and in addition to pay, they had an allowance for clothing and servants hire and were pensioned after retirement. The U.S. Army nurse would not receive the same benefits until the 1920s.

Early in the Army Nurse Corps history, nursing leaders who had not served in the army were requested to accept the position as superintendent. Thus, Jane Delano was asked to become superintendent of the Army Nurse Corps in 1909. She was then chairman of the American Red Cross Nursing Service and president of the Associated Alumni, later to be known as the American Nurses' Association (ANA). The reason that she agreed to serve as superintendent of the Army Nurse Corps was to improve the quality of nurses who would be members of the Army Nurse Corps Reserve. The charter of the American Red Cross of 1905 stated that the purpose of the organization would be to furnish volunteer aid to the sick and wounded in time of war and disaster in accordance with the conditions of the Geneva Convention. To become an American National Red Cross Nurse, an individual had to show registration if that was required by law in her state and she had to be over 25 years of age. The members of the American National Red Cross Nursing Department were also members of the Associated Alumni. These nurses would eventually become the reserve force of the army during World War I and World War II. Jane Delano had succeeded in her task: by 1912 there were 3000 nurses on the reserve list and she resigned as superintendent of the Army Nurse Corps. While superintendent, Miss Delano inspected the hospitals where nurses were stationed both in the United States and in the Philippines; this helped to bring about improvements both in the nurses' quarters and in the hospital conditions.

Isabel McIsaac, who was appointed to succeed Jane Delano, died suddenly in 1914 and was succeeded by Dora Thompson, the first superintendent to have served in the military. She had served in the Philippines and been on duty during the earthquake in San Francisco in 1906. Dora Thompson's persistence influenced the surgeon general to change the regulations so that the nurse was given authority next after the medical officer in the wards. From the time she became superintendent, the Army Nurse Corps continued to grow and prepare itself for emergencies. She and Jane Delano worked closely together to attempt to meet the needs of the army for nurses during World War I. The Army Nurse Corps increased from 403 in April 1917 to 21,480 on November 11, 1918. That this force was available was due to the vision and determined effort of Jane Delano and many nursing leaders.

When the U.S. Navy Nurse Corps was founded in 1908 there were initially twenty navy nurses serving in naval hospitals in Washington, Annapolis, Brooklyn, California, and overseas.

World War I

As the prospects of war increased, the Red Cross organized base hospitals on military bases, and the personnel to staff them were commissioned or enlisted in the Army Nurse Corps Reserve. Medical schools were selected as desirable parent institutions for base hospitals. In previous wars these hospitals had been built up slowly and painfully as war progressed with staff members who often were strangers to each other. The cohesion and training of staff from medical school hospitals created a nucleus around which base hospitals could function, since the professional component would be trained and accustomed to working together. These hospital units were activated and sent overseas starting in May 1917.

Both Jane Delano and Dora Thompson recognized that it would be necessary to waive certain requirements for entrance into the service during the war. Even with waiving requirements and lowering the age limit to 21, not enough nurses joined the service to maintain a ratio of one nurse to ten hospital beds as the war progressed.

The nursing committee of the Council of National Defense worked to obtain an accurate census of nursing resources in the country and to find an effective mechanism to make them readily available when needed. It tried to increase the supply of student nurses in training schools for nurses and to advise other nursing organizations and the military on problems of nursing as they would arise from time to time during the war. The committee members believed their mission was to guard the quality of nursing care in homes and hospitals as well as the teaching of nursing (3).

When nurses were first sent overseas, gaps in preparation became apparent. There was no outdoor uniform and no official identification, passport, or card issued to the nurses. By July of 1917 a uniform had been designed and issued by the American Red Cross. The nurse was to wear the uniform when off duty and have an identification card. A nursing headquarters was set with the headquarters of the American Expeditionary Forces (AEF). The nurses served with British, French, and American forces. Conditions overseas varied according to the hospital size and location. The status of the nurse was unclear: she lacked rank and thus was left to the mercy of the officer in charge of any area. The nurse was not to socialize with either enlisted personnel or officers, and she was proceeded by all others in regard to living quarters, dining, and transportation. Some nurses were left at train stations for two to three days or transported as third-class passengers because of this lack of status. When nursing organizations, the DAR, and women's organizations heard of the treatment of the nurses, they organized and requested the surgeon general to give the nurse rank and pay similar to that received by nurses in the Canadian Nurse Corps. The war was to end before that legislation could be introduced.

Nurses who joined the Army Nurse Corps during the war received no orientation to the army. They were given the regulations from the manual of the medical department and told to follow them. Many did not recognize that they were responsible for the budget, the rations, and the quarters, including all the bedding, desks, and chairs in the nursing quarters. It was a difficult task many performed admirably. By March of 1918 the manual for the medical department gave the nurse full responsibility for management of the ward, including enlisted personnel and all others giving nursing care. Because of this recognition of status, life on the ward was somewhat improved.

As the war progressed, the Army Nurse Corps was having difficulty meeting the requests for nurses to maintain a ratio of one nurse per ten beds. Dora Thompson and Jane Delano recommended the use of nurse's aides, and the surgeon general appeared to favor aides. The aide would have taken courses in dietetics, hygiene, and bed making and would supplement the supply of nurses. Nursing leaders, among them Annie Goodrich and M. A. Nutting, recommended an army school of nursing to supplement the nurse supply. The plan for the Army School of Nursing was based on the National League for Nursing Education's (NLNE) recently issued *Standard Curriculum for Schools of Nursing*.

The Army School of Nursing

The Army School of Nursing was planned as a three-year course of training, leading to a diploma in nursing, and would be given at various base hospitals. The base hospital would be assigned as a training camp, each one a complete unit having its own director, staff of lecturers, instructors, supervisors, and teaching equipment. Military hospitals could supply all clinical experiences except children's diseases, gynecology, obstetrics, and public health, which could be provided through affiliations. Dora Thompson wrote the surgeon general stating the plan for the Army School of Nursing as it related to maintaining the standards of nursing education, but she doubted it would meet the army's need for nursing personnel. She urgently recommended immediate measures toward the selection of groups of women who could be employed as nursing aides. In May 1918 the surgeon general agreed to have nursing aides trained in military hospitals.

The proponents of the Army School of Nursing took their plan to the twenty-fourth annual convention of the NLNE. With the NLNE were the American Nurses Association (ANA) and the National Organization of Public Health Nurses (NOPHN). Proponents of the plan thought that if the body of nursing voted for the Army School of Nursing, then possibly the Secretary of War would reverse his decision. Annie Goodrich, in her address, stated that the school, through its affiliation program, would return a large body of soundly prepared students to civilian hospitals. One of the arguments against the school was that educating large numbers of nurses would result in an excessive number of professional nurses after the war. Jane Delano argued that the training school could not produce the number of nurses needed nor could it be in operation quickly enough (39). Time proved her correct.

The Convention voted in support of the Army School of Nursing. Nursing leaders as well as important female civilians met with the secretary of war late in May to persuade him to change his decision. They were successful. It was decided that the Army School of Nursing would be approved.

The budget for the Army School of Nursing was approved in June 1918. That same month the advisory council met to discuss methods of recruiting, cooperation with civilian hospitals, and the numbers of training units that could be established. By late June, 321 applications had been received. The school did not develop rapidly enough to meet the army's needs. Among the reasons for delay was the unfamiliarity of the chief nurses with the training school field, delay in building quarters, and the lack of a graded, overt seniority system in the army.

During the summer of 1918 the major offensive of battle was begun in Europe. Col. Finney, surgeon with the American Expeditionary Force (AEF) and former physician to President Woodrow Wilson, returned to the United States in the summer of 1918 to request increasing numbers of nurses for the AEF. If nurses were not available he suggested that senior students from fifty medical centers and reserve hospitals be allowed to spend their third year overseas. Few senior students were sent overseas, but some were allowed to affiliate at army hospitals during their third year.

By October it was realized that there would not be enough nurses to care for both the military and the civilian patients. Only 487 students had been assigned to hospital units, while another 537 were ready for assignment. It was the influenza pandemic that saved the school from termination. Students were used to care for patients on the wards and were given only those instructions that would immediately increase their usefulness.

American casualties in World War I numbered over 321,000— 50,280 were killed in battle, 62,000 died of disease, and 206,000 were wounded; 101 nurses died in the AEF (38). Nursing care at that time in medical history was exceedingly important in the recovery of the sick and wounded. X-rays were used on the field of battle, or close to it, to find and remove shell fragments; thereafter it was nursing care that controlled the recovery process. The influenza– pneumonia pandemic of the fall of 1918 and Winter of 1919 accounted for two-thirds of all deaths by disease (38).

There were times when the ratio of nurse to patient reached one to fifty in the AEF hospitals. On November 11, 1918, there were 8587 nurses assigned to the AEF and 184,421 American soldiers occupying beds in 231 hospitals. Maintenance of morale among American nurses and their observance of social customs varied greatly among the various hospital stations in France. The chief nurses at larger hospital centers in France could meet and discuss problems and formulate rules of conduct for all nurses at the center. The chief nurses in smaller, more isolated hospitals did not have that advantage. Consequently, it was the nurse's own background that created the social environment. There was no concurrence as to acceptable conduct, thus the wide variation from unit to unit. When on leave the nurse was not allowed to travel singly or without a chaperone.

Nurses described what it was like while in the AEF. Some of the hospitals were only 6 kilometers from the front line. Nurses in these hospitals later describe spending

> . . . .most of the night jumping out of bed into our trench coats and snatching our helmets and gas masks and running down to the first floor, where we had to sit on the floor, not knowing just when a bomb would come crashing down on us. The planes flew very low and we could hear the engines very distinctly [4].

Other nurses described the operating room, where the operating tables were placed as close together as possible and were never empty. Each surgical team had two tables; one patient was waiting while the surgeon finished the other. Nurses also traveled as part of a shock team that performed triage. In the triage area the soldiers' wounds were redressed and the patient was sent to an evacuation hospital. To apply heat the nurse improvised a hood over the stretcher and used lanterns to supply the heat. The only real trouble, the nurses said, was that mice were found running around the cot when the patient woke up (21).

Few hospitals did not lose one or more of its nurses by death. They also had to contend with serious illness among the staff. Many of these hospitals had come as units from the United States. They had known the family of those who had died; thus it was difficult for them to maintain morale and write to the parents of those who had died.

Some nurses were seriously wounded during enemy action. The sick nurses were cared for in various ways: some hospitals had them remain in their quarters while in others an infirmary was created. Nurses who became disabled were evacuated to the United States. There were two convalescent homes for nurses in Europe.

Hospitals in the United States were equally short of nurses. Camp Devon, a 2000-bed hospital, had 6000 patients in the fall of 1918. The surgeon general authorized U.S. units to employ nurses for the influenza emergency, but many communities did not have nurses available to serve the military hospitals. Some hospitals were even difficult to locate, and nurses told of needing help to find them.

Julia Stimson in the War

Julia Stimson was appointed chief nurse of the American Red Cross in France in July 1918. The American Red Cross functioned as a bureau of nursing for the U.S. Army hospitals for the rest of the war. Among her responsibilities was to write letters to the families of every one of the seriously and dangerously ill patients. Miss Stimson wrote letters about her experience to her family. They were later published under the title *Finding Themselves*. She spoke of receiving patients with gas injuries and receiving as many as sixty-four in one night, with many patients having to have their eyes bandaged.

Newspaper accounts generally discussed care of the wounded in terms of "the Red Cross," creating the impression that the Red Cross had complete charge of all medical work for the army. The army was allowed to militarize all Red Cross hospitals in France once the United States had entered the war so there was frequently confusion as to who the nurse was serving. This caused some hardship with the American Red Cross because some nurses refused to join the Army Nurse Corps, went overseas as Red Cross nurses, served in the American Red Cross hospitals, and cared for the American soldier.

Julia Stimson was later named director of the Nursing Service of the AEF. She was responsible for over 10,000 nurses in Europe at the time of the Armistice. She established a good working relationship with Major General Ireland, the chief surgeon of the AEF. He would later become the surgeon general of the U.S. Army.

Julia Stimson agreed to remain in the army during the period of reconstruction and reorganization and until such time as ". . .we shall know definitely that the ANC (Army Nurse Corps) is going to continue as a progressive up-to-date organization or revert to its previous status. In the latter case, of course, I shall not remain in it" (37).

Thus, both she and Annie Goodrich believed at that time that the ANC was a progressive organization. One of the reasons for this belief was that both women thought the army system was better than that found in many other large hospitals. On their inspection trips they had found Army hospitals of more than 1000 beds, which they considered "great scientifically equipped hospitals that had come into existence almost overnight" (37). On returning to the United States in the summer of 1919, Julia Stimson was appointed assistant superintendent of the Army Nurse Corps and dean of the Army School of Nursing. Annie Goodrich had resigned as dean of the Army School of Nursing, and Dora Thompson took a leave of absence from her position as superintendent of the Army Nurse Corps because she needed a rest.

The war gave the Navy Nurse Corps an opportunity to serve in England, Ireland, Scotland, and on the French coast. The war was essentially a land war, so the demands for navy nurses was not as severe as the demand for army nurses. The Navy Nurse Corps had a peak strength of 1,500.

Post World War I

The military nurse corps always decreases in size and suffers all of the problems of the military during peacetime. The Army Nurse Corps did not obtain rank during the war and could obtain only relative rank by 1920. Relative rank meant a nurse could wear a symbol of rank on her collar and be addressed as an officer, but she still received less pay than her male counterpart. The physician normally disciplined the enlisted personnel if the senior enlisted man could not handle the discipline problem.

Nurses served throughout the United States and overseas but their numbers decreased. During peacetime, there were between 600 and 800 nurses serving the military until 1940, when their numbers started to increase in preparation for World War II. Among the changes was the decrease in the size of the Army School of Nursing. Julia Stimson had become dean of the school and superintendent of the Army Nurse Corps in 1919. After the Armistice, students in the school were contacted regarding their commitment to complete the course. Seventy percent of the students surveyed stated that they intended to remain in the school. Many of the schools had not followed the *Standard Curriculum*, so the school was consolidated in the fall of 1919 to four sites and later in 1920 to one site. It's difficult to determine whether the school was truly as good as the curriculum design or its initial graduates would indicate. Of 508 who completed the course, 420 applied for registration and only one failed to pass her state board examination. The Army School of Nursing continued until 1932 but was closed for economic reasons. The students who had gone to the Army School of Nursing did not have to serve on active duty unless there was a position available in the Army Nurse Corps; thus few served on active duty. As economic security became an increasingly important issue during the 1920s and 1930s there was very little opportunity for nurses to join the corps.

Julia Stimson was intensely proud of the corps, and she utilized her knowledge of the corps' work in France and the war department's records to bring the achievements of the ANC to the attention of the nursing profession and the public. When she spoke of the progress that nursing had made during the 1920s she emphasized that nurses were being taught to think for themselves and were no longer content to be "pickers up of pieces and subordinate handmaidens." Major Stimson observed that nurses were leaning to view themselves as teachers of health and as taking their place in the spreading effort toward preventive health. She spoke often of prevention as well as cure being part of the nursing role (36).

World War II

When the country prepared for World War II, so did the military nurses. The nurses who served in combat during this war were usually recognized only as military statistics; few knew of the conditions under which they served. Many nurses know of the soldiers left on Bataan and Corregidor, but few nurses know that nurses were left on Corregidor and served until captured. Both army and navy nurses were kept prisoners by the Japanese in the Philippines throughout the war. During their time of service on Bataan, they worked under terrific hardships. When the Japanese arrived they were surprised to find female officers with the American troops. Because they had not been prepared they allowed them to continue nursing. The nurses were taken to the civilian prison camp at Santo Tomas near Manila; here they ran the prison hospital and cared for soldiers until released in 1945. General Wainwright stated "their names must always be hallowed when we speak of American heroes" (41).

Nurses served wherever the American soldier was sent. They were often not far behind when troops landed on beachheads overseas. The nurses lived in tents and cheerfully endured their camp life. Ernie Pyle, the famed war correspondent, remarked on the composure of the Army nurses (32):

> Army doctors, and patients, too, were unanimous in their praise of them. . . The Carolina nurses, too, took it like soldiers. For the first ten days they had to live like animals, even using open ditches for toilets, but they never complained. . . .The touch of femininity, the knowledge that a woman was around, gave the wounded men courage and confidence and a feeling of security.

The nurses uniform in combat was steel helmets and fatigues. During the amphibious landing at Anzio, nurses too were among the killed. Five army nurses were among the first American women killed as a direct result of enemy action. By July of 1945 the Army Nurse Corps had fifteen killed in action, twenty-six wounded in action, sixteen initially missing in action but returned to duty, and five still missing in action (20).

During this war, the army also experimented and created the Mobile Army Surgical Hospital (MASH). They first appeared in late November 1942. A complement of surgeons, nurses, and corpsmen travelled with each unit, which could be ordered to move at a moment's notice. The extended use of air transport for the evacuation of wounded soldiers opened a new field of military nursing. Both the army and the navy had flight nurse programs. These flight nurses represented the elite of the corps and many nurses clamored for admission to the branch. The nurse was trained to convert transport planes to flying ambulances and to organize the loading and unloading of the sick and wounded. Once on board the plane, the nurse represented the sole medical care and had to be prepared to intervene when the patients' conditions warranted. Other nursing changes included extension of the nurse anesthesia program from a two-month to a four-month program, and they trained corpsmen as anesthesia technicians.

Once again, during World War II, the army was unable to forecast and recruit the number of nurses that would be needed. By early 1945 the army had an estimated shortage of 10,000 nurses. Walter Lippmann, in his December 1944 column, informed the public of the shortage, suggesting that many nurses were shirking their duty by not enlisting in the army. Because of this, a draft nurse bill was presented to Congress. That bill heightened the nation's awareness that the army was not effectively solving the recruitment problem. If nurses had been granted waivers for height and/or weight requirements more would have been available. Male nurses were not accepted (they would not gain commission status until after the Korean War). By April of 1945 conclusion of the war on the European front freed nurses for duty elsewhere, making the draft nurse bill less necessary. Politicians began to recognize that this might be a first step toward federal interference into personal and family affairs, and the bill was quietly withdrawn in May 1945. It was during this war that military nurses finally gained commissioned rank. In 1944, after many attempts had been made, it was recognized that nurses truly did work and endure tremendous physical activities in wartime situations. It was because of this recognition that the bill to give nurses actual commission status finally passed in 1944. They got commissioned status for the duration of the emergency plus six months.

When the war ended in Europe (May 8, 1945) there were 52,000 army nurses on active duty. On VJ Day (September 2, 1945) there were 57,000 in the Army Nurse Corps. During major battle offensives, army nurses assisted in developing the concept of recovery wards for immediate postoperative care of patients. The flight nurses helped to establish the incredible record of only five deaths in flight per 100,000 patients transported. It was during this war that the first basic training centers were established to provide military orientation for army nurses. This was also the first time following the war when the military nurses became eligible for all veterans benefits. Thirty-six percent of the nurse veterans used their GI bill to go to school. This was an early source of nurses with bachelors and masters degrees.

In 1947 the Army-Navy Nurses Act provided for permanent commissioned officer status for members of the corps. The Air Force Nurse Corps was established in July 1949, and 1199 army nurses who had been members of the Army Air Corps Flight Nurse Program transferred to the U.S. Air Force and formed the nucleus of this corps.

The Korean Conflict

The next military situation in which nurses served in a combat area was Korea. Only 10 percent of the Army Nurse Corps was assigned to Korea. It was the air evacuation that changed the survival of the wounded soldier. Nurses were assigned to MASH units that were to be 8 to 20 miles from the front line. There were usually sixteen nurses assigned to each unit. It was the use of helicopters, whole blood and rapid evacuation that improved the survival rate to 98%. Patients were evacuated rapidly from Korea to Japan.

Vietnam

The first ten army nurses arrived in Vietnam in March 1962. Between March 1962 and March 1973 more than 5,000 nurses served in Vietnam. Because of the Army Nurse Corps need for nursing personnel the Warrant Officer Nurse Program was authorized. Graduates of two-year associate degree programs were commissioned as Warrant Officers during the conflict (90) while on active duty. Also, 11 Army Reserve Medical Units were activated and served in Vietnam between April of 1968 and January 1970.

MUST(Medical Unit, Self-contained, Transportable) hospitals became operational in Vietnam. These inflatable rubber shelters with integral electral power, air conditioning, heating, hot and cold water, and waste disposal were transported by truck, helicopter, or cargo aircraft to create the mobile hospital that replaced the MASH units of Korea. The female nurse was once again recognized as an important morale factor to troops. All male nursing units were established then disbanded as the troops commented on how great it was to find female nurses serving in the combat area when they did not have to serve. Nurses also participated in collection of data on combat wounds and care of those wounds.

In Vietnam the concept of the hospital utilization had to be modified. There were no front lines nor was there a secure road network in the combat areas, so the helicopter was used primarily for evacuation. The helicopter and the communication system moved patients to the most readily accessible operating room. All hospitals were fixed installations in Vietnam, but that did not mean they were secure, nor that they could not be moved. In 1964 four Navy nurses were awarded the Purple Heart for injuries sustained during the Viet

Cong bombing of their quarters in Saigon. There was also one Army nurse killed: 1st Lt. Sharon Lane died on June 8, 1969 of shrapnel wounds received during an enemy attack on the 312th Evacuation Hospital in Chu Lai.

Summary

Throughout the history of America, nurses have played an important role in the care of military personnel and their families. During times of war, the courage and compassion of military nurses have been outstanding. Frequently, the talent and ingenuity demonstrated by nurses during the most critical stages of wars have led to the development of new techniques, skills and modalities of nursing care that have had a profound effect on the advancement of nursing practice in all settings.

Nurses in the military have always been committed to the cause of peace and the maintenance of health but they have also responded swiftly and competently when care of the wounded required their expertise.

References

1. Bollet AJ: The rise and fall of disease, Am Med 70:12–16, 1981

2. Brown A: Medical Nursing, 2nd ed. Philadelphia, W. B. Saunders, 1952

3. Council of National Defense: Report from the Committee on Nursing, September 9, 1917, Teachers College Archive, Columbia University, New York

4. Crawford M: Personal Accounts of Conditions in the AEF, US Base Hospital No. 7, Record Group 112 National Archives, Washington, DC

5. Cromelin M: Report of M. Cromelin to the Surgeon General, November 26, 1898, The United States Army Historical Unit

6. Dolan JA: Nursing in Society. 14th ed. Philadelphia, W. B. Saunders, 1978

7. Faddis M, Hayman J: Care of the Medical Patient. New York, McGraw-Hill, 1952

8. Fitzpatrick ML: The National Organization for Public Health Nursing, 1912–1952: Development of a Practice Field. New York, National League for Nursing, 1975, pp. 2, 37

9. Foote J (ed): State Board Questions and Answers for Nurses. Philadelphia, J. B. Lippincott, 1924

10. Freeman RB, Heinrich J: Community Health Nursing Practice, 2nd ed. Philadelphia, W. B. Saunders, 1981, p. 3

11. Haldeman JC, Abdellah FG: Concepts of progressive patient care. Hospitals 33:38–144, 1959

12. Hall L: A center for nursing. Nurs Outlook 11:805–806, 1963

13. Hanlon JJ: Principles of Public Health Administration, 5th ed. St. Louis, C. V. Mosby, 1969, pp. 14–15, 23, 30

14. Harmer B: Textbook of the Principles and Practice of Nursing. New York, Macmillan, 1924

15. Harrison E: Hygiene of the household. Am J Nurs 3:348–351, 1903

16. Hiestand WC: Riverholm: Nursing history in Rockland County. Dispatch, August–September, 1979

17. Himes NE: Medical History of Contraception. New York, Schocken Books, 1970, pp. 59–64

18. Hume E: Victories of Army Medicine. Philadelphia, J. B. Lippincott, 1943, p. 29

19. Illick JE: Child-rearing in seventeenth century England and America. In deMause L (ed): The History of Childhood. New York, Harper & Row, 1974, pp. 303–350

20. Kalisch PA, Kalisch BJ: The Advance of American Nursing. Boston, Little, Brown, 1978, pp. 1–5, 460

21. Kelly FM: A Spanish War nurse remembers. The Alumnae Jl. New York, City Hospital School of Nursing, July 1926, R6 112, E 230

22. Lambertsen E: Nursing Team Organization and Functioning. New York, Teachers College Press, 1953

23. Marram G, Barrett B, Bevis E: Primary Nursing: A Model for Individualized Care, 2nd ed. St. Louise, C. V. Mosby, 1979

24. Manthey M: Primary nursing. Nurs Forum 9:64–83, 1970

25. Maxwell AC: The Field Hospital at Chickamanga Park, Sixth Annual Report, 1899, p. 78

26. National League of Nursing Education: Proceedings of the Twenty-Fourth Annual Convention. New York, National League of Nursing Education, 1918, p. 162

27. Nightingale F: Notes on Nursing (reprint). New York, Dover, 1969, p. 138

28. Nutting MA, Dock L: A History of Nursing—The Evolution of Nursing Systems from the Earliest Times to the Foundation of the

First English and American Training Schools for Nurses, 2 vols. New York, G. P. Putnam's Sons, 1935, pp. 29, 32, 62–82

29. Palmer IS: Florence Nightingale: Reformer, reactionary, researcher. Nurs Res 26:84–89, 1977

30. Paul G: Nursing in Acute Infectious Fever. Philadelphia, W. B. Saunders, 1923

31. The Prescriber's Memoranda. New York, Wood & Co., 1881

32. Pyle E: Here is Your War: The Story of GI Joe. Cleveland, World Publishing, 1944, pp. 82–83

33. Richards L: Reminiscences of Linda Richards: America's First Trained Nurse. Boston, Whitcomb and Barrows, 1915

34. Roosevelt JW: In Sickness and in Health. New York, Appleton, 1896

35. Shields EA: History of the United States Army Nurse Corps (Female): 1901–1937, Doctoral dissertation, Teachers College, Columbia University, 1980

36. Stimson J: Changing Standards of Nursing. Speech given at Medical Night, Women's City Club December 11, 1929

37. Stimson J: Personal communication, September 20, 1919, The U.S. Army Historical Unit (on loan to NY Hospital Medical Library Archives)

38. Surgeon General of the US: Report of the Surgeon General, 1919, The United States Army Historical Unit

39. Thompson D: Administrative History of the Army Nurse Corps During the War Period, unpublished manuscript

40. Wagner D: The proletarianization of nursing in the United States, 1932–1946. Int J Health Serv 10:271–290, 1980

41. Wainwright J: General Wainwright's Story: The Account of Four Years of Humiliating Defeat, Surrender and Captivity. Garden City, New York, Doubleday, 1946, p. 81

42. Wald LD: House on Henry Street. New York, Holt, 1915

43. Wald LD: The treatment of families in which there is sickness. Am J Nurs, March, 1904

44. Lillian Wald Collection, Special Collections, Butler Library, Columbia University, New York, New York

45. Weeks CS: A Textbook of Nursing. New York, Appleton, 1885, pp. 13, 202

46. Wilson J: Fever Nursing. Philadelphia, J. B. Lippincott, 1899

47. Zander KS: Primary Nursing Development and Management. Germantown, Maryland, Aspen Systems, 1980, p. 21

2

Nursing Education in America— Diversity in Evolution

The Nineteenth Century and Care of the Sick

Nursing was developed by mankind to alleviate human suffering. However, if we look at how nursing was practiced in the nineteenth century, it actually heightened human suffering rather than alleviated it. The untrained nurse working in hospitals and homes, while unfit to care for patients, was the sole provider of care.

Economic and Social Background of American Nursing

In the late nineteenth century the United States was in the midst of the Industrial Revolution. Families toiled twelve to sixteen hours a day in poorly lit, unventilated factories. Young children frequently feel asleep at machinery and were maimed or killed. Labor was cheap and plentiful and safety laws were not considered necessary.

The population in cities surged with people seeking a better life. Many were newly arrived immigrants from Europe, while others were lured from farms in the surrounding rural areas. Cities seemed to grow daily and housing was poorly constructed and overcrowded. Paved streets and sidewalks did not exist. Mud was mixed with garbage, which was thrown into the streets daily. Epidemics of typhus, cholera, diphtheria, and tuberculosis regularly ravaged the population. There were no sanitary laws governing housing, hygiene, or food. The illness and death rates in cities were very high, especially for preschool children. In some slum areas two of three children died before reaching the age of five.

The Role of Women in the Nineteenth Century

Women's roles in society in the nineteenth century were very restrictive. They did not have any legal rights as individuals. They were classified as a possession of their husbands and were in the same category as chattel. Women were educated for two roles, that of wife and mother. It was, therefore, very difficult for a refined woman to earn a living. Some were employed as private governesses, private tutors, or teachers; others with special talent and extraordinary hard work became dressmakers or milliners (21).

Nursing was not deemed an acceptable employment for well-bred ladies. Hospitals were not considered appropriate places for refined women to visit and nurses were viewed as menial servants.

Nursing Care in the Mid-Nineteenth Century

Within the family, women provided the nursing care to ill members. Many brides learned home remedies from relatives and friends. A popular book that was purchased or received by many brides was the *Documtur Housewife: The Fruit of Experiences Freshly Gathered from Elderly Lips, and Preserved in Print.* This guide listed many useful recipes as well as a section on first aid and care of the sick (12).

If a family member was ill for several days or weeks, a night-watcher was hired to observe the patient during the night. Sometimes a relative or friend or elderly widow who knew the family would assume this responsibility. While such persons were unskilled, they could report new or changed symptoms. Other times a nurse would be hired to care for the unfortunate patient. Hired nurses generally did not receive any training prior to 1873. Nursing was in the same class as servants or maids, and it was considered drudgery, not a humanitarian calling. No rules governed inspection or discipline of nurses or nursing care, and registration and licensure would not be implemented until the next century. Anyone who worked in a hospital or a home caring for ill people was called a nurse.

Often nurses were women who were unemployed at anything else, such as inmates arrested for drunkeness, immorality, or vagrancy. These women spent two days in a workhouse and were paroled as soon as possible if they chose to do nursing in hospital wards. They received no training in even the basic skills of nursing or hygiene or nutrition. Few could read or write, so physician's orders and nursing reports were nonexistent. These nurses were unpaid, unsupervised, and undisciplined. Their lack of knowledge and commitment often led to unnecessary suffering and death of hospital patients.

Many of the hired nurses of this era were from the criminal class or were alcoholics, and they exploited and abused clients. Isabel M. Stewart and Anne L. Austin, in *A History of Nursing*, describe them as follows: "They slept on straw beds laid on bathroom floors, terrorized the helpless sick, took fees and were not to be trusted with medicines nor with food brought in by visitors" (43).

These women did not possess a spirit of self-sacrifice or caring for the people they treated. Some accepted bribes to hasten death, and they would promptly remove the bed clothes and linen and allow their clients to suffer from the elements.

Occasionally, interested physicians would provide minimal instruction at the bedside or lectures to nurses. However, these training sessions basically included medical information. The nursing care component was seen as following doctor's orders. Since nurses were classed within a servants role and were neither respected nor deemed competent, the highest praise of a nurse was that she did not harm the patient.

The lack of education of these hired nurses not only did not enable them to provide safe nursing care, but in times of epidemics, they actually hindered the recovery of clients. In the spring of 1833, Philadelphia was experiencing a severe cholera epidemic, and the nurses hired by Philadelphia General Hospital were of little use—some lay in drunken stupors on the dead victims while others fought over care of the sickest patients. The Hospital finally appealed to the Sisters of Charity to restore order and care for the sick (8).

The typical hired nurse who worked in the home was accurately portrayed by Charles Dickens in his novel *Martin Chuzzelwit* (1844) in the personage of Mrs. Sairy Gamp—an unsympathetic, incompetent woman who contributed to human suffering. She was uncouth, always tipsy, dirty, unkempt, and dishonest (11).

Nursing Education in the Religious Orders

Several religious orders undertook nursing care responsibilities or were closely allied with nursing. These orders recruited refined intelligent women who were sincerely interested in the care of the ill These sisters and deaconesses provided humanitarian care in hospitals, mental asylums, orphanages, workhouses, and homes.

Both the Sisters of Charity and the Sisters of Mercy were dedicated to the humanitarian calling of nursing the sick and poor. The Sisters of Charity, founded in 1633 by St. Vincent de Paul, began their work in the United States in 1809 under the direction of Elizabeth Bayley Seton. (Mrs. Seton was later canonized for her charitable works. She was the first native born American to receive Sainthood). The Sisters of Mercy were founded in Ireland in 1827 by Catherine McAuley. The first American convent was established in Pittsburgh in 1843 by seven sisters from Carlow, Ireland.

Traditionally, the Sisters of Charity received a systematic program of nursing training that included experience in the hospitals and in the home. In general, the care the sisters provided was far superior to any other nursing available. These nurses were motivated by their desire to help those in distress and devoted themselves to their tasks. They toiled to provide clean, orderly, emphatic nursing care (12).

Medical Education in the Nineteenth Century

Medical education in the 1800s was very rudimentary. Attendance at lectures was not required and at times could even be dangerous. Classes were usually very disorderly, with fist fights frequently escalating into a general melee. Furniture was destroyed and the unfortunate physician who happened to be lecturing quickly fled the hall. It was a common saying during this time that a boy who was not fit for anything else should become a doctor (21).

In fact, the majority of practicing physicians did not graduate from medical schools; rather, they learned their trade through the preceptor-apprentice system. Under this system a man was an assistant to a practicing physician for as long as three years. In addition to his medical chores the apprentice was also expected to help with farm and home chores. The total cost of his tuition to his preceptor was about $100 (12).

This was a large sum of money when we note that the salary of an average worker was $2.00 a day. Some of the typical costs of medical services in the mid-nineteenth century were as follows (37):

Office prescription	$0.25–$1.00
Consultation visit	$1.00–$3.00 (plus mileage)
Natural delivery	$4.00–$5.00
Surgery for fractures	$5.00–$25.00

The apprenticeship program was strongly supported by practicing physicians as it was very lucrative for them. Conversely, they did not support formalizing medical education via medical schools. The general quality of medical care was low, with an abundance of quacks.

The Nightingale System and Development of Hospital Schools in America

One strategy to improve the care of the sick in hospitals and homes was to establish a system of training nurses to provide competent nursing care. Interest in nursing education arose from a variety of sources and led to the opening of the first nursing school based on the Florence Nightingale model in 1873. In the transplantation of Nightingale's ideas, however, many significant aspects were changed. Unfortunately, these alterations led to an ensuing struggle for control of nursing education between hospital administrators and nursing educators.

Influence of Pioneering Woman Physicians

Early interest in the training of nurses was expressed by pioneering women physicians. This dynamic group of talented women strove to implement important changes in health care. Motivated by the lack of acceptance of their male peers and the poor quality of medical care for women and children, they succeeded in establishing a new type of hospital. Three such hospitals were founded between 1857 and 1862, and all included training schools for nursing in the initial planning.

The New York Infirmary for Women and Children was founded in 1857 by Dr. Elizabeth Blackwell (the first American female physician to graduate from a medical school in the United States), her sister, Dr. Emily Blackwell, and Dr. Marie Zakrzewska. The Infirmary was the first institution in the world established primarily for the care of women and children. It was staffed by female physicians and provided care in the hospital, dispensary (clinic), and the home. The nursing program, however, was not a complete success. It was a difficult four-month program in which students were provided with room and board and received weekly lessons from Dr. Zakrzewska (21).

Four years after the successful establishment of the New York Infirmary for Women and Children, the Women's Hospital of Philadelphia was founded. It was an adjunct of Women's Medical College of Pennsylvania. Dr. Ann Preston, a graduate of Women's Medical College, was a leading force in the opening of the hospital. In 1862, a six-month nursing program was initiated, and eventually all nurses who were hired for the hospital were trained in the school. Although the school did not award diplomas, graduates were recognized as being trained nurses. The first known graduate was Harriet Newton Phillips in 1869 (21).

Dr. Marie Zakrzewska (known as Dr. Zak to her colleagues), after working at both the New York Infirmary and the New England Female Medical College in Boston, succeeded in opening the New England Hospital for Women and Children on July 1, 1862. The nurse training program that began in 1872 has been considered the first general training school for nurses in America. Although it was actually the third program, it provided a longer, more organized program and was loosely based on the ideas of Florence Nightingale. While studying in Europe, Dr. Susan Dimock, one of the administrators of the nursing program, had visited the Kaiserswerth school and Florence Nightingale.

The training program was one year in length with twelve lectures given by five of the female physicians. Students worked from 5:30 a.m. to 9:00 p.m., with one free afternoon from 2:00 p.m. to 5:00 p.m. every second week. Melinda Ann (Linda) Richards was the first graduate of this program on October 1, 1873. She has the distinction of being the first nurse to graduate from a training school in the United States. Miss Richards was instrumental in the organization and administration of several training schools in the United States. Another notable graduate from New England Hospital for Women and Children in 1879 was Mary Eliza Mahoney. Ms. Mahoney was the first black nurse to graduate from a school of nursing. She also had a very distinguished career in many aspects of nursing (21).

Influence of the Civil War on Nursing Education

A substantial number of women who served as nurses in the Civil War were from socially prominent families. After the war, many wrote of their hospital experiences, and some, such as author Louisa May Alcott (1832–1888), published them. They increased public awareness of the need to develop training programs for nurses. Their support also provided a measure of respectability to the nursing role.

Other voices of support for nursing schools were added to the chorus of women who served in the Civil War. In 1869 Dr. Samuel D. Gross reported to the American Medical Association on the Committee on the Training of Nurses. He advocated the establishment of training schools in all hospitals. However, he believed that physicians and county medical societies should be responsible for these schools (12).

Another prominent Boston physician, Dr. Horatio Storer, wrote a pamphlet in 1868 entitled *Nurses and Nursing.* He also urged the development of schools to train nurses. He believed these schools should be an integral part of large hospitals and under the control of medical personnel (21).

Most of the support from the medical profession was dependent on physicians' controlling nursing education. A major reason was that physicians believed the dual purpose of the schools was to prepare competent assistants for physicians and to provide nursing services to the hospital. They viewed the nursing role merely as an extension of themselves. They viewed the nurse in a dependent role, making no independent tasks or judgments.

The Nightingale Model of Nursing Education

While the medical profession was busily placing the nursing role in a passive and subservient position, Florence Nightingale was carving a unique independent role for nursing. Miss Nightingale believed that "No man, not even a doctor, ever gives any other definition of what a nurse should be than this—devoted and obedient. This definition would do just as well for a porter. It might even do for a horse. It will not do for a nurse" (2).

Florence Nightingale is considered the founder of modern nursing. She symbolized a new era in health care, emerging from the Crimean War as a heroine to the English people. Through Miss Nightingale's unique talents for organization and administration, knowledge of health and nursing care, and determination to change the terrible conditions of the wounded soldiers at Scutari, she managed to reduce the death rate of the English soldiers from 42 percent to 2 percent in two months. She proved that competently trained nurses were the key to better health care (12).

Her vibrant interest in promoting a higher quality of health care by developing training schools for nurses was strongly supported in Great Britian. As a tribute to Miss Nightingale, a sum of £50,000 (approximately $220,000) was raised for the Nightingale Fund Training School for Nurses (21). Miss Nightingale established the school at St. Thomas Hospital in London in 1860. All of her expertise in the areas of nursing, nursing education, nursing administration, and health care were incorporated into this school. It became the model for all other schools worldwide. Miss Nightingale applied her learning experiences in nursing training at Kaiserswerth, Germany with Pastor and Frau Fliedner, her outstanding military nursing experience at Scutari in the Crimean War, her research in health care administration, nursing, and nursing care, and her own genius in creating a new role for nurses.

One of the hallmarks of the Nightingale School of Nursing was complete autonomy from the hospital: financial, organizational, and physical. The generous gift of £50,000 guaranteed a stable financial base and the opportunity to build a training school, hire competent faculty, design a pertinent curriculum, purchase equipment, and carefully select the students. She believed it was essential for nurses to teach and control nursing.

Hospital administrators and physicians did not agree with the Nightingale view of the nurse. They considered nurses akin to housemaids and believed that training in cleanliness and attention to personal needs were the primary roles of the nurse. They had previously been in charge of training nurses and were reluctant to relinquish their control. In fact only 4 of the 100 physicians at St. Thomas Hospital were in favor of the training school (21).

The three basic aims of the Nightingale school were to train hospital nurses, to train nurses to train others, and to train district nurses (public health nurses) for the sick and poor. She believed that nursing had a separate body of knowledge and role function from medicine. She viewed the nurse as a colleague of the doctor—working with him, but having a distinct sphere of responsibility (12). "It is the surgeon who saves a person's life—it is the nurse who helps the person to live" (2).

Nightingale planned a curriculum that included required classroom lectures and clinical experience. She believed "a hospital alone was not to be a center for the education and practice of nursing," students would also visit homes, where emphasis was on health teaching.

Overall, the Nightingale plan viewed the student as a learner, not a worker. The student's education was not to be compromised by overwork, inadequate theory, and clinical experiences or responsibilities of non-nursing experiences such as scrubbing or cleaning (12). "A nurse should do nothing but nurse. If you want a char woman (servant) hire one. Nursing is a specialty" (2).

Finally, Nightingale did not believe in graduation or registration; she was a strong advocate of continuing education. Thus, students who finished the year long course at St. Thomas Hospital did not receive diplomas; however, their names were recorded in a special book to validate their training.

Nightingale's schools prospered. She was always a busy writer and her books *Notes on Hospitals* (1859), *Notes on Nursing* (1860), and two books on community health nursing (1865) were widely read in Europe and the United States. Her ideas were a stimulus to the growing movement in America to develop training schools for nurses.

American Schools Based on the Nightingale Model

The late nineteenth century was witness to several social reforms in prisons, hospitals for the mentally ill, and health care. Following the Civil War, urbanization increased the demand for nurses. Many socially prominent and influential women who had served as nurses in the War were organizing support for training schools for nurses.

They were influenced by the writing of Florence Nightingale and planned their schools on the one at St. Thomas Hospital. An indication of the growing popularity of this cause was an editorial in 1871 in a popular lady's magazine, *Godey's Lady Book*. The editorial entitled "Lady Nurses" supported the need for upgrading nursing education so that it would be a profession that could attract women of refinement. These women would provide competent nursing care and be readily accepted as peers by all households (17).

Bellevue Hospital Training School

Louisa Lee Schyler was a New York City socialite who organized a group of prominent ladies into the State Charities Aid of New York. They visited various charitable institutions, such as hospitals and asylums, and discovered many areas that were in serious need of reform. She was shocked by the conditions she discovered in Bellevue Hospital in Manhattan. Most patients lay on the floor without linens or blankets or with soiled linens from deceased patients; others shared beds. The death rate was appalling: 15 of every 100 patients died in the hospital (12).

Miss Schyler was determined to establish a school of nursing to alleviate some of the human suffering she had witnessed. Although the plan was opposed by the medical staff, hospital administration, and politicians, Miss Schyler managed to raise more than $23,000 for the school in private donations (21).

The school had very strict admission requirements because they wished to attract refined ladies. On May 24, 1873 the school opened with twenty-nine pupils. It quickly prospered and gained more support from physicians. One physician noted that the school was so effective that Bellevue was soon able to replace all of the old nurses with trained nurses. As the old nurses left they hurled coarse language at hospital authorities and stones at the new nurses (21).

The course at Bellevue was two years in length, including one year of service. Lectures were given irregularly by the nursing superintendent in charge of the school and by various physicians. In 1874

Linda Richards became the night superintendent and initiated the practice of record keeping by students. Students were paid a stipend of $10 per month for the first year, with a slight raise the second year. The difference in stipend recognized the increased clinical service pupils provided. It also highlighted the confusion in the basic aim of the school: nursing education or service to the hospital. The lack of a stable financial base was a major disadvantage that compromised control of the school of nursing.

Connecticut Training School

The second training school to open in the United States was founded by Georgeanna Woolsey Bacon, who was strongly supported by her husband, Dr. Francis Bacon, and a wealthy philanthropist, Charles Thompson. Mrs. Bacon and her two sisters had served as nurses in the Civil War, and all three siblings subsequently became active in nursing: Abby published one of the first books on the subject in 1876, *A Century of Nursing with Hints Toward the Organization of a Training School*; and Jane helped reorganize the nursing staff as director of Presbyterian Hospital in New York (21).

The Connecticut Training School in New Haven opened in October 1873 with four pupils. The school was established as a separate organization with a board of directors. They contracted with the hospital to provide nursing in exchange for educational services. Therefore, there were at least two important changes from the Nightingale model: the emphasis was on nursing service rather than nursing education and the training was not controlled by nursing. In addition, part of the budget of the training school was obtained through fees paid by families who employed students as private duty nurses in their homes. It is notable that a group of nurses and physicians published one of the first nursing textbooks in 1877. The school remained an independent body until 1906, when control was assumed by the hospital.

Boston Training School

This school was initially supported by funds from voluntary contributors. The school directors were able to maintain control until 1896, when, as a result of financial problems, the school came under control of the Massachusetts General Hospital. Linda Richards served as an early superintendent, and she reorganized the program to improve the educational component.

Comparison of American Training Schools with the Nightingale Model

The number of training schools for nurses grew rapidly from 4 in 1873 to over 400 by the turn of the century. The rapid growth was a result of the realization by hospitals that training schools were the most economic means of supplying nursing staff in the hospital and homes. While the initial programs were based on the Nightingale model, there were significant differences and weaknesses that altered the history of nursing education. The primary weakness was the lack of autonomy caused by an unstable financial base. This caused schools to "sell" students' services to hospitals and private homes in an effort to provide a steady income. It also gradually eroded the control that schools had over various aspects of the training program. For example, if schools could not afford to hire faculty, the hospital provided educational services, usually irregularly scheduled lectures by physicians.

As the hospital assumed more control of the training school, the quality of education declined. Students became primarily workers not learners. They worked mainly with sick patients and on wards as the hospital needed them, regardless of their classroom theory or schedule. Their experiences were restrictive, uncoordinated, and inferior in many respects to their European counterparts using the Nightingale model.

By the 1890s pupils were working an average of 70 hours a week. About two percent of their time was spent in the classroom and ninty-eight percent in clinical practice. Lectures were usually in the evening, and students were required to make up any clinical time lost by attending lectures (21).

Early Training Schools for Black Nurses

Four prominent training schools for black nurses were founded between 1886 and 1891. They experienced difficulties similar to the early white schools, including a patchwork curricula that developed over the years and an inadequate financial base, which was partially supported by fees from students' services in private homes. These schools also suffered from the additional prejudice toward blacks at the time. It had been a crime for blacks to learn to read and write during the era of slavery. As blacks became more educated, they faced the additional burden of exclusion from many training schools. The rejection was based on state law, local law, training school regulations, or covert discrimination. Separate schools for blacks were necessary to provide adequate training for black nurses (40).

Spelman Nurse Training School

This school was housed in a female school, Spelman Seminary in Atlanta, Georgia, and opened in March of 1886. Nursing was taught as a postgraduate course or in addition to other studies. Two types of programs were offered: a two-year "professional" course and a shorter "nonprofessional" course. The latter provided instruction to care for the sick in their own homes. The program followed an academic year and was taught by Dr. Sophia B. Jones, a black Canadian surgeon educated in the United States. The program at Spelman was gradually lengthed, and by the turn of the century, it was a four-year academic course. Public examinations were a tradition at Spelman, and nursing students participated in the areas of theory and clinical application (40).

Provident Hospital and Hampton Institute

Provident Hospital was founded in 1891 in Chicago and followed a curriculum similar to other schools in the 1890s. Hampton Training School for nurses, also founded in 1891, was originally known as Dixie Hospital but was later incorporated into Hampton Institute. The education model was not Nightingale's plan; rather, it provided community emphasis. The hospital was interracial and succeeded in providing competent care to all patients (40).

Tuskegee Institute

Influenced by the establishment of the training school at Provident Hospital, this school opened in 1892 in Tuskagee, Alabama. Of the four black schools described, only Tuskagee was developed primarily to provide service, not education. It is now the oldest existing school of nursing for blacks in the United States (40).

Entrenchment and Expansion of Diploma Schools

From 1873 to 1933 the U.S. population doubled and the number of hospitals increased forty-two times, from 149 in 1873 to about 6334 in 1933. This remarkable increase was due to (1) major scientific and technological advances that helped preserve life, (2) an expansion of supportive services, and (3) a growing confidence in hospital care (21).

As health care became more complex, it also became more expensive. Hospital administrators soon discovered that nursing schools were a cheap source of labor, and most hospitals—whether large or small, urban or rural, specialized (for example, children, tuberculosis) or generalized, well-endowed, or with a small budget—desired a training school. From 1873 to 1893 the number of training schools increased from four to thirty-four, and by 1902 there were 492 training schools with more than 11,000 students (21). This rapid growth occurred with minimal legal or professional controls. Many schools lacked essential elements of curriculum: education consisted, as before, of haphazardly scheduled medical lectures by physicians in which the nursing role was not discussed and theory and clinical practice were not coordinated. The major emphasis was on technical proficiency and the number of clinical hours worked.

Many schools had no nursing faculty and many used students to completely staff the hospital. By 1900, student nurses were working, in addition to female wards, the male wards, childrens' wards, operating rooms, dispensaries (clinics), diet kitchens, laundry, and central supply (sterilizing and wrapping instruments). They worked an average of ten to twelve hours a day, six and one-half days a week. The school year lasted approximately eleven months, with two to four weeks vacation a year, and all time lost due to illness had to be made up before graduation. The students had no say: if they complained or refused to accept additional responsibilities they were threatened with dismissal. Thus, students endured much abuse to earn their diplomas.

The initial founders of the training schools often expressed concern for the students' health and education, but there was little they could do. The decision-making power was in the hands of the people providing the financial support—the hospital. In fact, by 1900 most of the schools had become an integral part of the hospital. Control of nursing had slipped away from nursing and been passed to hospital administrators and medical staff.

This subversion of nursing education would become nursing's Achilles heel for the next century. As training schools continued to proliferate, the need for wresting control of nursing education away from hospitals became a rallying cry for nurse educators. Many began to discuss the unimaginable: nurses controlling nursing. How? A new route to nursing education through colleges and universities was a cry in the wind in the early twentieth century, but it grew stronger as the exploitation of student nurses continued.

The zenith in the growth of hospital schools of nursing occurred in the late 1920s, the number reaching almost 2300. This phenomenal growth, however, was halted by the Great Depression. Many hospitals went bankrupt and closed their doors. Hospital schools of nursing, therefore, closed too. Many of the smaller and weaker schools vanished, and by 1936 there were 1472 state-accredited schools.

The 1930s curriculum was somewhat strengthened in that the number of hours of service had been decreased and the number of hours of theory had been increased, but it was still very narrow in scope. Courses still focused on technical dexterity and ignored liberal education.

Baccalaureate Programs in Colleges and Universities

When the United States entered World War I in 1917, schools of nursing were asked to increase their enrollments. In an effort to attract college educated women for leadership roles in nursing, schools were also requested to accelerate their programs to accommodate these women. Many school administrators were reluctant to cooperate, so a special program was developed to facilitate their learning. The highly successful Vassar Training Camp program provided these nurses with an intensive three-month course at Vassar and then entrance into the nursing program of their choice for the remaining time.

The inadequacies of hospital schools were recognized more publicly at this time and an investigation of nursing education was encouraged. In response to this pressure and other concerns, two landmark studies were conducted during the 1920s: The Goldmark Report (1923) and the Committee on the Grading of Nursing Schools series (1928 and 1934) (See Chapter 6).

Both landmark studies spotlighted lack of a stable financial base as a primary cause of the problem. And both recommended placing nursing education in higher education. Isabel Hampton, first superintendent of the Johns Hopkins Training School for Nurses, deplored the proliferation of schools and poor quality of education. She supported state-funded schools of nursing. Adelaide Nutting, a protege of Isabel Hampton who became the first nursing professor in America at Teachers College, Columbia University in New York City, also advocated public funding for nursing education. In her 1926 book, *A Sound Economic Basis for Schools of Nursing*, she urged government support to nursing should be similar to that given to teacher education. She compared the development of state-supported schools with the Normal Schools for teachers (42).

While some nursing leaders favored wresting control of nursing education from hospitals and placing it in colleges and universities, the majority of nurses did not support it. Why? One reason could be the expense of college education. Another reason could be that their clinical training background limited their knowledge of the appropriate level of professional education.

Strong opposition to collegiate schools of nursing was also generated by physicians and hospitals. Physicians maintained that nurses were already overtrained. They argued that hiring college-educated nurses would be too costly and further that women with brief training in bedside procedures would be as satisfactory as present nurses. Many hospital schools of nursing supported the present narrow scope of nursing education as necessary. They believed that nursing theory and intelligence were unnecessary: a dull nurse was more effective than a bright one. Unfortunately, these latter groups are able to publicize their ideas more readily than nursing leaders supporting higher education for nurses (21).

Early Nursing Programs in Colleges and Universities

Despite the general opposition to collegiate nursing education, there were some dynamic, visionary people who established early programs.

University of Minnesota

This program was established by Dr. Richard Olding Beard in 1909. It was the first undergraduate nursing program that was organized as an integral part of a university. The standards for admission were the same as for other academic programs. The three-year program was under the college of medicine and offered a diploma. Although degrees were not granted to graduates for several years, it was a major advancement in nursing education. Other courses, which were offered to students in other colleges, were outside of the academic system. They were merely courses offered by nurses. There were no standards for admission or faculty appointments.

Teachers College, Columbia University

This pioneering school has been affectionately called the "mother house" of collegiate education in nursing. It nurtured the beginning stirrings of higher education nursing programs for undergraduate and graduate degrees. The program was founded by a group of nurses led by Isabel Hampton Robb. The dean of the school, James E. Russell, was supportive of their cause. The initial programs were to provide additional education to diploma school nurses. The first program was established in 1899 as an eight-month course in hospital economics. Eventually, Teachers College pioneered in masters and doctoral education for nurses.

In 1907 Adelaide Nutting left Johns Hopkins for Teachers College and became the first nursing professor, in the world. In 1910, through a generous endowment, the Department of Nursing and Health was created. Programs were established for nurses in the areas of teaching, administration, supervision, and public health nursing. Teachers College was a pioneer in education for nurses.

Yale University School of Nursing

This program is considered the first autonomous collegiate school of nursing in the United States. It was founded in 1923 through a five-year grant from the Rockefeller Foundation. Annie W. Goodrich, former director of the Army School of Nursing, was the first dean. The Rockefeller grant encouraged Miss Goodrich to create a truly professional nursing program. Some of the new aspects of the curriculum were the coordination and consolidation of classroom theory and clinical experience, emphasis on health prevention, the elimination of non-nursing tasks (scrubbing, dusting), and the inclusion of public health and community nursing. In recognition of its success, the Rockefeller Foundation endowed the program for $1,000,000 in 1929.

By the mid 1930s the emphasis of the program had changed. The Yale School of Nursing now admitted people with baccalaureate degrees only. The program was 30 months and granted a masters in nursing degree. At that time Yale's enrollment was about 500 women and almost 5000 men (21).

Other Early Collegiate Schools

Western Reserve University established a School of Nursing in 1923 through an endowment by Frances Payne Bolton, a philanthropist and strong supporter of nursing. It offered a B.S. degree. Vanderbilt University School of Nursing was founded in 1930 with generous endowments from the Rockefeller Foundation, Carnegie Foundation, and Commonwealth Fund.

A small number of students attended collegiate schools and the standards of nursing education were not raised significantly during this early period.

Development of Postgraduate Education in Nursing

Several programs had been established in colleges and universities by the late 1930s. The largest and highest quality offerings were degree courses in public health nursing. Many nurses agreed that practice in public health required advanced learning beyond the diploma school. The narrow approach to nursing, focusing on the care of the acutely ill hospitalized client (a deviation from the Nightingale model), did not prepare students to work with the chronically ill and provide health teaching in the community.

In general, diploma education did not lay a foundation for advanced learning. The standards for admission were usually lower than most colleges and universities, and it was outside the mainstream of professional education. As a result, "advanced" education in nursing or postgraduate education developed in a very haphazard manner. Postgraduate education was composed of a variety of programs—nondegree (specified number of courses) and specialized baccalaureate programs to prepare nurses to teach in diploma schools, to be administrators of hospitals or practice a clinical specialty in hospitals, or to be public health nurses in the community.

Some masters programs were also developed. The names of the degrees varied, and with the exception of the public health programs, most of the specialized baccalaureate programs did not have any nursing courses. Students did not receive advanced knowledge in nursing, only the functional speciality (teaching, administration). The clinical specialty programs encouraged a more technically expert nurse rather than practice at a higher level.

While these programs were taught on college and university campuses, they were not actually an integral part of the academic setting. Students in non-degree programs were not admitted to the college, and the nurses teaching these courses did not qualify for a faculty position. The program did not qualify for credits toward a degree.

In the specialty baccalaureate programs, there were many inconsistencies in admission criteria, number of credits for a degree, and graduation requirements. The courses in general were on a nonprofessional level and again did not lay a foundation for higher degrees.

Nursing education seemed to be in a muddle. A solution that had been advocated by visionary nursing leaders to establish a baccalau-

reate degree as the basic education for nurses. The generic baccalaureate program was defined as a four-year program combining liberal
arts and professional nursing content and leading to a baccalaureate
degree in nursing. It would also lay a strong foundation for advanced
education on the masters level. Future nursing students would be
viewed as learners, not workers. They would not have to provide
service for their education. This goal seemed very far away in the
1930s and 1940s. However, as World War I had publicized the inadequacies of nursing education and sparked the investigation of nursing education so would World War II. This time, however, the spark
would not be extinguished. It would burn brightly and light the way
for nursing.

World War II and its Effect on Nursing Education

With the surprise bombing of Pearl Harbor by the Japanese on December 7, 1941, the American industries and training of personnel
were immediately accelerated to meet national emergency. Nursing
became a vital part of this effort. In 1942 there were 42,000 nurses in
practice. The United States government requested an additional
125,000 nurses within the next two years (65,000 the first twelve
months and 60,000 the second year) (4).

Frances Payne Bolton, Congresswoman from Ohio, philanthropist, and a long time supporter of nursing, introduced the Bolton Act
into Congress, creating the Cadet Nurse Corps. This bill subsidized
nursing education by providing funds for student nurses to cover
tuition, fees, books, uniforms, and stipends. More than $176 million
was eventually allocated by the government for the Cadet Nurse
Corps (23). Lucile Leone Petry, a former dean of Cornell University,
New York Hospital in New York City, and a staff member of the
U.S. Public Health Service, became the director of the program.

Women who volunteered for the Cadet Nurse Crops spent the
first nine months in a college or university learning the basic sciences and fundamentals of nursing. The next fifteen to twenty-one
months were spent in a nursing school. Since boards of nursing required 36 months of training, the nurse cadets worked in civilian or
military hospitals for six months to qualify for licensure exams.
Many were then sent overseas to care for American wounded soldiers, while others remained in civilian hospitals. The Cadet Nurse
Corps was an outstanding success and all quotas were exceeded (21).

The national nursing associations quickly organized into the National Nursing Council for War Service. This Council helped coordinate nursing resources; recruitment and education were two of their primary responsibilities. All schools of nursing were asked to evaluate their curriculum in an effort to accelerate nursing education from 36 months to 30 months.

The evaluation process revealed the many deficiencies in the hospital programs. These findings motivated nurses to renew efforts to improve nursing education after the war.

Post World War II: Changes in Nursing Education

In 1944 Congress passed a benefit package, the G.I. Bill of Rights, for all veterans of World War II. This bill included educational funds for veterans who chose to advance their education. More than 2.5 million veterans including nurses used their G.I. benefits to finance their college education (9).

Nursing education was part of this rush to college. More than fifty percent of nurses returning home from military service planned to seek additional education in a clinical specialty, teaching, administration, or public health nursing.

Nurses were very confused about the quality of the programs and the appropriate program to enter. The National League of Nursing Education (NLNE) published a list of postgraduate courses to provide a guide to evaluate them. It was not an evaluation of the programs, only a listing.

Nursing leaders were also very concerned about the status of nursing education. One of the last acts of the National Nursing Council for War Service before it disbanded was to authorize three studies of nursing. One of these studies involved an investigation of nursing education. The Carnegie Foundation sponsored the study, which was conducted by Esther Lucile Brown, a noted researcher and educator. The study explored the organization, administration, control, and financing of nursing education to meet the needs of hospitals and communities (see Chapter 6).

The Brown Report entitled *Nursing for the Future*, was published in 1948 (6). The twenty-eight recommendations included both diploma and postgraduate education and also mirrored some of the conclusions of the landmark studies of the 1920s.

Recommendations included bringing basic nursing education into colleges and universities, upgrading postgraduate programs to the level of other college programs, including psychiatric preparation in all basic nursing programs, public financing of nursing education, and instituting a system of accreditation of schools.

The response to the recommendations of the Brown Report was overwhelming. In support of including psychiatric nursing preparation for all nurses, increased monies from the National Mental Health Act of 1946 were allocated to nursing education by Congress.

Another priority was the establishment of a system of nursing accreditation. The National Nurse Accrediting Service was established and published its first list of accredited schools in 1949. The list highlighted two main concerns: poor showing of the diploma schools and the confusion of placing all postgraduate programs in the same category. Nondegree, baccalaureate and masters programs were not differentiated (7).

The promotion of a generic baccalaureate nursing program was gaining support, but it still encountered many obstacles. One was the lack of federal funding to establish programs and the other difficulty was the number of postgraduate programs, including baccalaureate programs, that awarded specialized nursing degrees in nursing education, nursing administration, and other areas.

The problem of specialized baccalaureate education was finally settled when nursing accreditation criteria were changed by the N.L.N. to include only generic baccalaureate programs that integrated public health nursing. Specialized baccalaureate programs had five years to amend their curricula, from 1959 to 1963. While this accreditation change endorsed the generic program, such programs did not grow in number until 1964, when a comprehensive federal aid program was passed by Congress.

The acceptance of basic nursing education at the baccalaureate level was, however, only a beginning. Another major task had to be completed: the identification of the professional nursing content at the baccalaureate level. The early programs did not teach nursing within the college. Some combined two years of liberal arts courses with three years of diploma school education for a baccalaureate degree in nursing. Others awarded sixty to ninety credits for diploma school education acquired before entering college and added two years of liberal arts for a baccalaureate degree in nursing.

The identification of nursing content was a joint effort of the National League for Nursing's Subcommittee on Baccalaureate Education and Research funded by the 1964 Nurse Training Act. As nursing content was identified and sequenced, challenge exams were instituted for diploma school graduates who wished to enter baccalaureate programs and receive credit by examination. In the 1970s, special educational tracks were developed to accommodate the RN (diploma school and later associate degree program) [A.D.N.] graduates in the baccalaureate track.

These tracks followed a variety of patterns, but they all had the same aim: to recognize the strengths of the RN by evaluating previous learning through proficiency or challenge exams, to help socialize the RN (as an adult learner) into a collegiate setting, and to provide counseling as to the proper sequencing of courses (18). During the mid and late 1970s, completion programs for RNs were developed. These two-year programs were developed to meet the special needs of the working adult RN who wished to return to school. Classes were arranged during evening and weekend hours, with ample opportunities to challenge courses for college credit.

Another creative educational pattern which emerged during the 1970s was the establishment of external degree programs. These college degree programs, such as the Regents External Degree Program in New York, let students continue working as they earned college credits. Programs were basically designed to help the RN obtain an associate degree or baccalaureate degree in nursing.

The acceptance of college programs is indicated by the decline of diploma schools (21): in 1953 diploma schools constituted 82.2% of the number of nursing schools; in 1976 that percentage dropped to 28.4. In contrast, both baccalaureate and associate degree programs increased markedly, especially A.D.N. programs.

Support of Baccalaureate Education in Nursing by National Nursing Organizations

The number of years that elapsed between the Goldmark Report in 1923, the Brown Report in 1948, and the final acceptance of basic nursing education at the baccalaureate level indicates the depth and strength of the struggle. Also of significant importance is the lack of a clear statement supporting baccalaureate education from any modern national nursing organization until 1965.

An early statement supporting baccalaureate education for nursing was issued in the 1890s by the American Society of Superintendents of Training Schools (which later became the National League of Nursing Education). The support by the Society was instrumental in establishing the nursing program at Teachers College. The NLNE officially endorsed the generic baccalaureate program in 1948. In 1950, however, it was changed to a long-term goal, rather than a short-term one. It was further diluted in 1954 when the statement encouraged articulation among all levels of nursing education—diploma and collegiate (7).

The NLN explained that the 1950 statement had caused animosity among nurse educators (diploma and collegiate) and there was a danger of splintering and weakening nursing. Also, the American Hospital Association (AHA) and the American Medical Association (AMA) would consider withholding support from the NLN accrediting program if the 1950 statement were further promoted. At the time, the diploma schools constituted the majority of the membership, and a combined effort, therefore, by diploma schools, the AHA, and the AMA forced a major policy change (7).

There were two other unsuccessful attempts, in 1955 and 1965, by various members of the NLN to issue a statement of support for baccalaureate programs. In 1982 the executive board of the NLN published a mild endorsement of collegiate education. It still stirs up much controversy among the membership and the issue is still unresolved.

What about the American Nurses Association (ANA)? At the 1960 convention the issue was introduced, and it produced so much controversy that it could not even be introduced at the next convention in 1962. By 1965, however, the ANA officially endorsed generic baccalaureate education. An official statement was published in the September issue of *American Journal of Nursing*. This was followed in 1969 (revised in 1978) by a position paper on graduate education (7).

The failure to resolve the education issue has resulted in a schism in nursing education. Nurses are still prepared in both hospital and collegiate settings, but there has been a steady decline in the number of hospital settings and an increase in the number of associate and baccalaureate degree programs based in colleges and universities.

Graduate Education in Nursing

In the early development of graduate education in nursing (masters and doctoral programs), there was widespread disagreement about its purpose and scope. From 1939 through 1956 the question "What should be taught on the masters level?" could be answered by another question, "What should be taught on the baccalaureate level?"

Due to the variety of patterns in nursing education, both questions could be answered in numerous ways. Nursing had spawned two systems of basic education, diploma schools and generic, four-year baccalaureate programs. (Note: associate degree programs did not impact on masters education until the late 1960s.)

Diploma schools supported specialized baccalaureate education as an advanced level of learning. Collegiate programs, on the other hand, promoted a baccalaureate degree, which provided a general basis for the beginning practitioner. Masters programs were viewed as the level for specialization for teaching and administration.

In addition a wide variety of baccalaureate curricular patterns had developed that combined diploma school and two years of liberal arts courses in a college or university to lead to a baccalaureate degree. A popular model was the five-year program: two years of liberal arts in a college or university and then three years at a diploma school. The nursing education was the same as any student attending the hospital school of nursing, and the program led to a baccalaureate degree in nursing.

Another model granted sixty to ninety blanket college credits to students from a diploma school program before they entered college. Then, the college provided two years of liberal arts. In both of these patterns the nursing content and the liberal arts content are not integrated. Some of these latter programs led to a baccalaureate degree in nursing. If, however, the two years of liberal arts included teaching or administration courses, the program was often considered a specialized baccalaureate program and the college awarded a baccalaureate degree in nursing education or nursing administration (7).

The original aim of transferring nursing education into colleges and universities was to elevate the level of nursing content. In other words the college would control the education and integrate liberal arts content with professional nursing content. For example, studying psychology would help the nursing student understand human relationships. This information could be applied to her nursing role with clients as well as with her peers. The student was encouraged to grow in both her professional and personal life experiences. Unfortunately, the five-year model (three years diploma school and two years of liberal arts) predominated in the educational scene.

An extensive study in 1952 by Dr. Margaret Bridgman (a noted researcher in education and president of Skidmore College) and the NLN Accrediting Service revealed many weaknesses in collegiate programs. Essentially, many were not providing a baccalaureate level education and, thereby, not laying an adequate foundation for masters education (5).

The issue was finally settled in the late 1950s, when nursing accreditation standards were changed to include only diploma schools and generic baccalaureate programs that integrated public health nursing. This eliminated the practice of granting blanket credits for diploma school graduates. Accreditation rules later also specified that all the education must be controlled by the collegiate nursing faculty. Thereafter, the number of specialized baccalaureate programs and five-year programs declined.

Also, the interest in identifying the professional level of nursing content, i.e., building a body of knowledge, sparked an interest in research. It was soon realized that there were few trained nursing researchers. The masters program was viewed as the place for educating competent nurse researchers as well as for designing and implementing research projects.

Masters Education in Nursing

Origins: 1939–1952

The origins of masters education in nursing are very vague. Accurate information and statistics about these programs were not available until the mid-1950s. A major reason was that initially the accreditation procedures grouped all post-diploma programs under the category of postgraduate education.

Another factor is that the organization of masters programs varied. They had numerous titles, requirements, and credit systems. Also, students entered at various times throughout the year and remained for an indefinite time. Many courses and programs were listed as baccalaureate and masters levels simultaneously. The only difference was the degree for which the student was striving. In 1939–1940 approximately 3087 students were enrolled in post-diploma programs, and possibly, 73 of these student were in masters programs (1).

In 1945 a list of programs leading to a degree was published by the NLNE (nondegree programs were omitted). This list helped to guide nurses who were returning from the war and wished to enroll in postgraduate education. At this time there were sixteen colleges and universities offering seventy-eight different programs and conferring seven different degrees. Some of these programs were masters level, but it is difficult to be completely accurate (35).

The publication of Nursing for the Future by Esther Lucile Brown in 1948 and the establishment of an accreditation system in 1949 provided impetus to clarify the nature of collegiate education. In 1950 the National Nursing Accrediting Service discussed two long-term goals for masters education: one involved the need for regional planning to use the limited faculty and facilities as effectively and efficiently as possible; the other identified the need to develop criteria for masters level education. (There was also a similar recommendation for baccalaureate programs.)

Meanwhile, Dr. R. Louise McManus, chairperson of the Division of Nursing Education at Teachers College, decided it was time to move specialized education to the masters level. She chaired a voluntary, informal group of representatives from five area schools, including Long Island University, New York University, Rutgers University, St. John's University, Skidmore College, and Teachers College, Columbia University. (The University of Pennsylvania later asked to join.)

The schools decided to have baccalaureate education as a beginning level and masters programs as the specialized degree. Each school planned their own basic baccalaureate program. All diploma school graduates who wished to enter these programs would have to pass NLN achievement tests (25).

The results of this decision were far reaching. At a conference of post-diploma programs in 1952, sponsored by the NLN, a resolution was passed that supported phasing out specialized baccalaureate programs within five years. While this goal was delayed, it was accomplished by 1963, and the generic baccalaureate program became the model for basic preparation in professional nursing.

Transitional Stage: 1953–1964

During these eleven years, masters education was finally recognized as the advanced level of nursing education. At the first meeting of the Council of Member Agencies of the newly organized NLN in 1953, directors of six masters programs in nursing suggested that the NLN sponsor a conference on graduate education. The idea was well received, and a large group of administrators of graduate programs in nursing met in 1954 and 1955. They began to formulate the first guidelines for organization, administration, curriculum, and testing in masters education in nursing. The task was completed by the newly created NLN Subcommittee on Graduate Education in Nursing and published in 1957. The guidelines were revised in 1960, 1962, and 1967 and recognized the distinct characteristics of the masters program vis-a-vis baccalaureate education. Its primary purposes were specialization and research (7).

One area of disagreement was the emphasis of the masters content—specifically, the need for both clinical and functional role preparation in all programs for teachers, administrators, and clinical specialists. After prolonged disagreement, the faction supporting both clinical and functional preparation won. In the late 1960s, however, when programs in clinical specialization were proliferating, the double preparation was eliminated, and clinical programs did not include functional courses. Some administrative programs followed this pattern, too. However, in the 1980s double preparation is again gaining favor. If a clinical specialist chooses to teach or be an administrator, some preparation in either of these areas is preferred.

Meanwhile, back in the 1950s, the long delay in recognizing masters programs in accreditation procedures was ended in 1956. Finally masters programs were separated from other postgraduate courses. Another giant step was taken the following year, in 1957, when accreditation procedures were changed to accredit only diploma school programs, basic baccalaureate programs, and masters programs. A five-year period was given for phasing out specialized baccalaureate programs. The number of specialized baccalaureate programs fell from 16 in 1957 to 1 in 1963. Conversely the number of masters programs grew from 25 to 32 (30).

Regionalization

The 1950s also witnessed the birth of regional planning in graduate education in nursing: the Southern Regional Educational Board (SREB) and the Western Interstate Commission on Higher Education (WICHE). Both organizations believed that the key to better nursing was strong masters programs to prepare faculty.

The majority of collegiate nursing schools were concentrated in the northeastern part of the country. Three-quarters of the nurses who attained a masters degree in nursing in the 1950s were graduates of Teachers College.

Monies for regionalization plans were obtained through private sources, such as the Commonwealth Fund and the Carnegie Foundation, and federal funds (Public Law which passed in 1956).

SREB initiated its first five-year project in 1954 by forming a consortium of six colleges and universities in the South. Through intercollegiate cooperation, six masters degree programs were developed in 1959.

WICHEN, a regional program to promote graduate and professional education in the health fields, was established in the western part of the country in the early 1950s. The Western Interstate Commission for Higher Education in Nursing (WICHEN) was established in 1955 to promote masters programs. They used SREB as their model, and by the end of the 1950s the West could boast six new masters programs. Funding came from both public and private sources.

Both SREB and WICHEN made major contributions to graduate education; all of their programs were research based and WICHEN organized a special project to define advanced clinical content in nursing.

Maturing of Masters Education: 1964–1975

The 1960s and early 1970s were the years in which masters education matured and became an important credential for nurses in leadership positions. The biggest impetus to master development and nursing education, in general, was the passage of the Nurse Training Act of 1964 (Title VIII of the Public Health Service Act). From 1964 to 1971, over $334 million was appropriated by Congress for nursing education (39). It represented the first comprehensive aid package that provided for construction, faculty development, student grants, and loans. It allowed all levels of nursing education to expand rapidly.

As nursing matured during this decade it began to reexamine the nursing role, to identify its distinct body of knowledge. Increasing emphasis was placed on the scientific basis for nursing, and the advanced clinical role was being explored and expanded for the first time. WICHEN published the results of several years' research into defining the content of advanced clinical areas. SREB also held yearly research conferences to identify advanced clinical content.

The result at the masters level was increased interest in research and an expanding number of graduate programs in clinical specialties. By 1966 the majority of programs in the West had shifted to a clinical focus (3).

The federal budgetary cutbacks of the 1970s and 1980s curtailed some programs and sent others scurrying to find alternate financial sources. The emphasis in the 1980s in graduate education seems to be the expansion of programs with functional majors, while still supporting clinical specialization.

Doctoral Programs in Nursing

Doctoral education in nursing has suffered the same growing pains in its development as the baccalaureate and masters programs that preceded it.

The first doctoral program in nursing was established in Teachers College about 1920, but the growth of doctoral programs has been slow. Due to the delayed growth of masters programs, an adequate pool of candidates was not available until the 1960s. Also, there has been a lack of a clear body of nursing knowledge and a clear direction as to the nature and orientation of the doctorate. In other words, "What is to be learned on the doctoral level?"

In the early years of doctoral education, before 1961, there were only three programs in the United States: Teachers College awarded a doctorate in education, Boston University offered a doctorate in nursing science, and New York University awarded the doctorate of philosophy degree.

There are now approximately twenty-three programs offering doctoral programs. (The latest to open is a Ph.D. program at the University of Virginia in the fall of 1982.) There are still three basic types of degrees being offered: doctor of nursing (Science) (D.N.[S].), doctor of education (Ed.D.), and doctor of philosophy (Ph.D.) (28).

The development of a doctorate in nursing or nursing science has been a controversy for three decades. Should nursing have its own professional terminal degree? The same arguments were presented on the masters level for a masters in science (M.S.) or master in arts (M.A.). Other professions have such degrees, such as masters of jurisprudence (law). The issue is unresolved today.

Dr. Helen Grace, a nurse educator, provides an interesting historical perspective to doctoral education in nursing. She identifies three phases of development from 1926 through the 1980s (16).

The first phase is called the *functional specialists* (1926–1959) because most of the nurses receiving the degree were teachers or administrators. Of the 132 nurses who earned the doctorate during this time, 80 received Ed.D. degrees. Probably most were from Teachers College.

Nurse scientists (1960–1969) is the name of the second phase. Three new programs opened in the 1960s, accounting for 449 nurses who earned doctorates during this decade. There was strong financial support from the Division of Nursing of the U.S. Public Health Service. Specifically there was funding for the nurse scientist program. This program awarded grants to finance the education of nurses in disciplines closely related to nursing. These graduates would then be qualified to implement doctoral programs (16).

The final phase of doctoral development was in the 1970s, *doctorates* in and of *nursing*. Sixteen new programs opened during this dynamic decade. Twelve offered a Ph.D. and four awarded D.N.Sc. (16).

In 1975 Dr. Virginia Cleland, a noted nurse researcher, suggested a moratorium on new doctoral programs. She believed the present programs should be strengthened, assuring qualified faculty and identification of the nature and direction of the doctorate (36).

The purposes of doctoral study for the future may be in research, nursing theory development, and the nature of clinical practice.

Nursing Research

The development of nursing research and nursing theory are closely allied. They are both part of nursing's movement toward a professional status. Both nursing research and nursing theory have the same goal, defining nursing to improve the quality of nursing care the client receives, and theory is dependent on research, in that adequate research knowledge and skills are prerequisites to building nursing theories.

What is research and why is it necessary in nursing? Research is a scientific method of collecting and interpreting data to gain new knowledge. It is necessary in nursing because this approach provides the best way to validate or prove our nursing knowledge.

Historically, nursing knowledge was acquired in three ways: tradition, authority, and trial-and-error. Nursing care was, therefore, based on actions and procedures that other nurses did (tradition), someone told you to do (authority), or you tried on a haphazard basis (trial-and-error). If there were several ways to do one nursing procedure, no one knew the best or most effective and efficient one. They had not been scientifically tested. A nurse chose one at random. If nursing is to be considered a profession, nursing actions and procedures must be chosen on a scientific basis. This testing of nursing knowledge will help build the unique body of knowledge.

The need for research in nursing was recognized as an early problem. It was, however, not able to be integrated into all collegiate levels of nursing education until the 1970s.

Early Support for Nursing Research

As early as the 1930s, there was concern about developing nursing research. Sigma Theta Tau, an honor society in nursing, initiated a research fund to help awaken nurses to the need for research. At this time there were very few properly trained research workers. Much of the "research" was really a collection of statistics. Most research studies or theses were descriptions of a problem on a unit (e.g., care of valuables on a medical unit, organization of a linen closet on a surgical unit). These studies did not analyze data, they merely presented the material. There was also no evidence that the solution presented to the problem was the best one; it was merely one used by the "researcher" (7).

At a special forum on nursing research in 1941, sponsored by the Association of Collegiate Schools of Nursing (ACSN), the status of nursing research was discussed. It was agreed that there was little encouragement of research in nursing practice and nursing education. Any studies that were done were not published or shared with other nurses to be evaluated. Last, there was an endless circle of inadequate research training in all levels of nursing, including nursing faculty (15).

Growing Support for Nursing Research

After World War II, two major influences seemed to spark interest in nursing research. The Brown Report, in 1948, recommended placing nursing education in colleges and universities, and there was a need for research in curriculum and design and content. It is interesting to note that the study of nursing by Dr. Brown was conducted by people outside nursing, reflecting the deficit of research talent within the field of nursing.

The second influence was the expectation of significant federal funding after the Cadet Nurse Corps funds expired in 1948. In anticipation of these funds, plans were drawn up for programs to improve nursing service and nursing education through research. Unfortunately, the funds were not allocated and only a small sum was obtained through private foundations.

In the early 1950s, Teachers College established the Institute of Research and Service in Nursing Education. It was the first known unit ever created to study and develop nursing education through research, on a full-time basis. This unit, plus the scholarly journal *Nursing Research,* which was launched in the early 1950s, helped to promote a higher standard of nursing research and the sharing of the results. The first issue of *Nursing Research* with Helen Bunge as its editor, was mailed to 8500 subscribers (21).

The 1950s was also the decade that the American Nurses' Association became involved in a long-term research project to study nursing functions in a variety of settings across the United States. It was a prelude to the publication of standards for nursing practice. Initially, the research was done by non-nurses, but as more nurses became qualified in research, they assumed the responsibility. The ANA was also involved in the establishment of the American Nurses' Foundation. This fund was organized to provide research grants for scientific and educational projects. The Foundation presently provides a variety of funding, including grants to nursing doctoral students and monies for post doctoral research activities.

Support from Regionalization Projects (SREB and WICHEN)

One of the first decisions of SREB and WICHEN was to plan "research-based" curricula, i.e., they would integrate a research plan for the design and content of the curricula as well as a research course within the curricula. Both projects helped annual research conferences and contributed a major share in defining nursing content on the baccalaureate and masters levels. WICHEN, especially, contributed to advanced clinical content. A research center for WICHEN was founded at the University of Colorado to coordinate research.

Influence of Federal Funds for Research

The government has allocated funds for various research projects and grants since the end of World War II. From the 1940s through 1956, funds for nursing research grants and fellowships to train nurses in research skills had totalled $625 million. These funds, from the Department of Health, Education and Welfare, represented small grants to many people and institutions.

The United States Public Health Service (USPHS) has provided many different types of grants. These were usually channelled through the Division of Nursing. From 1958 through 1966, special faculty research development grants were available. These grants nurtured individual research projects for faculty and curriculum development, and most were awarded to graduate nursing programs. By 1966, most masters programs had incorporated research experiences into their curricula and the federal program was phased out (14).

The USPHS-funded projects totalled almost $7 million from 1955 through 1963. These grants were instrumental in promoting research in all areas of nursing education and nursing practice (13). Two specific projects were the Special Predoctoral Fellowships in 1956, which provided funds to qualified nurse researchers for individual and collaborative interdisciplinary research grants, and the Nurse Scientist Program in 1962, which allocated funds to graduate nursing students preparing to be researchers and to institutions in developing research competence. Over $2 million was allocated for these two programs (21).

Both federal and private funding helped support SREB and WICHEN in the early years as well as national conferences on research.

The 1970s and early 1980s witnessed deep cuts in federal funds to all nursing programs, but past research monies have strengthened nursing in providing competent researchers and in integrating research in education and in practice. New federal legislation is being drafted for ongoing support of nursing research and education.

Trends in Nursing Research

Studies in nursing research during the past four decades can be viewed on a continuum, from a narrow focus to a broad interdisciplinary focus. In the 1940s many of the research studies involved clinical experiences in a particular area; for example, care of the patient with tuberculosis in a particular hospital medical unit. The studies had a very narrow focus and were rarely shared with other nurses.

In the 1950s and early 1960s the research studies concentrated on the functions and role of the nurse: "What should the nurse do?" Qualifications for practice as well as the number of nurses and other personnel needs for adequate staffing were studied. There was a severe nursing shortage during this time and the belief was that an adequate number of personnel would guarantee a high quality of nursing care (14).

Research in the late 1960s and 1970s was influenced by interest in identifying a body of nursing knowledge and the popularity of the clinical nurse specialist. Studies were broadened to include both clinical and administrative aspects of nursing, nursing care, and nursing education. The research component in undergraduate and graduate curricula was strengthened and provided a growing pool of qualified nursing researchers.

The decade of the 1980s promises a surge in research at all levels of nursing, nursing administration, and nursing practice, and nursing administration. One impetus is the continuing need to strengthen nursing's body of knowledge. Another reason is the growing acceptance of research as being cost effective. In a decade of budgetary cuts, research can provide the most effective modes of nursing. Finally, with the growing number of doctoral programs, an increase in nursing research will be accomplished as increasing numbers of nurses develop their research skills.

Heightened interest in nursing research is evidenced by the growing number of research conferences and symposia across the United States. These conferences like those sponsored by Sigma Theta Tau, are very important since a major weakness has been the lack of sharing of nursing research with peers. It is hoped that the 1980s will be the decade wherein nursing research becomes the usual procedure rather than the exception.

Nursing Theories

The development of nursing theories is a new and exciting area in nursing. It is a method of defining and identifying the unique role and functions of nursing. This uniqueness is nursing's body of knowledge, the special knowledge that nurses need to do nursing. It also means that the boundaries or limits in nursing are clarified, i.e., "When is a nurse doing nursing and when is she not doing nursing?"

Other professions have theories that define their practice too. For example, "when is a psychologist practicing psychology and when is he not?" "When is a physician practicing medicine and when is he not?"

So far, nursing theories seem very similar to nursing research in the role they perform for the profession. Both help define the uniqueness of nursing. But how are they different? Research investigates a specific nursing procedure or action. It is limited in scope. An example of a research project would be to test different methods of teaching new mothers about baby care. The different strategies would be tested to determine which one was the most effective. One group would be taught in a group session with a nurse. A second group would learn the same information in a group session using a film and then have a discussion with a nurse. (In each situation we assume the nurse is doing nursing.)

A nursing theory, however, is much broader in scope. It describes a systematic approach to practicing nursing. Rather than describing a specific procedure, it describes the characteristics of the relationship between the nurse and the client. This relationship determines the nurse's actions in all nurse-client situations. For example, listed below are two statements describing a nurse-client relationship. These statements could be part of a nursing theory. If we believe the following statements, then both conditions must be present in any nurse-client relationship for the actions to be defined as nursing.

1. A nurse does those activities for a client that he cannot do for himself.
2. A nurse helps a client achieve as much independence as possible for himself.

Now let us examine the three situations listed below. In which situation does the nursing actions include both statements listed above?

A nurse is teaching a client in a hospital to change a dressing before he goes home. The nursing actions will be different in each situation.

Client A: Nurse changes the dressing for the client for several days while client watches.

Client B: Nurse changes the dressing for several days. Allows client to do procedure before going home.

Client C: Nurse changes the dressing for several days. Allows client to change the dressing as many times as necessary until he is confident in the procedure before he goes home.

According to our two statements, only the nurse with client C is doing nursing. Only the third nurse does the dressing while the client is unable to do it (statement 1) and also helps him to learn to change the dressing himself to be as independent as possible (statement 2). The nurses in situations A and B are not doing nursing according to our "theory." They have not acted to fulfill statement 2. They might be considered technically skillful but are not practicing professional nursing.

Application of the theory could be in a variety of settings (hospital, home), with a number of illnesses, and with many types of clients. If the characteristics of the relationships have been determined, then our unique nursing role will be defined.

Theory and research are related. Theories describe the relationships and research tests them in the real world to see if they are true, i.e., do they work.

Theories are composed of statements that are related to each other and describe various relationships. In addition, these statements must define and describe at least the four essential concepts in a nursing theory—person, health, nurse, and society (environment). Statement 2—"A nurse helps a client achieve as much independence as possible for himself"—actually describes the relationship among the nurse-client-health. In other words, a nurse helps a client to be healthier by being as independent as possible.

Statements link concepts. What are concepts? They are a label or a name given to an idea or mental image. The concept of "health" creates many images related to our past experiences in feeling well, being ill, and measures to get healthy.

If we were to diagram a nursing theory, it would appear as thus:

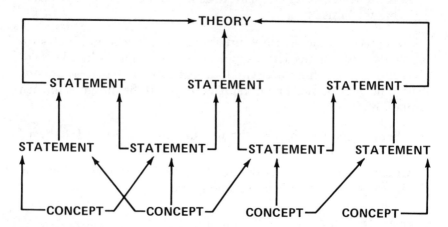

Concepts are linked to form statements. Statements are related to form other statements. A theory is composed of interrelating statements.

In nursing literature the term "proposition" is sometimes used for "statement." They are interchangeable. Another common term used in theory development is "conceptual model." It is sometimes incorrectly used to mean a theory. A conceptual model is a loosely organized set of concepts and statements. It becomes a theory when it has been tested and proved valid.

Origins of Nursing Theories

Florence Nightingale could probably be considered the first nursing theorist, as she was the first person to define and describe nursing in her book in 1859 *Notes on Nursing: What it is and What it is Not.* Nursing has been elaborating and redefining the nurse ever since.

A century later, during the 1950s, nursing was searching for its identity in a complex, rapidly changing world. Many nurses believed nursing was a profession, but nursing had been unable to clearly define its unique knowledge base.

The ANA had published some definitions of nursing functions in 1932, 1937, and 1955, but they were nonspecific. Therefore, a few nurses decided to write their own definitions and descriptions of nursing. Virginia Henderson and Hildegard Peplau were two prominent nurses who individually began this task.

Miss Henderson published her first definition of nursing in 1955, revising it in 1966 (5).

> The unique function of the nurse is to assist the individual, sick or well, in the performance of those activities contributing to health or its recovery (or to a peaceful death) that he could perform unaided if he had the necessary strength, will or knowledge. And to do this in such a way as to help him gain independence as rapidly as possible.

Dr. Peplau's book *Interpersonal Relations in Nursing* in 1952 described four phases of the nurse-client relationship. Her work stimulated many research studies in the area of interviewing skills and communication.

During the 1960s there was increased interest in defining nursing, especially as it applied in the clinical area. Clinical nurse specialists were required to define their higher level of functioning. Also, as more masters programs included research courses, there was a strong desire to test the ideas of nurses. During this time some nurses, like Dr. Martha Rogers, began to write their descriptions of nursing. Their ideas were initially difficult to test because some definitions and relationships were broad, but they represented a beginning, and over time, they have been expanded and tested.

Beginning of Theory Development

In the late 1960s and early 1970s there were many conferences that discussed the need for theories. They also discussed the basic elements of a theory and methods for evaluating them.

Finally, in the 1970s some new nursing theories began to be developed and tested in clinical practice. Two examples are Dorothea E. Orem, who published her self-care nursing theory in 1971 (and her revised theory in 1980), and Sr. Callista Roy, who published her adaptation theory in 1976 (and her revised theory in 1981). Progress is very slow in the testing of the theories. A study by Daryl T. Nagel at the University of Texas at Austin revealed that many nurses believe that theory development may continue for two decades.

It is important to recognize that theories cannot be perfect. All have strengths and weaknesses and many are revised as necessary. In nursing, some of our theories will eventually be validated; those that cannot be validated should be revised or discarded.

Interest in theory development, as in nursing research, is on the rise, and again there are many national conferences and symposia to discuss various aspects of theory development. Nursing literature in this area is also expanding.

Our future survival may depend on whether we can distinguish our role from the growing number of paraprofessionals and the expanding roles of other professionals. The development of strong nursing theories can be a powerful unifying force within nursing and reflects the growing sophistication of the profession.

Associate Degree Nursing Education

A relatively recent and controversial event in the history of nursing education was the establishment of the associate degree nursing program. Developed by Dr. Mildred Montag of Teachers College in 1949, this model of education was neither a form nor an evolution of programs already in existence (20). The associate degree program was the first and, to date, the only nursing education program to be developed as a result of planned research and controlled experimentation. Several historical events and societal trends influenced its beginning: the shortage of nurses during World War II, the Canadian experiment in nursing education, the development of the community college movement, the recognition of differentiated functions in nursing, and several independent studies that identified priorities for nursing.

Early Development

United States involvement in World War II created a shortage of nurses, particularly on the home front. To provide more nurses for the military, nursing education was accelerated and enrollments were increased. Congress enacted legislation creating the Cadet Nurse Corps, which provided financial incentives to schools of nursing that could prepare students in less than the traditional three years. This experience demonstrated that nurses could be adequately educated in two and one-half years in programs that incorporated both general and nursing education.

At about the same time, Canada was also investigating alternative models of nursing education. The Metropolitan School of Nursing at Windsor, Ontario, conducted an experiment to determine whether a professional nurse could be prepared in less than three years. Although it provided only nursing courses, this innovative program was independent of the hospital. The report of this study concluded that "when a school has complete control of students, nurses can be trained at least as satisfactorily in two years as in three years and under better conditions" (22).

After the war, several independent studies examined the role, preparation, and functions of nurses; the problems confronting nursing education; and the future of American nursing. Both the Brown Report, *Nursing for the Future* (6), and the report of the Ginzberg Committee, *A Program for the Nursing Profession* (10), recommended that nursing functions be subdivided among two groups of personnel—professional and practical. In addition, the Brown Report called for preparation of all registered nurses within the mainstream of higher education.

In her doctoral dissertation, published in 1951 as *The Education of Nursing Technicians* (27), Mildred Montag set forth her belief that the functions of nursing could and should be differentiated and that these functions lie along a continuum, with professional at one end and technical at the other. Montag proposed the need for a new type of worker, the "nurse technician," with nursing functions less in scope than the professional nurse and broader than the practical nurse. Montag listed the functions of this "bedside" nurse as (1) to assist in the planning of nursing care for patients, (2) to give general nursing care with supervision, and (3) to assist in the evaluation of the nursing care given. Montag advised that "separate and distinct programs" be set up for professional and technical workers yet insisted that education for nursing belonged within the established educational framework of the country (27). The institution determined appropriate for this purpose was the community college.

The emerging community college system, which already was providing education at the technical level for other occupations and had initiated some programs in nursing, was the logical setting to place technical nursing education. Community colleges offered a unique American approach to education, and after World War II, the number of community colleges in this country almost doubled from 610 in 1940 to 1100 in 1970 (24). In addition to developing technical and other semiprofessional programs in many new fields, community colleges offered transfer opportunities to senior colleges and universities. The low tuition was also an attractive feature. More importantly, the "open-door" philosophy of the community college permitted access to higher education for all, regardless of age, marital status, sex, or race.

The proposed technical nursing curriculum was to be an integrated one, striking a balance between general education courses and nursing courses, with careful selection and supervision of clinical laboratory experiences. These experiences were to be based on specific learning objectives. The emphasis would be on education, not on service to the hospital. An associate degree was to be awarded at the end of the two-year period, at which time graduates would be eligible to take the state board examinations for registered nurse licensure. The program would be considered to be terminal and not the first step toward a baccalaureate degree. Graduates would be expected to perform technical nursing functions at the beginning level on graduation.

In 1952, an advisory committee established by the American Association of Junior Colleges and the National League for Nursing was charged with conducting cooperative research on nursing education in the community college. This pilot project was administered by Teachers College, Columbia University and was directed by Mildred Montag. The original project included seven junior and community colleges and one hospital from each of six regions of the United States.

The goals of the Cooperative Research Project were (1) to describe the development of the associate degree program, (2) to evaluate its graduates, and (3) to determine its implications for the future of nursing. The results of the Project demonstrated that associate degree nursing technicians could carry out the intended nursing functions, that the program could be suitably set up in community colleges, and that the program attracted students (26). Furthermore, it placed the entire responsibility for the educational process on the educational institution and the student rather than on the hospital or service institution.

When the Cooperative Research Project was concluded in 1957, other community colleges were assisted in developing nursing programs by the National League for Nursing. The success of the Cooperative Research Project and subsequent efforts sparked the rapid growth of associate degree nursing programs, a growth that paralleled the expansion of the community college movement itself.

Associate Degree Nursing Education Today

The associate degree nursing program is now a well-established type of educational program in nursing. Associate degree nursing education has expanded from its modest beginning in 1952 to over 707 programs in 1980 (34), producing more graduates annually than either diploma or baccalaureate programs. The graduates of these programs are gainfully employed in a variety of settings, including hospitals, outpatient departments, physicians' offices, and nursing homes.

The inception of associate degree education in nursing brought with it a change in the kind of student who enrolled. Traditionally, nursing students were a homogeneous group composed mainly of single, white females below age nineteen who were usually from middle-class homes (20). The student body in an associate degree program is a heterogeneous one. Associate degree programs attract a diverse group of older indivuals, married women, minorities, and men. Persons of quite varying academic backgrounds are found in associate degree nursing programs. Recent years have seen individuals who already possess baccalaureate or higher degrees in other fields seeking admission to associate degree programs. Flexible scheduling patterns provide opportunity for many to attend school and complete degree requirements on a part-time basis.

Over the years, the associate degree nursing curriculum has been revised. There is a tendency to place more emphasis and time on nursing courses and clinical experiences than on general education, sometimes through the addition of summer sessions or intersessions. Some programs have added courses in leadership and physical assessment in an attempt to meet the demands of employers.

The entire concept of the associate degree nursing program as terminal has also changed. More graduates seek additional education beyond the associate degree, and the "ladder" concept in nursing education has become popular. Registered nurse, baccalaureate, and "two-on-two" programs are increasing as the associate degree graduate insists that barriers to articulation between two-year and four-year institutions be removed.

There have also been changes in philosophy as to what the technical nurse is and does. There has been little acceptance of the "technical" title. Resistance has come from the students and graduates of associate degree programs as well as from the nursing community at large. In 1976, the Council of Associate Degree Programs of the National League for Nursing moved to change the name of the graduate of associate degree programs from "technical" to "associate degree" nurse. The "technical" title was also rejected by the National Student Nurses' Association as implying a less qualified nonprofessional.

The entry level competencies of the associate degree nurse were rewritten and described in 1978 by the Council of Associate Degree Programs of the National League for Nursing. As outlined in this document (31), the role seems much broader than that conceived initially by Montag. The Council defined five interrelated roles: provider of care, communicator, client teacher, manager of client care, and member within the profession of nursing. In addition, several assumptions basic to the scope of practice were enumerated. Associate degree nursing

1. Is directed toward clients who need information or support to maintain health.

2. Is directed toward clients who are in need of medical diagnostic evaluation and/or are experiencing acute or chronic illness.

3. Is directed toward clients' responses to common, well-defined health problems.

4. Includes the formulation of a nursing diagnosis.

5. Consists of nursing interventions selected from established nursing protocols wherein probable outcomes are predictable.

6. Is concerned with individual clients and is given with consideration of the person's relationship within a family, group, and community.

7. Includes the safe performance of nursing skills that require cognitive, psychomotor, and affective capabilities.

8. May be in any structured care setting but primarily occurs within acute and extended-care facilities.

9. Is guided directly or indirectly by a more experienced registered nurse.

10. Includes the direction of peers or other workers in nursing in selected aspects of care within the scope of practice of associate degree nursing.

11. Involves an understanding of the roles and responsibilities of self and other workers within the employment setting (31).

Based on an inspection of the above, it appears that in the years since associate degree nursing education first emerged, proponents have modified the functions to coincide with the times as well as the expectations of the employer.

Unfortunately, the expectations of the employers and supervisors of associate degree graduates have not always been consistent with the functions originally delineated. Because of staffing problems, poor understanding of the abilities of technical nurses, and the traditional concept of nursing roles (based on the diploma model), which prevail, inappropriate utilization of these workers has often resulted. Associate degree graduates have been assigned as team leaders and put "in charge"—positions for which they were neither prepared nor intended to function. This is not surprising considering that a major issue for the nursing profession today is the lack of differentiation of all levels of practice. Beause all hold registered nurse licensure, associate degree and diploma graduates are used interchangeably with baccalaureate graduates by hospital and nursing administration. This improper utilization of nurses, regardless of educational preparation, continues to be a disturbing and consistent problem for the profession.

Another related professional issue, particularly problematic for associate degree nursing is the ANA's Entry into Practice Resolution. If the proposed changes are implemented, a number of questions need to be answered relative to the consequences for associate degree nursing. Will there be separate licensing examinations for associate degree and baccalaureate graduates? If so, will this result in different titling for each group? Will A.D.N. programs become, in effect, L.P.N. programs? What would become of existing A.D.N. programs? How will the curriculum change? How would interstate licensure be affected? Another fundamental conflict relates to the point-of-entry into the profession of nursing. Will it be at the A.D.N. (technical) level or at the B.S.N. (professional) level?

Many such questions have been raised publicly and privately by nurses as well as other interested regional and national groups. Clearly this proposal remains a volatile issue and will continue to require serious deliberation by all concerned.

Implications for the Future

The net result of the entry-into-practice controversy will have wide-spread implications. Interestingly, it has been noted that the ongoing debate over the technical role and functions has already forced the profession to reconsider the role, functions, and utilization of the professional nurse (38). This kind of introspection is an important step in the evolution of the profession.

In addition to the outcome of this debate on the future of associate degree nursing, other influencing factors will probably precipitate further changes. Despite a downward trend in nursing school enrollments nationwide, admission figures indicate that associate degree nursing education programs are currently receiving more applications for admission than they can accommodate. Will this lead to more selective admission policies for associate degree programs? If so, how will the characteristics of the student body in A.D.N. programs change? As higher education becomes more expensive and less financial assistance is available to students in the form of scholarships and loans, will associate degree education become an even more attractive route into the nursing profession? As more and more of these graduates seek career mobility, will an articulated system of nursing education become a necessity?

The answers to all of these questions remain to be seen. Obviously, there are differing predictions about the future of associate degree nursing education. The one point on which most nurses agree, however, is that the associate degree nurse has made a profound impact on nursing education in this country.

Practical Nursing

The early development of practical nursing in this country was largely unplanned and for many years proceeded independently of professional nursing (32). Before 1860, nursing services in America were provided by practical nurses who were self-taught and gained their knowledge by experience. There was no specific training for practical nurses until the end of the nineteenth century.

Early Programs for Preparation of Practical Nursing

In 1892, the first program to offer preparation for practical nursing was started through the Y.W.C.A. in Brooklyn, New York. Known as the Ballard School, the program was approximately three months in length and trained its students to care for invalids, the elderly, and children. Students were referred to as attendants. At the same time, a similar program was established in Boston by the Massachusetts Emergency and Hygiene Association. In 1907, the Brattleboro School for Practical Nurses opened in Vermont. The focus of all of these programs was home nursing care, including cooking, laundry, and other light housekeeping duties. Few of the early schools provided hospital experiences (32).

During World War II, however, when the demand for nurses was great and the supply short, the American Red Cross undertook the recruitment and preparation of nonprofessional nurses. A planned curriculum was developed consisting of lectures and supervised clinical experience in the hospital setting. Those who completed the program were utilized in a variety of health care settings, including hospitals and clinics. This method of supplementing nursing resources proved successful, and although many were convinced that there was a permanent place in nursing for the "subsidiary worker," some were more skeptical.

In 1947, the Joint Committee on Auxiliary Nursing Service, a representative group of six national nursing associations, published a pamphlet entitled *Practical Nurses and Auxiliary Workers for the Care of the Sick*. This document identified the need to recognize the specific functions of practical nurses and other ancillary personnel. Much controversy ensued, and many professional nurses expressed their reluctance to accept the nonprofessional worker in the patient care situation. Opinion on the subject was divided.

Despite any misgivings, practical nursing proliferated and it became necessary to stop untrained individuals from functioning as practical nurses. Individually, states began to establish laws to control practical nursing. By 1955, most states had adopted some type of law regarding the licensing of practical nurses and had established mechanisms for program approval by the state board of nurse examiners. Although many states enacted licensure laws governing practical nursing, a large number of individuals who had been functioning in this capacity were granted license by waiver, thereby never really having any formal training. In these instances, employing institutions gave preference to those practical nurses who were prepared in approved schools. Consequently, it became important that preparation be obtained in an approved training program and that the practical nurse realize the signficance of obtaining licensure.

Practical Nursing Today

The growth rate of programs and numbers of students increased steadily over the years, but it now appears to have leveled off. According to the National League for Nursing, in 1980 there were 1299 practical nursing programs in the United States producing 41,892 graduates (33). The schools providing practical nurse preparation vary widely. A program may be offered by a high school, trade or technical school, hospital, junior or community college, university, or independent agency. Practical nursing education was heavily supported by federal government for some time.

The curriculum also varies considerably from state to state and among schools. The time allotted is generally one year or approximately 2000 hours of instruction. The focus is on the teaching of basic skills, with some theory added. Usually about one-third of the time is spent in the classroom and two-thirds in clinical areas. On graduation the student is eligible to take the licensing examination to become an L.P.N or L.V.N.

Recently there has been a movement to combine practical nurse education and associate degree programs in the community college. All students are grouped together for "core" courses during the first academic year of study. At the end of this time, the student has the option of exiting from the educational program and seeking licensure as a licensed practical nurse or continuing for an additional year, earning the associate degree, and becoming eligible for registered nurse licensure. In line with this trend, other career ladder opportunities that facilitate the upward mobility of licensed practical nurses have been made available by some colleges, universities, and diploma schools.

The graduate of an approved school of practical nursing has excellent potential for employment. Nearly 89 percent of the practical and vocational nurses newly licensed in 1980 were employed in nursing six to eight months after licensure. The majority are employed in structured health care settings, such as hospitals (74.6%) and nursing homes (16.3%). The remainder work in doctor's offices, private duty, public health agencies, schools, and industry (33).

Over the years, practical nursing has progressed through a series of role definitions, and representative nursing organizations have attempted to clarify and delineate the functions of the practical nurse. In general, it has been agreed that the licensed practical nurse functions under the direction of a registered nurse or physician and is involved with preparation, implementation, and evaluation of the nursing care plan. The *Statement of Functions and Qualifications of the Licensed Practical Nurse* recently issued by the National Federation of Licensed Practical Nurses lists the standards of practice expected of these individuals (29).

I. Accepts assigned responsibilities as an accountable member of the health care team

II. Functions within limits of educational preparation and experience as related to assigned duties

III. Functions with other members of the health care team in promoting and maintaining health, preventing disease and disability, and caring for and rehabilitating individuals who are experiencing altered health states

IV. Knows and utilizes the nursing process in planning, implementing, and evaluating health services and nursing care to the individual patient or group
   A. Planning
      1. Assessment of health status of the individual patient, family, and community groups
      2. Analysis of information gained from assessment
      3. Identification of health goals
   B. Implementation
      1. Observing, recording, and reporting significant changes that require intervention or different goals
      2. Applying nursing knowledge and skills to promote and maintain health, to prevent disease and disability, and to optimize functional capabilities of an individual patient
      3. Assisting the patient and family with activities of daily living and encouraging self-care as appropriate
      4. Carrying out therapeutic regimens prescribed by a physician or other qualified health care provider
   C. Evaluation
      1. Determine the relevancy of current goals in relation to the progress of the individual patient, family, and community
      2. Determine involvement of recipients of care in the evaluation process
      3. Determine the quality of nursing action in the implementation of the plan
      4. Reorder priorities or new goal setting in the care plan

V. Participants in peer review and other evaluative processes

VI. Participates in the development of policies concerning the health and nursing needs of society and in the role and functions of the LP/VN (29)

In the past few years, the National Association of Practical Nursing Education and Service has introduced legislation to add "supervises others" to the list of functions of the practical nurse. Although this responsibility has not been included to date in any licensing law, the addition has been proposed because of the inappropriate utilization of practical nurses by employing institutions. In addition to being placed in charge nurse positions, practical nurses are frequently pressed to perform other functions beyond their level of preparation. This is a matter of serious concern not only for practical nurses but also for the entire profession.

Another matter of great concern for practical nursing is the ANA Entry into Practice Resolution. If implemented, practical nursing as it is known today would be eliminated. The future of practical nursing is, therefore, most uncertain and will depend on the developments that arise as American nursing education continues to evolve.

Summary

The development of nursing education in America has been characterized by great diversity. As educational models and patterns continue to evolve, the one common theme that emerges is the growing belief that education for nursing is the prerogative of educational institutions, not service agencies and that nursing requires a liberally educated person as well as a competent clinical practitioner.

References

1. Association of Collegiate Schools of Nursing: Report Compiled by Membership Committee on Activities Reported by Members, 1940–41, May 24, 1941. Unpublished microfilmed material, Central Files. New York, NLN, 1941

2. Barritt ER: Florence Nightingale, Her Wit and Wisdom. New York, Peter Pauper Pess, 1975

3. Belcher HC: Nursing Education and Research. Report of Regional Project 1962–66. Atlanta, SREB, 1968, pp. 21, 83

4. Bernays E: The nurses contribution to American victory. Am J Nurs 45:683–686, 1945.

5. Bridgman M: Purposes, Conditions and Trends in Graduate Nurse Education. Extracts from Consultation Materials. Unpublished microfilmed reports, Central Files. New York, National League for Nursing, 1953

6. Brown EL: Nursing for the Future. New York, The Russell Sage Foundation, 1948

7. Brown JB: History of Masters Education in Nursing in the United States, 1945–1969. Doctoral dissertation, Teachers College, Columbia University, 1978

8. Bush LP: Reminiscences of the Philadelphia Hospital and re-marks on old-time doctors and medicine. Philadelphia General Hosp Rep 3:312–313, January 1890

9. Butts RF, Cremin LA: A History of Education in American Culture. New York, Henry Bolt and Company, p. 582

10. Committee on the Function of Nursing: A Program for the Nursing Profession. New York, Macmillan, 1948

11. Dickens C: Martin Chuzzlewit. New York, Macmillan Co., 1910, pp. 312–313

12. Dolan JA: Nursing in Society, 14th ed. Philadelphia, W. B. Saunders, 1978

13. Freeman R: Public funds for nursing. Am J Nurs 63:M28–M32, 1963

14. Gortner SR: Research in nursing: The federal interest and grant programs. Am J Nurs 73:1052–55, 1973

15. Gowan Sr MO: Research in the Association of Collegiate Schools of Nursing. Unpublished microfilm material, Central Files. New York, NLN, 1941, pp. 2–3, 12

16. Grace HK: The development of doctoral education: An historical perspective. *In* Chaska HL (ed): The Nursing Profession. New York, McGraw-Hill, 1978, pp. 112–123

17. Hale SJ: Lady nurses. Godey's Lady's Book 82:188–189, 1871

18. Hale SL, Boyd BT: Accommodating RN students in baccalaureate nursing programs. Nurs Outlook 29:535–540, 1981

19. Henderson V: The Nature of Nursing, New York, Macmillan, 1966, p. 15

20. Kaiser JE: A Comparison of Students in Practical Nursing Programs and in Associate Degree Nursing Programs. New York, National Leaugue for Nursing, Pub. No. 23–1592, 1975

21. Kalisch PA, Kalisch BJ: The Advance of American Nursing. Boston, Little, Brown, 1978

22. Lord AR: Report of the Evaluation of the Metropolitan School of Nursing. Canadian Nurses Association, 1952, p. 54

23. Major federal programs for nursing education. Am J Nurs 64:21, 1964

24. Medsker LH, Tillery D: Breaking the Access Barriers: A Profile of Two Year Colleges. New York, McGraw-Hill, 1971

25. McManus RL: Personal interview, 1976

26. Montag ML: Community College Education for Nursing. New York, McGraw-Hill, 1959

27. Montag ML: The Education of Nursing Technicians. New York, G. P. Putnam's Sons, 1951

28. Murphy JF: Doctoral education in, of, and for nursing: An historical analysis. Nurs Outlook 29:645–649, 1981

29. National Federation of Licensed Practical Nurses: Statement of Functions and Qualifications of the Licensed Practical Nurse. New York, NFLPN, 1980, pp. 7–8

30. NLN: Accreditation Status of Institutions Offering Programs in Collegiate Nursing, 1950–1963. Unpublished mimeographed files of Mrs. Gudrun Willard, New York, NLN

31. National League for Nursing: Competencies of the Associate Degree Nurse on Entry into Practice. New York, National League for Nursing, 1978

32. National League for Nursing: Licensed Practical Nurses in Nursing Service, Pub. No. 11–1180. New York, National League for Nursing, 1965, p. 8

33. National League for Nursing: Nursing Data Book, Pub. No. 19-1882. New York, National League for Nursing, 1982, pp. 142–145

34. National League for Nursing: State Approved Schools of Nursing—RN, Pub. No. 19-1900. New York, National League for Nursing, 1982

35. NLNE: Advanced Programs Leading to a Degree in Universities and Colleges, 1945

36. News. Am J Nurs 75:763, 1975

37. Nowak JB: The Forty-Seven Hundred. Caanan, New Hampshire, Phoenix, 1981

38. Rines A: Associate degree education: History, development and rationale. Nurs Outlook 25:0, 1977

39. Scott, J: Federal support for nursing education, 1964 to 1971. Am J Nurs 72:1855–61, 1972

40. Sloan PE: Commitment to equality: A view of early black nursing schools. In Fitzpatrick ML (ed): Historical Studies in Nursing. New York, Teachers College Press, 1978, pp. 68–85

41. Some Problems in Grading Our Schools of Nursing, Trained Nurse and Hospital Review, 77:507–509, 1926

42. Stewart IM: The Education of Nurses. New York, Macmillan, 1943

43. Stewart IM, Austin AL: A History of Nursing. New York, G. P. Putnam's Sons, 1962, p. 137

3

Credentialing—Chaos to Accountability

Credentialing of appropriately qualified nurses has been a dominant, recurrent theme in contemporary nursing history. Over time, nursing organizations have demonstrated extraordinary commitment to the development of standards intrinsic to credentialing procedures. Additionally, organized nursing played a central role in implementing those procedures.

Although credentialing mechanisms have undergone numerous adaptations since their inception, the meaning of credentialing remains essentially unchanged. Credentialing is usually defined as the process by which specific qualifications are formally endorsed. Generally accepted credentialing procedures include licensure, certification, accreditation, and documentation of formal education.

In nursing, all four processes are presently operative. Documents are awarded to individuals who satisfactorily complete the required course of study in an educational institution. Professional nurse licenses are issued by governmental agencies to persons whose qualifications conform to the standards mandated by state laws. Certification by professional nursing associations is available, on a voluntary basis, to graduate nurses who demonstrate specified aptitudes in designated specialty areas. Another kind of certification is offered by educational institutions that prepare graduate nurses for advanced, specialized practice. Accreditation is the recognition given to nursing education programs and nursing service agencies by professional accrediting bodies. Voluntary in nature, accreditation involves adherence to the prescribed criteria of the particular professional organization.

The underlying purpose of nurse credentialing is protection of the public through implementation and maintenance of high educational and practice standards. Generated by the profession itself, credentialing mechanisms pertaining to individual nurses and educational programs reflect nursing's ongoing commitment to the public welfare.

The Necessity for Credentialing

Nursing's concern with credentialing has surfaced at various intervals in the history of modern nursing. Its roots, however, can be traced to the period following the Civil War, when hospital-based nurse training programs first evolved in this country.

The development of nurse training schools coincided with postwar changes that had a profound effect on the social, political, and economic structure of American life. These very changes ultimately influenced the course of nurse training. At the time the first training schools appeared, women had become increasingly visible as wage earners. Economic instability precipitated by the high cost of the war resulted in an economic depression, which began in 1873. The financial problems existing in many families made it necessary for large numbers of women to seek work. Nursing was one of the few occupations judged by society to be suitable for women. Reflecting the highly valued womanly traits of gentleness and compassion, nursing presented little threat to the male-dominated world of work. As the number of women entering training schools increased, the need for more training schools was recognized. Paralleling these events was the growing agitation for women's rights. Various women's groups were focusing on the need to improve the political, educational, and occupational status of women.

Following the establishment of the first three major schools, the number of training schools steadily increased. Hospital authorities gradually became cognizant of the advantages inherent in a ready supply of inexpensive labor, and as new hospitals emerged, training schools were incorporated into many of these facilities. By 1893, there were thirty-four nurse training schools in existence, but striking inconsistencies related to admission requirements, course content, and length of program were evident. Although diplomas or certificates were awarded to nurses who completed the various programs, these credentials failed to validate any uniformity of preparation.

Prevailing conditions were largely unsatisfactory for the graduate nurse. Private home nursing was then the major area of employment for trained nurses, and this manner of work provided little or no opportunity for socialization with peers. The lack of communication between schools and the absence of alumnae associations served to isolate the working nurse. Consequently, little unity existed among nurses nor was interest in each other's welfare an overriding concern. Forced to compete with the untrained for jobs, trained nurses were seriously hampered by limited physician support and the lack of public knowledge regarding differences in educational preparation.

Despite their educational flaws and the problems confronting their graduates, training schools continued to proliferate. No mechanism was readily available to control this rapid expansion, and a plethora of irresponsible training programs eventually appeared. Graduates of earlier programs who subsequently assumed leadership positions as superintendents of the more prestigious schools became increasingly alarmed by the absence of uniform educational requirements and the external manipulation of nursing education. The flagrant disregard for standards demonstrated by some schools and the unchecked growth of all manner of schools provided impetus for the movement toward reform.

The decision for nurses to take matters into their own hands was not inconsistent with the national climate of the time. Odious business practices and corrupt political activities had already invaded areas other than nursing. Those whose self-serving interests included the exploitation of specific occupational groups were being identified and censured.

Nursing leaders such as Isabel Hampton, Adelaide Nutting, and Lavinia Dock recognized that the dispersion of nurses was detrimental to the attainment of goals. Steps were taken to develop alumnae associations at several prominent training schools, and the earliest of these were begun at Bellevue in 1889, the Illinois Training School in 1891, and the Johns Hopkins Training School in 1892. The introduction of alumnae associations provided forums for the expression of concerns and the development of strategies for change. By 1893, organization on a wider scale had become a major objective of nursing's leadership group. The need for nursing to control its own professional standards was identified as a priority, and unification was advanced as the means to achieve desired outcomes. Within one year, the first American nursing organization was successfully launched and the movement was begun that would ultimately effect enactment of the earliest legal credentialing measure for trained nurses in the United States.

Credentialing of the Individual Nurse

It is appropriate to refer to the movement for legally approved standards as the nurse registration movement. Although licensure was the credentialing mechanism put into effect when the laws were passed, the term "registration" was the term commonly used to identify issues related to the movement, the movement itself, and the initial laws that were enacted. The term "registration" reflects the influence of Great Britain. The Medical Act of 1858 had provided for the registration of British physicians, and registered status eventually became the goal of a highly visible segment of the British nursing community. In view of the communication network that existed between the registrationists in Britain and the nursing leaders in the United States, it is likely that the term was automatically adopted here.

The earliest known reference to registration for nurses is generally attributed to Dr. Henry Wentworth Acland, a British physician. As early as 1867, Dr. Acland had attempted to inaugurate a system of credentialing in England that would assist the public to identify nurses who were appropriately trained. His efforts produced no results and the issue lay dormant for many years. In 1887, Mrs. Bedford Fenwick, former matron of St. Bartholomew's Hospital in London, embarked on a campaign for nurse registration that would ultimately affect nursing education throughout the world. Although Florence Nightingale's system for training nurses was already well established, it had not won universal acceptance from British physicians. Consequently, nursing care in Great Britain varied in quality and was frequently inferior. Convinced that legalized standards would upgrade nursing education, improve nursing's image, and attract more desirable candidates, Mrs. Fenwick founded the British Nurses' Association in 1888 for the purpose of achieving legal sanction. Subsequent attempts by the British Nurses' Association to effect a registration law generated fierce opposition from powerful adversaries and repeatedly met with defeat. During the struggle, British nurses were divided into two hostile factions, a factor that later prompted the emphasis on unity among American nurses.

Despite its controversial nature, registration remained Mrs. Fenwick's goal. In 1892, she recognized the benefits nursing would derive from affiliation with the World's Columbian Exposition to be held in Chicago the following year. Women were to play central roles in the management of various aspects of the Exposition and a significant number of exhibits were to focus on the contributions of women's work. Placed in charge of the British women's exhibit, Mrs. Fenwick initiated the plan for convening an International Nursing Congress as part of the International Congress of Charities, Correction, and Philanthropy scheduled to meet during the Exposition. It was for the purpose of arranging this Nursing Congress that she traveled to the United States in October 1892. During her visit, Mrs. Fenwick met with Isabel Hampton, superintendent of the Johns Hopkins Training School; Lavinia Dock, Miss Hampton's assistant; and Adelaide Nutting, a graduate of Johns Hopkins. Miss Hampton was already a distinguished nursing educator by virtue of the superior nurse training system she introduced at Johns Hopkins. Having been appointed chairman of the Nursing Congress, Miss

Hampton believed that the exposure provided by the Congress would awaken an interest in nursing reforms among physicians and the general public. According to Isabel Stewart, the four women conversed at great length about the status of nursing and desired improvements (33). The result of this historic meeting was to have a direct influence on the future organization and registration of American nurses.

Support for an organized system of nurse training and the registering of diplomas appeared in one nursing periodical early in 1893 (8). That same year, references to registration appeared in several addresses delivered at the Nursing Congress. The immediate outcome of the proceedings in Chicago, however, was the organization of the American Society of Superintendents of Training Schools for Nurses (hereafter called the Superintendents' Society), whose membership comprised many of the foremost nursing educators of the day and whose fundamental aims were equal and acceptable standards of education for all trained nurses. Collectively, these guardians of nursing constituted an illustrious group that would soon establish discriminating guidelines for reform. Individually, a number of these women would later assume leadership positions in the movement for legal regulation in their respective states. In 1894, however, the limited membership of this elite society precluded their implementation of an overt campaign for registration. The time for such action was not yet at hand; no approved educational standard had been developed, and no collegial bond existed between nurses.

From its inception, the Superintendents' Society considered the founding of a national organization for nurses as one of its priorities. The unrestrained growth of unsound training schools fueled the erratic state of nursing education and gave the matter of national unification increasing urgency. Protection of the public and the welfare of the individual nurse were issues of vital concern. Lavinia Dock identified the purposes of a national organization in her classic address of 1896 (6):

> To unite and fraternize all the best of our profession that they will learn to stand together, move together, work together . . . To acquire influence, moral dignity and force as a body, and to undertake successfully the solution of those varied complications which . . . time and circumstances are fast bringing into nursing questions.

National organization became a reality on February 12, 1897, with the founding of the Associated Alumnae of Trained Nurses of the United States and Canada (hereafter called the Associated Alumnae). Alumnae societies that would later evolve into state associations became the designated units for membership. The steps culminating in the creation of the national association illustrate the infinite wisdom with which the Superintendents' Society designed their plan for progress. State associations would eventually provide the means for achieving legal regulation, and the coordination of strategies was to be the responsibility of the parent organization, the Associated Alumnae. The justification of nursing's emphasis on state promotion of registration laws is contained in the "states' rights" provision (tenth amendment) of the Constitution of the United States. A national licensing proposal would, therefore, conflict with the right of each state to enact such legislation.

The gathering momentum for registration manifested itself between 1898 and 1902 in selected publicity campaigns and activities that centered on the formation of state associations. State organization was a viable expectation because of the establishment of additional alumnae societies and, in some instances, the combining of these societies. On November 9, 1899, Sophia F. Palmer, superintendent of the Rochester City Hospital, and Eva Allerton of the Homeopathic Hospital in Rochester addressed the New York State Federation of Women's Clubs on the subject of state legislation for nurses. Designed to stimulate public awareness, these talks may well have been the first to petition support for registration from a body of laypersons.

The launching of the *American Journal of Nursing* in 1900 added a powerful voice to nursing's agenda. The indomitable pro-registration position of the Journal's first editor, Sophia F. Palmer, was reflected in the many editorials appearing during the early years of publication. Each monthly issue was utilized as a vehicle for disseminating information on the urgency of the movement and the progress being made. It was Miss Palmer's conviction that the absence in this country of a periodical created by nurses for nurses was a deterrent to the growth of the profession. The *American Journal of Nursing*, as nursing's official organ, expertly filled this void and succeeded in keeping nurses in touch with significant questions and developments.

Although many physicians supported nursing's legislative aims, others were less appreciative of the perceived assertiveness demonstrated by nurses seeking legal protection. Opponents believed that nursing was going too far in its bid for internal control. Medical journals of the time contained numerous articles denouncing nursing organizations for fostering their own self-interest and threatening the authority of medicine and the rights of hospitals.

The registration movement thrived despite this negative criticism, and efforts to unite nurses through state associations continued unabated throughout 1900. New York was first to establish a state association in April 1901. Virginia organized in June of the same year; Illinois followed in August and New Jersey in December. Although three of the four initial states to organize included registration in their objectives, the priority given to legal regulation was most apparent at the Third International Congress of Nurses held in conjunction with the World's Pan American Exposition at Buffalo, New York, in 1901.

The major thrust of the proceedings was the legal improvement and control of nursing education and practice. The resolution unanimously adopted by those present stated (5): "It is the duty of the nursing profession of every country to work for suitable legislative enactments regulating the education of nurses, and protecting the interests of the public, by securing State examinations and public registration, with the proper penalties for enforcing the same."

The transactions of the Congress sparked the determination of both American and foreign nurses, and many embarked on campaigns to advance nursing associations and legislation.

With organization as its cornerstone, the registration movement in the United States has followed a well-defined path toward fruition. Originating with the Superintendents' Society, it progressed through the planning phase via the Associated Alumnae and to final implementation by state associations. The cohesiveness of the leadership provided an outstanding model for the rank and file and underscored the importance of unity in the execution of change.

Licensure and Registration

Mrs. Bedford Fenwick, while not an American, deserves recognition as the prime mover of legal regulation for nursing. By virtue of the ideals she communicated, and the force and extension of her influence, nurses in this country were motivated to initiate the necessary measures for accomplishment.

In the United States, it was Sophia F. Palmer and Lavinia Dock who gave substance to the movement and provided the essential leadership. As editor-in-chief of the *American Journal of Nursing,* Miss Palmer regularly and explicitly aired statements in favor of registration. She brought relevant letters, discussions, and announcements of meetings to the attention of her readers and published proposed registration bills to provide examples for nurses in other states. Her effective contributions to the promotion of a registration law in New York State later earned her an appointment to the New York State Board of Nurse Examiners, on which she served as its first president.

Lavinia Lloyd Dock served organized nursing in many elected ca-

pacities throughout her career, and her intelligence and high principles are clearly evident in the many addresses she delivered and
articles she wrote. During her tenure as foreign correspondent for
the *American Journal of Nursing*, she fostered international col-
legiality and focused attention on issues of consequence to the nursing world. An admitted revolutionary, Miss Dock frequently demonstrated radical behavior in her defense of women's rights and
condemnation of social injustice. In espousing equality for women,
she was one of the few nurses to openly take a stand on this question
at a time when it was unpopular to do so. She displayed similar zeal
in her crusade for the regulation of nursing. In both New York and
New Jersey, she assisted the registration movement with recommendations that were realistic, timely, and well researched.

Isabel Hampton Robb was equally committed to legislative reform and viewed it as the means for achieving professional distinction for nursing. Although her role in the actual attainment of laws
was supportive rather than activist, Mrs. Robb was nevertheless a
key figure in the earlier development and timing of the registration
movement. By designing a sound organizational pattern for American nursing and supervising its logical progression, she ultimately
provided the framework for a unified approach to legislation. Mrs.
Robb's profound interest in the advancement of nursing generated
her overt approval of nurse registration, and her stature as a leader
increased the value of her endorsement.

The completion of the organizational phase made it possible for
nursing's leaders to direct their attention to the enactment of legislation. Accordingly, their next step was the promotion of strategies
that would actualize their goal. Foremost was the need to apprise
the nursing community of the anticipated beneficial effects of registration and arouse a spirit of unified commitment to its attainment.
The second strategy was the wider circulation of publicity designed
to enlist the support of the general public. Nurses were requested to
write letters to newspapers, physicians, and influential legislators
protesting the activities of unreliable training schools and reinforc-
ing the need for legal controls to curb their proliferation. It was
considered politically expedient to obtain the sanction of organized
medicine and other prominent groups in order to increase the likelihood of favorable actions by the various legislative bodies. Third, it
was advised that each state nurses' association appoint a legislative
committee that would, with the advice of legal counsel, draft a suitable bill for approval by the association. Once this was accomplished, arrangements could be made, through appropriate channels,
to have the bill introduced in the legislature. Fourth, the manner in
which nurses conducted themselves when implementing their tac-

tical measures was a matter of some importance to the leadership. Discretion and decorum were identified as expected behaviors even in the face of hostile opposition. It was recognized that compromise would be a necessary component of the struggle to achieve registration. Nevertheless, nurses were urged to maintain their right to self-regulation since internal control was viewed as intrinsic to the effectiveness of the laws. The final strategy was the continual sharing of information regarding procedures and progress, and victories and defeats. A uniform approach to registration was considered highly desirable and more likely to occur in a collegial environment.

Consistent with the need for uniformity was the question of an appropriate title for the nurses who met the legally prescribed criteria for registration. Clearly, a universal title that could be incorporated into the proposed legislation in each state would minimize confusion, enhance conformity, and facilitate the movement of nurses from one state to another. "Registered Nurse" had been adopted by British registrationists in the early 1900s, and, after considerable debate among members of several state nurses' associations, it was finally selected as the appropriate title in this country.

Early Legislation

New York, with its concentration of superior training facilities and dedicated nursing leaders, undeniably led the rest of the states in introducing the protocols that would assure the enactment of legislation for trained nurses. New York's leadership position was not surprising in light of the state's many previous accomplishments in the areas of education and legislation for women. The founding of Vassar College in 1861 provided women with the opportunity for higher education. This was followed by their admission to Barnard College in 1889 and Cornell University in 1892. Medical education was also opened to women with the establishment of the Women's Medical College of the New York Infirmary in 1867. The improvement in the education of women teachers and the inclusion of women in the legal profession were other conspicuous examples of the early strides made in New York. Legislation that enabled women to undertake business ventures, enter into contractual agreements, and control their own property were additional prototypes of progressivism.

Irrespective of these imposing achievements and the New York State Nurses' Association's effective promotion of legal controls, New York was neither the first nor the second state to enact a registration law. North Carolina earned the distinction of being first when its bill became law on March 3, 1903 (23). New Jersey's bill was signed into law on April 7, 1903 (32), and on April 27, 1903, New York followed suite (21). Virginia, the only other state to enact a registration law in 1903, did so on May 14 (1).

It was Mary Lewis Wyche who was most responsible for the organization and registration of nurses in North Carolina. Miss Wyche had established North Carolina's first training school for nurses in 1894 at the Rex Hospital in Raleigh. After attending the Buffalo Congress in 1901, Miss Wyche returned to Raleigh to begin her campaign for a state association and a registration law (36).

As chairman of the legislative committee of the North Carolina State Nurses' Association, Miss Wyche was instrumental in framing the law that was introduced in the General Assembly by John C. Drewry early in 1903. The bill listed eligibility requirements that firmly specified the quality and quantity of training acceptable for licensure and registration. Included in the provisions were a minimum age requirement of twenty-three; the formation of a State Board of Trained Nurses, comprised of four licensed nurses and three physicians who would be responsible for the examination of candidates; and a waiver of examination clause for nurses with four to five years of experience who submitted documentation of their moral fitness and professional capabilities. The proposed law also granted the Board the right to censure for cause, allowed licensed nurses to use the title "Registered Nurse," and prevented anyone from practicing professional nursing without a license or from falsely representing themselves as thus qualified (36).

The bill was uncontested in the North Carolina House of Representatives and approved on January 28. In the Senate, however, the Committee on Public Health defeated the nurses' proposal and presented a considerably altered substitute version. Efforts to convince the legislature of the merits of the nurses' bill were to no avail. Opposition from a group of physicians and legislators was particularly vehement, and the nursing association was unable to generate adequate public support. The nurses conceded on a number of salient points and the substitute bill was approved by the General Assembly and signed by Governor Charles B. Aycock. The law, in failing to prohibit the untrained from practicing nursing, merely protected the RN title and was thus substantially weakened. Despite the significant deficiencies in this initial nurse registration law, its attainment was unprecedented in this country and was considered by many to be a major breakthrough.

New Jersey's nurses were next to submit a bill to their state legislature. Introduced on January 26, 1903, by Assemblyman Harry Scovel of Camden, the bill was subjected to numerous delays initiated by the opposition in the hope that the bill would be "killed" before the legislature could act on it (9). Irene T. Fallon, president of the New Jersey State Nurses' Association from 1902 to 1903, was determined to see the bill survive. Together with Sophia A. Bruckner, who had assisted in drafting the bill, Miss Fallon made frequent trips to the State House at Trenton to promote the bill and convince undecided legislators to vote in favor of its passage. With the assistance of several prominent political figures, Miss Fallon and Miss Bruckner were successful in defeating their opponents. The bill was passed in the legislature and subsequently signed by Governor Franklin Murphy.

Considered by many the weakest of the first four laws, New Jersey's registration act neglected to provide for state examinations, omitted the establishment of a state board for nursing, and substituted the title "Graduate Nurse" for "Registered Nurse." The licensing provision was based on nebulous requirements and allowed for licenses to be issued by county clerks (27). Acutely aware of the law's shortcomings, the New Jersey State Nurses' Association focused their attention on amending the law. A 1907 attempt failed, but on April 1, 1912, a new law widely supported by medicine and the public was signed by Governor Woodrow Wilson. Although still permissive, the 1912 enactment called for stronger educational controls, formation of the State Board of Examiners of Nurses, recognition of the RN title, and licensure by waiver of examination (20).

In New York, the campaign for registration began in April 1902, with the formation of the Committee on Legislation of the New York State Nurses' Association. Its chairman was Eva Allerton, who is generally acknowledged as the driving force behind the successful enactment of New York's nurse registration act. After obtaining recommendations from prominent members of the Board of Regents and State Senator William W. Armstrong, Miss Allerton's committee drafted the bill, which was introduced by Senator Armstrong in the New York State Senate on February 23, 1903 (13). The advice of the Regents was particularly relevant because of the Board's unique supervisory role in safeguarding professional education and practice in New York State.

The bill's registration requirements stipulated a minimum age of twenty-one, two years of training in a hospital registered by the Board of Regents, and evidence of appropriate moral behavior. Additional provisions included formation of a five-member board of examiners, who were appointed from a list of nominees submitted by the nurses' association, permission to use the title "Registered Nurse," waiver of examination clause, and penalties for violation of the law (26).

Protesting the bill were a number of physicians who objected to nursing's self-regulation, some hospital authorities whose training schools would be jeopardized, and a group of nurses who were in conflict with the proposed composition of the examining board. A substantially weaker bill, which had been introduced in the State Assembly, was supported by the opposition. The ensuing hearings conducted in Albany in March 1903 were attended by supporters and opponents of the nurses' bill. After several weeks of debate, a compromise bill was negotiated, approved by the legislature, and signed by Governor Benjamin Barker Odell. The amended version did not appreciably alter the intent of the original; the insertion of clauses called for more stringent penalties for violators and re-registration every three years probably strengthened the bill. However, the counterproductive activities of the adversaries undoubtedly prevented New York from being the first to enact a registration law.

The legislation enacted in New York was considered the most efficient of the early registration laws. Compared with other states that were seeking legal controls, New York had several distinct advantages. First, its educational system and licensing laws were unequaled anywhere in the nation. Second the aggregation of trained nurses in New York exceeded the number in other states and was reflected in the New York State Nurses' Association's increased membership and power as a political pressure group. Third, the presence in New York of an impressive number of outstanding nurse leaders and reputable training schools generated a locus of influence unsurpassed elsewhere. In years to come, New York's registered nurses would continue to demonstrate exceptional leadership ability in the promotion of more effective regulatory mechanisms.

Attainment of legal controls for nurses in Virginia followed events similar to those in the three states already delineated. Under the leadership of Sadie Heath Cabaniss and Agnes Dillon Randolph, the Virginia State Nurses' Association framed the bill that was submitted to the legislature in January 1903. Despite resistance from opponents, the major provisions of the bill remained intact. Approved by the Virginia General Assembly on May 1, 1903, the bill was signed within two weeks by Governor Andrew Jackson Montague. Although educational requirements were minimal, the law did provide for the establishment of an all-nurse examining board, waiver of examination for those qualified, and censure for cause (11).

The Illinois Graduate Nurses' Association, fifth to seek registration in 1903, failed in its attempt to enact a law. Harriet Fulmer, president of the Association, and Isabel McIsaac, superintendent of the Illinois Training School, collaborated in the preparation of the bill introduced in the Illinois State Senate on January 20, 1903. Meeting with serious opposition from the Illinois Board of Health, the nurses agreed to a compromise measure that was finally approved by the legislature in April. Governor Richard Yates vetoed the bill, however, and Illinois thus became the first state to deny its nurses the opportunity to legally elevate standards (7).

In describing the first five legislative campaigns, emphasis has been placed on those specific nurses whose activities were of primary significance. However, recognition is also due the many unidentified nurses who supported the work of their state associations. Their willing participation was fundamental to the attainment of the first four laws, and the example they set encouraged the extension of the registration movement to other states. Another factor that motivated expanded interest was the phenomenal increase in the number of nurse training institutions. The United States government placed the number at 724 by 1904.

Maryland was the only state to enact a nurse registration law in 1904. Through the influence of Miss M. Adelaide Nutting, a state association was founded and a registration bill formulated. Support for nursing's goals was widespread in Maryland, and many esteemed individuals advocated enactment of the proposed law. Virtually unopposed and unaltered in the Maryland legislature, the bill was signed by Governor John W. Smith on March 25 (25).

Although their specifications varied and their effectiveness was limited, the early laws were nevertheless regarded as enormous accomplishments. The recognition attained by nursing in so brief a time span was a remarkable achievement when compared with the slower progress made by other professions such as medicine and law. Many factors combined to provide a favorable climate for nursing's rapid acquisition of legislative reform. First, the timing coincided with the increase in state legislation for human welfare. Protection of the public, as reflected in the enactment of labor laws and higher standards for professional licensing, was assuming greater importance. Second, the number of women in business, education, and the professions was on the rise. Presumably, the attempt by a group of women to seek legal recourse was no longer viewed with the degree of alarm manifested in prior years. Third, skilled nursing was becoming more highly valued as a primary component of patient care. In increasing numbers, physicians and hospitals were seeking the services of trained nurses. Fourth, the course of action taken by nursing was appropriately planned and carried out. Organizational steps, publicity, and campaign strategies had been explicitly designed to advance the legal sanctions of educational standards for nurses. Fifth, nursing's leaders approached the prospect of legislation with realistic expectations. They frequently reiterated that concessions would be required, and they repeatedly affirmed that the initial laws provided the foundation for stronger enactments in the future. Their argument that small gains were better than none undoubtedly provided the impetus for the acceptance of compromise. Finally, the campaigns for nurse registration were conducted with the dignity befitting an aspiring profession. The exemplary behavior demonstrated by the nurses involved in the presentation of legislative proposals earned the respect of legislators, peers, and other professionals.

In 1905, Indiana, California, Colorado, and Connecticut enacted registration laws, but attempts to secure such legislation in Iowa, Pennsylvania, and Massachusetts were defeated. By 1907, nursing associations had been organized in twenty-eight states, fifteen of which had achieved registration. Two years later, thirty-three state associations were in existence, and twenty-four of these had attained legislation. By this time, the state-to-state variations in the laws were becoming increasingly obvious and disturbing to nursing's leaders. Nevertheless, the registration movement continued. Thirty-three acts were passed by 1912, forty by 1915, and forty-five by 1917. Twenty years after the enactment of the first four laws, legislation regulating nursing training was operational in forty-eight states, Hawaii, and the District of Columbia. All denied the untrained the use of the RN title, and all specified a period of time when qualified trained nurses were eligible for registration without examination. None, however, prohibited the untrained from practicing nursing.

Despite this permissive feature, the laws were beneficial to a significant degree. Preliminary requirements for entry into nurse training were upgraded, additional subjects were added to basic curricula, and the evaluation of student performance improved. Teaching previously done by physicians declined and was replaced with instruction provided by nurse educators.

Elevated educational standards concomitantly improved nursing competence in the practice setting. Registered nurses were not only more highly skilled, they were more highly valued for their proficiency. Besides initiating improved educational and practice standards, however, the registration laws were credited with enhancing nursing's professional status. Legal sanction, it was believed, dignified nursing and gave it professional legitimacy. In view of organized nursing's social commitment and its emphasis on appropriate education, its early conviction that it qualified as a profession was justified. In recognizing the need for legal controls and initiating the strategies for their achievement, nurses demonstrated the self-motivation and self-direction expected of professionals.

Many physicians endorsed nursing's professional standing, while others disagreed. On more than one occasion, nursing was accused of trade union activities. This criticism was based on the premise that nursing's legislative demands were, in actuality, schemes to control the supply and wages of nurses. In light of nursing's dedication to registration as the means for promoting competence, such allegations were clearly unsupportable. Nursing organizations did not impinge on the freedom of nurses to work nor did they dictate where or under what circumstances nurses could work. According to Justin Miller (17): "The purpose of professional licensure is to secure to society the benefits that come from the services of a highly skilled group and . . . to protect society from those who are not highly skilled yet profess to be."

The disciplinary tools provided by the early laws apparently assisted in promoting professional responsibility. Although somewhat vague in describing grounds for censure and the procedures to be followed, the laws did mandate the suspension or revocation of RN licensure for those guilty of misrepresentation. The most common violations of the law consisted of untrained nurses falsely identifying themselves as registered or trained. Guilty of misdemeanors, the imposters were subject to fine or imprisonment. Others who submitted fraudulent credentials when applying for registration were similarly liable.

Problems facing the early state boards included the failure of some qualified nurses to apply for registration, the indifference of some training schools to provisions in the law, and the ambiguity in the wording of the laws. Validation of the moral fitness of candidates applying for licensure without examination was a particularly thorny issue. The inability or unwillingness of nurses to document the unprofessional conduct of peers was a decided handicap. Additional difficulties stemmed from the laws' indefinite terminology describing educational requirements, the lack of consistency in those requirements between states, and differences in the composition of the various state boards. Another persistent dilemma was the threat of amendments designed to curb nursing's self-regulating powers. When state examinations were begun, further disadvantages were identified. The absence of clear-cut guidelines for validating proficiency compromised the effectiveness of the tests. Nurses preparing the examinations were, in many instances, inexperienced in constructing test questions. The questions were frequently subjective and unclear, which in turn complicated the grading of responses. Since each state board gave its own examination, reliability varied from one state to another (31).

Although all of the limitations were of consequence to nursing's leaders, the flaw that generated the most concern over time was the permissiveness of the laws: they neither defined nor effectively limited the practice of nursing. The freedom of the unqualified to work as nurses without restraint was an issue that continued to confound organized nursing well into the mid-twentieth century.

Despite seemingly overwhelming defects, the laws did produce several desired results. By 1912, an appreciable number of inferior nurse training programs had been abandoned. Although appropriately prepared nurses were still faced with competition generated by the graduates of those programs, it was anticipated that their number would eventually be conspicuously reduced. Registration was not only an effective medium for distinguishing between qualified and unqualified nurses, it also provided the necessary data for evaluating the supply and distribution of trained nurses. The importance of statistical information was reflected in the numerous studies of nursing that followed. Investigations like *Nursing and Nursing Education in the United States* (1923) (more commonly called the "Goldmark Report"), "Nurses, Patients, and Pocketbooks", (1928), and Nursing Schools Today and Tomorrow (1934) relied on statistics to support conclusions (see Chapter 6). The adoption of a system of reregistration assured the currency of those data and, at the same time, re-endorsed the licensee's right to practice as a RN.

The registration laws also influenced the movement of nurse training into institutions of higher learning. Dissatisfied with the apprenticeship educational system fostered by hospital training schools and recognizing the importance of separating educational needs from institutional needs, several outstanding nurse leaders and university educators promoted collegiate education for nurses. Dr. Richard Olding Beard, in a 1909 address to the Superintendents' Society, advocated university education for nurses and reasoned that registration laws provided the effective means by which such educational advancement could be attained. By 1916, undergraduate education was available in ten universities. Predictably, the idea of replacing hospital training with university education was not enthusiastically received by the American Hospital Association (34). Undaunted, some nurse leaders continued to support collegiate education as the appropriate preparation for nursing practice. One of the recommendations of the 1923 "Goldmark Report" reinforced the need for increasing the number of university nursing programs. The Association of Collegiate Schools of Nursing, organized in 1933, continued to foster baccalaureate nursing education. In 1948, Esther Lucile Brown recommended the preparation of two distinct categories of nurses: one professional and the other technical (34). In 1965, the American Nurses' Association (ANA) advocated higher education for licensed professional nurses and associate degree preparation for technical nurses (3). Contrary to those proposals, hospital training schools prevailed and, until the late 1960s, persisted as the predominant providers of nursing education in this country.

In evaluating the effectiveness of the initial licensing legislation, some critics might hastily condemn its omission of collegiate education. However, any attempt to mandate higher education for nursing, at that time, would have been unrealistic. The system of nurse training inaugurated by Florence Nightingale did not encourage university education. Since Miss Nightingale's methods were adopted, with significant variations, by the better American schools, it follows that the hospital became the principal setting for training nurses. Furthermore, university education for women in general was still in its infancy, and the number of undergraduate institutions able to accommodate nursing programs was limited. Additionally, the political impotence of women, as reflected in the absence of suffrage, resulted in their inability to influence the election of officials sympathetic to their goals. Nurses, therefore, were forced to acquiesce to the demands of more powerful groups. Insistence on the inclusion of university education or overly restrictive provisions in the early legislative proposals would have further alienated the opposition and delayed passage of any laws.

Reforms

Irrespective of the restraints that impeded the progress of higher education in nursing, the initial laws constituted the basic legislation on which subsequent reforms were predicated. An outstanding example was the development and implementation of the State Board Test Pool Examination (SBTPE). The introduction of a national qualifying examination for nurse licensure and registration in the United States was largely the work of R. Louise McManus of Teachers College, Columbia University. Between 1944 and 1950, the SBTPE gradually became the accepted testing mechanism for all states, the District of Columbia, and Hawaii (31). Among the states, however, the minimum passing scores frequently differed. Identified as a barrier to interstate licensure for some candidates, the problem was resolved when nearly all states agreed on a uniform passing grade of 350 for each of the five segments of the examination.

Although the SBTPE has been judged reliable as a knowledge-testing tool, its format was recently altered: in July 1982, a newly designed examination was given. Departure from previous procedure is also observable with respect to the organization accountable for preparation of the test. Formerly constructed under the auspices of the National League for Nursing (NLN), the SBTPE is no longer within that body's jurisdiction. Instead, the National Council of State Boards now has major responsibility for planning, approving, and evaluating the examination, which is called the NCLEX.

With regard to the status of the Council of State Boards, a notable change has occurred in recent years. Responding to speculation concerning the propriety of the relationship between the Council and the ANA, members of the Council voted, in 1978, to become a discrete, autonomous body. Professional associations and their licensing procedures were being subjected to public and federal scrutiny in the 1970s. The fact that the Council was subsidized by the ANA was a serious issue, one that was open to charges of conflict of interest. The controversial nature of the alliance motivated the Council to re-examine its position. The outcome of the deliberations was the establishment, in 1979, of an independent organization—the National Council of State Boards (30).

Besides providing the impetus for improved testing mechanisms, licensure and registration precipitated constructive changes in the laws themselves. Amendments to and revisions of existing legislation were repeatedly advanced by state nurses' associations in the years following the initial enactments. Beginning as isolated campaigns confined to one or two states, legislative activity increased as additional state societies took steps to improve their laws. From approximately 1917 to the early 1920s, limited revisions were carried out in North Carolina (1917), California and Illinois (1919), and New York (1920). In others, only amendments were obtained. Generally superior to the earlier laws, but still permissive, the new legislation focused on educational standardization. The revised laws in California and New York also provided regulations governing the training and registration of attendants.

The Role of ANA

Beginning in 1915, the ANA (formerly the Associated Alumnae) took a more active interest in state legislative affairs. The Association's Committee on Legislation was established for the purpose of examining the variations in the existing laws. By 1919, that Committee had evolved into the Legislative Section of ANA, whose tasks included the development of a model law that could serve as a guide for state associations seeking legislation. The failure of any state to enact a mandatory nurse licensure act was a source of considerable dismay to organized nursing's leaders; the continuing discrepencies in the laws had become intolerable. In 1935, representatives of ANA, the National League of Nursing Education (formerly the Superintendents' Society), and the National Organization for Public Health Nursing combined to establish the Joint Advisory Committee on Legislation. After concluding a detailed study of the status of nurse licensure in forty-one constituencies, the Joint Advisory Committee issued its statement endorsing compulsory licensure for all nurses receiving financial remuneration for their services. The Committee also provided assistance to state societies preparing new laws. Publicity supportive of mandatory nurse licensure increased in the literature but, despite the rational arguments advanced by the nursing profession, actual results proved disappointing. Following the success of New York's nurses in obtaining the first compulsory nurse practice act in 1938, attempts in other states were largely unproductive. By 1951, only five states plus Hawaii had enacted such legislation. Because of the acute shortage of nurses during the World War II years, New York's laws did not become effective until 1949. Undoubtedly, the delay was generated by the concern that restrictive legislation would further limit the availability of nursing personnel. Once implemented, the law provided a basic definition of nursing and limited its practice to registered professional and practical nurses only.

Current Status

External resistance to mandatory nurse licensure persisted throughout the 1950s and, in some cases, still survives. Permissive legislation prevails in Texas, Oklahoma, and the District of Columbia. Indiana, after a long struggle, finally enacted a mandatory law, which became effective in 1982. Even after compulsory laws had been enacted in a majority of the states, those laws did not universally pertain to practical nurses. Lack of clarity in the provisions defining professional nursing practice produced inconsistent interpretations and reduced the laws' effectiveness. In 1972, New York provided the most appropriate solution to the problem of ambiguity. Through enactment of the Laverne-Pisani Bill, the sphere of the registered nurse was explicitly drawn and the nature of nursing practice clearly defined (22).

Increasing enactment of improved nurse practice acts has generated a resurgence of activities formulated to crush nursing's independence and limit its professional responsibilities. Organizations with vested interests have repeatedly attempted to alter the intent of the laws. At the same time, the federal government and concerned consumer groups were examining the licensing procedures of the health professions, with particular attention to the accountability of licensing boards. The concept of institutional licensure and the implementation of sunset laws evolved as a direct result of these inquiries. The promoters of institutional licensure assert that individual licensing for health care providers (excluding physicians) is no longer justifiable. Individual licensure, they argue, cannot guarantee ongoing competence. The licensing of employing institutions, on the other hand, would place responsibility for assuring quality on the agency rather than the individual. Thus, the employing facility could decide, without regard for educational qualifications, how its personnel were to be utilized. The plan, proponents maintain, would reduce consumer costs and increase efficiency. In responding to the proposed licensing measure, one well-known nursing educator declared (29):

> *Vested interests endeavor to do away with registered nurse licensure and, at the same time, diligently engage in legislative activities directed toward indiscriminate licensing of disparate and nebulously defined populations, providing such populations are made subject to the control of some medical priesthood.*

Sunset laws have been enacted in a majority of states to facilitate the review of state examining boards. Should the boards fail to meet statutory standards, the evaluating body can recommend termination. Since reinstatement requires new legislation, the state has the option of allowing the "sun to set" on the particular board's tenure. The advent of sunset legislation has produced considerable uneasiness among nurses in states where their examining boards might be in jeopardy.

To some degree, these repeated assaults on nursing's control over its own professional quality stem from nursing's failure to assert itself as a political force in this country. A sense of affiliation among nurses seems to have dissipated over time. This lack of cohesiveness is reflected in the small percentage of nurses actively supporting their principal professional organization. Of the 1,375,208 registered nurses in the United States, only 181,212 are members of ANA (2). The ANA is unquestionably weakened by this obvious disinterest. Conversely, organized medicine's political strength is enhanced by the support received from members; approximately 50 per cent of America's licensed physicians belong to the American Medical Association (AMA) (24). Additional circumstances, of course, underlie the differences in power between the AMA and the ANA. The AMA has greater wealth, superior political maneuverability, and more authority over its members. The ANA's potential for influence is considerably handicapped by the absence of those resources. Without a membership that is more representative of the total registered nurse population, the ANA and its constituent state associations face greater pressures in challenging those groups seeking to obstruct nursing's progress. Other factors must also be acknowledged as contributing to nursing's powerlessness. Nursing remains predominantly a woman's field, subject to the social stigma traditionally applied to women seeking professional equality. Furthermore, since nurses are mainly employees rather than independent practitioners, their authority is severely compromised.

Although the efficiency of professional licensure is being questioned by selected groups, it nevertheless remains the principal credentialing measure for nurses. Similar to the goals of 1903, appropriate recognition of the qualified is still one of organized nursing's primary concerns. In the past, a single mechanism was sought that would distinguish between the competent and incompetent. Presently, two categories of licensed nurses are recognized: professional and practical. Complicating the credentialing issue is the triad of routes to RN licensure. Graduates of diploma, associate degree, and baccalaureate degree programs are equally eligible for the NCLEX and are awarded the same RN license on satisfactory completion of all requirements. In view of current educational and scientific advancement, some professional nurses have taken the position that a baccalaureate degree should be legally mandated as the minimum educational requirement for practice as an RN. Professional nursing practice has become more complex and less mechanical. Nurses are expected to make decisions relative to the responses of patients, intervene with appropriate nursing actions, and evaluate the effectiveness of their nursing care. These responsibilities, some nurse educators believe, require the kind of educational base available through baccalaureate education. Continuation of three entry levels for the same license implies that there is no distinction in preparation and perpetuates the disregard for educational qualifications often demonstrated by employing institutions when assigning their personnel. However, efforts to enact a professional nurse licensing law requiring a baccalaureate degree for practice as an RN have thus far met with defeat. Nevertheless, diploma schools have declined while associate degree and baccalaureate programs have increased (35).

The proclivity among nurses for advanced education and the evolution of a multitude of diverse opportunities for acquiring such education present additional challenges to existing credentialing methods. The emergence of expanded roles in nursing, i.e., clinical specialists and nurse practitioners, and the involvement of nurses in primary care delivery have generated renewed interest in credential-ing and promoted the growth of voluntary credentialing mecha-nisms that acknowledge superior achievement.

Certification

Certification as a method for recognizing nurses with special apti-tudes is not a new phenomenon in the history of American nursing. It was utilized as a credentialing measure for public health nurses early in this century. The rapid growth of public health nursing as a specialized area of nursing practice was stimulated by the work of Lillian Wald and her associates in the Henry Street (Nurses') Settle-ment. Begun in 1893, that agency provided direct nursing services to individuals and families through its home visiting program. Based in the community that it served, the Henry Street Nurses' Settlement proved to be an outstanding example of nursing's ability to meet the health needs of select populations. Physical care and health teaching were the principal activities of the early visiting nurses and the ex-cellent quality of their work soon attracted the attention of others involved in the public health movement. Various subspecialties like maternal and child health care, contagious disease nursing, and school nursing emerged within the field of public health nursing. Fearing that the existing mode of hospital-based training was inade-quate for the preparation of nurses capable of assuming these diver-sified roles, nursing leaders encouraged the development of post-graduate education in public health nursing. Another issue of growing importance was the absence of standards for the practice of public health nursing. Leaders were concerned that the proliferation of public health agencies might generate the utilization of unquali-fied nursing personnel. The founding of the National Organization for Public Health Nursing in 1912 provided the means for the estab-lishment of specific criteria for public health nursing practice in the United States.

Demand for the services of public health nurses rose steadily, and by 1916, a significant number were being employed by state govern-ments, local health departments, and other official agencies. At the same time, it was becoming increasingly evident that many of these nurses lacked suitable educational backgrounds for the responsibili-ties they were expected to undertake. The National Organization for Public Health Nursing intensified its promotion of postgraduate study as the most appropriate educational preparation for public health nursing, and the number of programs quickly multiplied across the nation (10).

Certificates were issued to nurses who satisfactorily completed the particular program of study. In some states, however, certification was awarded by waiver to registered nurses already practicing as public health nurses. In California, for example, this was the accepted procedure if the nurse's basic education had taken place in an institution approved by that state's Department of Public Health. By 1921, California had altered its certification process by initiating examinations that determined the eligibility of candidates. Because public health nurses were being increasingly employed by government agencies, several states enacted legislation specifying qualifications for practice. Other states included public health nursing requirements in regulations governing health departments (16). Ostensibly, the movement toward standardization promoted efficiency, and official sanction added weight to the credentials of the public health nurse.

The National Organization for Public Health Nursing functioned in an advisory capacity to public health agencies and fostered educational standards for public health nursing until its dissolution in 1952. By this time, recognition of public health nursing as a specialty area of practice had been attained. In the late 1950s, the ANA began to examine the feasibility of implementing a certification mechanism that would acknowledge the professional achievements of nurses in various areas of clinical practice. Presumably, the emergence of additional specialties in nursing and the growing emphasis on quality assurance in the health professions generated the need to institute this credentialing process. Throughout the 1960s, the ANA took steps to refine its certification procedures and develop appropriate criteria. In 1975, ANA certification was awarded for the first time to ninety-nine nurses who qualified as either pediatric practitioners in ambulatory health care or gerontological specialists. Requirements included RN licensure, a specified period of practice in the particular specialty, documentation of outstanding clinical proficiency, peer endorsement, and satisfactory performance on a certification examination. Within a short time, certification was extended to provide recognition for practitioners of psychiatric, medical-surgical, maternity, and community health nursing. Further expansion of the ANA's program in the late 1970s created additional certification categories, several of which called for evidence of advanced education.

Responding to societal expectations regarding the ongoing competence of health care providers, a number of state nurses' associations developed their own programs for recognizing clinical expertise. Examples include the certification procedures established in the early 1970s in Kansas, Utah, North Dakota, and Colorada. Contrary to the ANA's criteria, advanced educational preparation was not required in these states. Rather, certification credits could be accumulated through such activities as informal study, continuing education courses, and active participation in professional organizations. Although these criteria varied from state to state, validated clinical excellence was expected in all instances. In 1971, a voluntary plan for the certification of psychiatric nurse specialists was introduced in New Jersey. Evidence of graduate education, advanced clinical practice, and a passing grade on a certification examination were required. New York initiated its certification programs for psychiatric-mental health practitioners in 1975. Utilizing criteria consistent with those of New Jersey, New York's process has since been applied to additional specialty areas.

Besides being available through professional nursing associations, certification is attainable through a variety of postgraduate educational programs. Specific certificate-granting programs have been developed in selected areas of specialization. Usually shorter in length than traditional graduate education, these programs tend to focus heavily on clinical practice. Certification is also obtainable in conjunction with educational preparation at the masters level. In this instance, two credentials are awarded: a certificate and a degree.

Supporters of certification have frequently asserted that its standards exceed those of licensure and advanced education. Identified by proponents as a method for regulating and protecting specialized practice, certification has been purported to assure expert quality for the public. In relation to the individual practitioner, certification has been deemed an effective credential for enhancing independence and career mobility. On the other hand, detractors have criticized certification as an attempt by professional organizations to promote their own interests, a device to exclude consumers from certifying boards, and, since performance-based testing has not been incorporated into the criteria, an unsatisfactory method for guaranteeing ongoing competence. Critics have further maintained that the many routes to certification are often redundant and bewildering.

Despite the disparate viewpoints it generates, certification is likely to be retained. Clinical specialization has grown in popularity within the profession, and the number of certified practitioners has increased dramatically over the past decade. It is still too early to predict the long-term effect of this proliferation; however, it must be remembered that certification is principally an internal, voluntary, professional credentialing mechanism. Except for those instances wherein specific nurses are certified through state controls, certification does not carry any official sanction. In their expanded roles, nurse specialists are, at times, called on to function beyond the boundaries permitted by law. Although often necessitated by circumstances, these increasingly independent nursing activities might be viewed as illegitimate. Some physicians have taken the position that the extension of nursing's authority encroaches on medical practice.

As malpractice suits increase, nurses are becoming more acutely aware of their vulnerability under the law. Accordingly, some state nurses' associations have begun campaigns to revise or amend existing nurse practice acts. However, the need for legislation that recognizes the changing scope of nursing practice has yet to be universally acknowledged by state legislatures. The ANA's 1980 publication *Nursing—A Social Policy Statement* can be useful to state organizations grappling with credentialing decisions. By providing a definition of nursing, delineating nursing's responsibilities, and establishing standards for specialization, the ANA has reinforced nursing's social commitment. Nevertheless, until state laws are updated nationwide, many nurses will continue to practice in advanced roles without legal approval. In light of the many questions surrounding the certification process, the emphasis placed on its effectiveness seems excessive to some observers and probably diverts attention from the need to strengthen legal credentialing procedures.

Credentialing of Nursing Education and Service

The movement toward evaluation and credentialing of educational programs in nursing originated in the early twentieth century, shortly after the initial nurse registration laws were enacted. The need to assess the educational quality of nurse training programs was quickly recognized when many candidates applying for registration failed to qualify because of inadequate preparation.

In New York, a system of registration for professional schools was already in effect under the auspices of the Board of Regents. Periodic inspections of these schools were carried out by appointed representatives in order to guarantee that educational requirements were being met. In 1903, nurse licensure became effective in New York State. The following year, Sophia F. Palmer, then president of the State Board of Nurse Examiners, recommended creation of the office of Inspector of Training Schools and further proposed that the position be filled by a qualified nurse. Complying with Miss Palmer's request, the Board of Regents established the office in 1906 and

Anna Alline was appointed to the post of inspector. Since the New York law stipulated that nurses applying for licensure had to be graduates of schools approved and registered by the Board of Regents, inspection of training schools presumably promoted the maintenance of standards.

States that had enacted registration laws followed the example set by New York. In several instances, nurse inspectors were hired; in others, inspection became a function of state boards of nursing. Not a voluntary process, inspection, it was generally believed, led to the expansion of curricula, better teaching methods, and improvements in the living conditions of students. In most cases, however, it had little effect on the exploitation of students as workers. At that time, few hospitals were well staffed by graduate nurses; students were expected to provide the necessary care to patients—frequently at the expense of sound educational principles. Certain schools resisted adherence to the law and a number of them accepted unqualified applicants in order to meet in-service needs. Isabel McIsaac, reporting on the situation in 1912 remarked (15):

> "Looking back it would seem that in the beginning the registration of schools should have been the first consideration rather than the registration of nurses."

Concerned nurse educators advised prospective students to investigate the standards of the schools to which they might apply. Through the medium of the *American Journal of Nursing,* applicants were advised to select the larger training schools since they were more likely to provide thorough theoretical and practical education. Graduates of these schools usually received greater recognition in the form of more responsible positions. The importance of the graduate's eligibility for licensure and registration was also stressed as a consideration in the selection of a training school.

By 1911, higher standards for the registration of nurse training schools in New York State were incorporated in the syllabus issued that year. In Illinois, a classification system for training schools was implemented. Evaluation was based on the bed capacity of the hospital, the effectiveness of the training program, and the level of interest in the student's welfare. Schools were then ranked according to their ability to meet state guidelines. Shortly thereafter, California initiated an accreditation system and the names of approved training schools were published in a survey conducted by the Bureau of Registration of Nurses. The following year, the Louisiana Board of Examiners also published a survey of their accredited training schools in which schools were given a rating of A, B, or C, with A being assigned to the schools with the highest standards.

Disparities in the educational preparation of nurses among the various states seriously hampered the interstate mobility of some trained nurses. What was legally acceptable in one state was frequently unacceptable in another. Consequently, licensed graduates from states with lower standards were prevented by law from acquiring licenses to practice in states with higher standards. Identified as a major impediment to nursing's progress, this lack of consistency became a national issue for organized nursing. As early as 1914, Adelaide Nutting had pointed out to the National League of Nursing Education (NLNE) that the need existed for a nationwide plan to rate schools. In 1915, a subcommittee of the ANA's Committee on Legislation began to collect, from states with registration laws, data relevant to each state's criteria for approving training schools. Findings indicated inequities in the quantity and quality of instruction, requirements for admission, and length of program. Ensuing recommendations centered on the development of uniform qualifications for the accreditation of schools and a standardized curriculum that could be adapted to the needs of individual states. Within two years, both objectives were achieved. A *Standard Curriculum for Schools of Nursing* was published by NLNE in 1917, and the ANA completed its report on the minimum requirements suitable for the accreditation of training schools in 1918. The latter document listed the educational qualifications necessary for entry into training, guidelines for the arrangement of theoretical and practical components within the training school's curriculum, criteria relevant to the teaching faculty, and rules pertaining to residential services for students. Apparently the report was unsuccessful in promoting significant responsiveness from nursing programs, for in 1919, the NLNE's Committee on Nursing Education addressed the issue of a classification system for schools of nursing. The prior introduction by the medical profession of a system of grading medical schools had achieved notable progress in the reduction of substandard schools preparing physicians. Similar results were anticipated by nursing leaders. It was further expected that the plan would facilitate the eventual implementation of an accreditation process. Precipitated by the Goldmark Report of 1923, the Committee on the Grading of Nursing Schools was established in 1926 for the purpose of initiating an appropriate inquiry into and evaluation of nursing schools in the United States. Substantially expanded in scope, the work of the committee eventually covered additional aspects of nursing and took eight years to complete. During that time, two grading surveys were conducted and various reports were produced. But, due to a number of factors, including the way in which statistical data were used in the surveys, schools were neither graded nor classified nor were the findings ever made available to the public. The overall impact of the study in terms of its initial purpose was difficult to assess. Its conclusions, however, provided a definition for distinguishing between appropriate and inappropriate training schools. According to Mary M. Roberts (28):

> *"It seems probable that the continuous release of vivid, well-illustrated, and informative material, through professional and other media, month after month throughout the life of the committee, did more to raise the general level of nursing education than the carefully detailed reports of the schools."*

Miss Roberts' opinion has since been challenged by those who claim that the study was ineffective in changing the attitudes of hospital authorities.

By the late 1930s, numerous accreditation procedures had evolved in nursing. The Association of Collegiate Schools of Nursing, through selective membership protocols, endorsed university programs that met its standards; the National Organization for Public Health Nursing focused on the status of educational programs in public health nursing; and the Catholic Hospital Association's Council on Nursing Education took responsibility for assessing nursing education in Catholic schools. The proliferation of diversified nursing organizations, each with its own accreditation program, was identified as burdensome, repetitious, and costly for educational institutions. Acknowledging that distinctions existed between the mandatory aspect of state approval of schools and the voluntary nature of professional accreditation, NLNE strongly reinforced the importance of the latter mechanism in motivating educational advancement in nursing. Taking the lead in promoting a single, national, professional agency for the accreditation of training programs, NLNE embarked on a study to determine the feasibility of the proposal. Conferences held at that time were attended by representatives from the various nursing organizations and from other professional groups as well. Emphasis was placed on the principle that professional education should be accredited by that particular profession. It was further stressed that accreditation be national in scope and realistic in design. Because of inherent and understandable differences between schools, ranking was deemed inappropriate and on-site visitation was viewed as a necessary component. The urgency of the issue was another factor recognized by those who participated.

Fifty-seven schools were asked to cooperate in NLNE's pilot project. All selected schools had satisfactory reputations but varied in geographic location, size, source of funding, and affiliation. Fifty-one schools were actually studied and the outcomes apparently motivated further development of the accreditation plan. By 1939, NLNE was prepared to initiate its program, and publicity encouraging schools to voluntarily seek accreditation was published in the *American Journal of Nursing*. The response was less than favorable and only 123 schools had complied by 1949. This lack of interest was attributed to the expense involved in the credentialing process. Most schools could ill afford the cost and, therefore, declined the opportunity. In the meantime, those in disagreement with NLNE's accrediting function criticized it as an attempt to control educational institutions, restrict the number of nursing students, and convert nurse training into collegiate education. The American Hospital Association, for example, withheld approval of the NLNE's program because it was not convinced that accreditation would promote better nursing education.

In 1948, a new effort to implement a national accrediting system was undertaken. This time, the six major nursing organizations joined together to found the Joint Committee on the Unification of Accrediting Activities. By the following year, the efforts of the Joint Committee had produced the National Nursing Accrediting Service (NNAS), whose principal function was to be the evaluation and accreditation of nursing programs throughout the country. The NNAS established separate boards of review for collegiate programs, diploma schools, public health nursing education, and postgraduate programs. The accrediting process that emerged provided the framework for the modified system that was later adopted and, in varying degrees, still survives (14).

Accreditation of Educational Programs

At the same time that the Joint Committee was seeking to coordinate accreditation services, another national committee was involved in designing a classification system for basic programs in nursing. Representing various health care organizations, the National Committee for the Improvement of Nursing Services was formed to survey and classify schools according to predetermined criteria. Esther Lucile Brown's study, published in 1948 under the title *Nursing for the Future*, had provided the impetus for the organization of that committee and was also credited with accelerating the movement toward unified accreditation in nursing (see Chapter 6). Compared with accreditation, which was a long-term, diversified process involving all levels of nursing education, classification was considered a short-term, comprehensive mechanism related to basic education. Published in the *American Journal of Nursing* in late 1949 and in the committee's report, *Nursing Schools in the Mid-Century*, the classification list showed many schools in an unfavorable light. Responding to the protests generated by the classification process, the National Nursing Accrediting Service (NNAS) initiated a temporary accrediting procedure that motivated wide acceptance. By the end of 1952, approximately 600 nursing programs had acquired temporary accreditation (14). Hailed by many nurse leaders as an enormous achievement, the work of NNAS inspired renewed commitment to accreditation as a viable method for stimulating educational reform.

The consolidation and restructuring of nursing's principal organizations in 1952 was to have a significant impact on the future direction of the accreditation process in nursing. That year marked the reorganization of the ANA and its merger with the National Association of Colored Graduate Nurses. The National Organization for Public Health Nursing, Association of Collegiate Schools of Nursing, and NLNE fused with the newly organized National League for Nursing. Only the American Association of Industrial Nurses chose to retain its independence as a separate society. In 1953, NLN assumed full responsibility for accrediting educational programs in nursing when it absorbed the National Nursing Accrediting Service.

Implementation of accrediting services by NLN required on-site evaluation visits and was thought to be an unwarranted expense by many administrators of diploma schools. Questions were raised with respect to the purposes and effects of NLN's accreditation program. Some critics declared that it fostered associate and baccalaureate degree education to the detriment of hospital schools. Other opponents argued that accreditation promoted rigid standardization, which in turn restricted creativity and innovation. Representatives of NLN countered that accreditation applied to all programs, its goals being the elevation of standards for nursing education, appropriate recognition of schools striving to upgrade their educational programs, and protection of the public.

Over the years, the NLN has consistently reviewed and revised its accreditation procedures, in keeping with trends in education and credentialing. Criteria for accreditation have been strengthened and many schools have made notable curriculum improvements. Principally a peer process in the way criteria are applied and voluntarily sought by educational programs, accreditation is available through each of four corresponding councils of NLN: the Council of Associate Degree Programs, the Council of Baccalaureate and Higher Degree Programs, the Council of Diploma Programs, and the Council of Practical Nursing Programs.

With respect to nursing programs offered by colleges and universities, it is important to differentiate between professional accreditation of specific programs within institutions and institutional accreditation, which focuses on the educational institution as a whole. The first type is performed by members of the related profession; the second is carried out by an appropriate regional accrediting body. Thus, associate, baccalaureate, and masters degree programs in nursing are accredited by NLN, whereas the institutions in which these programs reside are accredited by agencies like the North Central Association, Middle States Association, or any one of four other such territorial associations. In the case of hospital-based programs, these too are accredited by NLN but the hospital itself is accredited by the Joint Commission on Accreditation of Hospitals (JCAH). General institutional accreditation is germane to the United States and dates back to the 1900s, when educational facilities themselves introduced the concept in order to elevate standards and discourage governmental intervention in educational policy-making.

State boards of nursing, as licensure-granting agencies, are also vested with the power to credential basic educational programs in nursing that prepare graduates for licensing examinations. More an approval mechanism than an accreditation process, state board recognition is awarded to those programs meeting the minimum requirements established by the respective states. Before any nursing program can be accredited by NLN, it must first attain state board approval and must be located in an accredited institution.

The six steps involved in NLN's accreditation process are as follows (19):

1. Determination of eligibility for NLN evaluation
2. Initiation of the process
3. The self-study and the writing of the self-study report
4. The accreditation visit
5. Evaluation by the appropriate board of review
6. Continuing self-study and ongoing program development and improvement

Eligibility is established when it is ascertained that the program is legally qualified to issue credentials such as a degree or diploma, is offered by an accredited institution, is approved by the appropriate state board, and is currently in operation. The actual process begins when the program's administrator has fulfilled all planning arrangements, and authorization from NLN has been obtained. Inherent in the self-study component is a period of introspection on the part of those involved in the particular program. Strengths, weaknesses, and educational resources and innovations are identified, and students, faculty, and other personnel assume active roles in the self-evaluation process. Following submission of the self-study report, NLN reviews it to determine if the information is presented in accordance with established guidelines. The accreditation visit by peers is then utilized to validate the findings of the self-study report. Visitors are nurse educators from similar types of programs who conduct the visit in accordance with specific NLN regulations. Finally, decisions regarding accreditation are made by a board of review after all data have been appraised. Accreditation, whether it be for the first time or continuing, may be awarded unconditionally, granted with recommendations, or denied. A mechanism for appeal is provided to programs in situations wherein there is disagreement with the board's conclusions (19). Boards of Review and Appeal were formally appointed. They are now elected from the membership in a given council, such as the Council of Baccalaureate and Higher Degrees.

In cooperation with the American Public Health Association, NLN participates actively in the evaluation and accreditation of agencies providing community nursing services. Begun in 1966 through the joint effort of both organizations, the credentialing of community health agencies was generated by increasing concern over the status of health care in this country. As in the care of educational programs, the accreditation of service organizations is a voluntary, self-initiated, peer process designed to promote high standards and assure competence. Except for differences in the NLN Council involved in the accreditation and the criteria pertaining to on-site visitors, essentials of the accrediting procedure are similar to those described for nursing education. However, the additional component of accountability for practice standards is an important aspect of the process. Factors such as the particular agency's responsiveness to community health needs, effectiveness in implementing service programs, reliability in informing consumers of available resources, and commitment to the appropriate utilization and education development of its staff are intrinsic to the self-study phase and the review board's decision (18).

Accreditation of Hospitals

Hospital nursing services are also subject to the scrutiny of a professional accrediting body, but in this instance the responsibility lies with the Joint Commission on Accreditation of Hospitals. Organized in 1951, JCAH is principally a coalition of physicians and hospital administrators whose tasks include the development of standards for hospitals and related institutions and the assessment and accreditation of these facilities. Standards for patient care established by the JCAH shortly after it was founded have been integrated into the criteria for accreditation. In 1968, the ANA's nursing practice standards were incorporated into the JCAH's accreditation guidelines. Identified as a positive force in the promotion of constructive change, JCAH's accreditation standards have provided the means for more efficient utilization of nursing personnel. The seven standards presently applied to nursing center on the qualifications and roles of nurse administrators, the appropriate functions of registered nurses, the organization of nursing departments, the application of the nursing process, the availability of in-service education, the policies affecting nursing practice, and the periodic evaluation of nursing staff and nursing care (12).

Current proposals by JCAH to revise its standards in 1983 have generated heated reactions from organized nursing. It is anticipated that the projected elimination of nursing standards and the substitution of three ambiguous goals will reduce the quality of nursing care, dilute nursing's role, and ease restraints now applicable to non-nursing employees. These goals are:

Goal I
An organized nursing department/service assumes responsibility, with commensurate authority for reasonably assuring that the quality of nursing care delivered to patients is consistent with currently available knowledge and nursing skills.

Goal II
The organized nursing department/service maintains a high standard of professional performance and conduct.

Goal III
Quality patient care is achieved and maintained through a department/service program for monitoring patient care, and identifying and resolving important problems. This program is integrated/coordinated with the hospital's overall quality assurance program.

Described as a threat to the safety of patients, the planned change reintroduces the spectre of external control of nursing. Once again, nursing is being forced to defend its well-established right to self-regulation. Determined nurses are vigorously rejecting the JCAH proposal and working toward its defeat.

Over the years, nursing has repeatedly demonstrated responsible behavior in the formulation and implementation of standards designed to improve the quality of nursing education and practice. Credentialing in nursing evolved as a natural consequence of those efforts and provided the basis for validating conformity to the established criteria. However, the privilege of professions to institute and self-administer quality controls has been recently examined and questioned by outside forces. The increasing interest of the federal government in credentialing mechanisms, for example, is reflected in the two major reports issued by the United States Department of Health, Education and Welfare in 1971 and 1977. The validity and reliability of various credentialing procedures were explored in order to determine whether they did indeed promote accountability for protection of the public. Growing consumerism, public resentment of spiraling health care costs, and governmental subsidization of many programs within the health care professions were some of the circumstances motivating those investigations. The multiplication of a variety of credentialing measures was suspected of serving the self-interests of professional groups rather than the needs of society. The governmental reports recommended the consolidation and improvement of credentialing along with the possible elimination of redundant mechanisms. The implied threat of official interference with existing policies evoked considerable attention. Questions were raised about the degree to which state boards were meeting their social responsibilities, and activities instrinsic to licensure were identified as needing reform. The structure and functions of state boards were judged to be inflexible and obsolete. Criticism was particularly harsh with respect to the continued recognition of minimum standards for initial licensure, the weaknesses of disciplinary specifications, and the absence of mandatory measurements of ongoing proficiency for re-registration. The omission of statutory provisions calling for evidence of continuing education was viewed as irresponsible by some critics. Controversy generated by the issue has yet to be resolved nationally. Although states like California, Florida, Minnesota, and Illinois (as well as several others) have enacted legislation enforcing various continuing education requirements, the movement has not spread to all states.

A significant result of the continuing education conflict has been the proliferation of a variety of continuing education programs. Interestingly, the appropriate accreditation of these programs has become a new concern for organized nursing. ANA, NLN, and state nurses' associations have all been involved in the approval of educational programs offered for continuing education credit. In addition, these same organizations have been connected with the development and promotion of educational presentations of their own. The selection of courses has thus become confusing for nurses interested in accumulating the proper credits. On the basis of its long-term and effective affiliation with the accreditation of nursing programs, the NLN is not amenable to relinquishing this function. The ANA, on the other hand, has presumably assumed an accrediting role because of the close link between continuing education and registration. The competition generated by these divergent views creates problems within the profession and casts doubt on nursing's ability to manage its own affairs.

In an effort to bring order out of chaos, the ANA supported the creation of a committee to study credentialing systems in nursing. Inaugurated in 1974, the Committee for the Study of Credentialing in Nursing was originally charged with examining the issue of accreditation. The investigation ultimately expanded to include licensure, registration, and certification (see Chapter 6). Final recommendations published in 1979 by the study Committee included the establishment, by 1982, of a national nursing credentialing center. Among its many duties, the proposed center would coordinate activities related to nurse licensure, register and certify nurses, and act as the accrediting body for nursing education and service. The committee further advocated that licensure be designated as the appropriate credential for professional nurses prepared at the baccalaureate level, that registration be voluntary and pertain to graduates of associate degree programs only, and that certification (also voluntary) be awarded to licensed nurses with evidence of advanced skills (4).

Without apparent prior sanction from state constituencies, the ANA in 1980 appointed the Task Force on Credentialing in Nursing for the purpose of implementing the study's recommendations. The unrest produced by both the findings of the study and the abrupt actions of the ANA most likely induced the Task Force to offer several alternative functional models for the proposed center. Although it is unclear which model will be selected, it is probable that licensure and registration will no longer be included in its functions, and, pending funding, it is expected that the center will be operational by the designated date.

The NLN has been particularly critical of the center as initially proposed. Among its expressed concerns were issues related to the questionable thoroughness of the study's methodology, the absence of consumer representation in the activities of the center, and the degree of power that would be vested in the administrators of the center. Credentialing of individuals by the same organization that credentials educational programs has been described as a conflict of interest. Furthermore, the NLN has consistently supported the licensing of practical nurses and the prevailing three levels of entry to

RN licensure. The promotion of associate and baccalaureate degree education explicit in the study's recommendations presumably jeopardizes NLN's position. While many nurses might disagree with NLN's views on multiple routes to licensure, its expertise in accreditation has rarely been challenged.

The proposed credentialing center's further limitations include the possible distortion of current licensing and registration procedures, the increased potential for enforcement problems, and the additional likelihood of conflict with state authorities managing licensing mechanisms. The higher cost involved in the center's credentialing proposals is another factor that cannot be ignored. Overall, the negative implications merit prudent evaluation by the nursing community.

Unquestionably, credentialing in nursing is presently a complex and baffling issue, and conflict is basic to its existence. Clear solutions to the many problems generated by the rapid growth of credentialing mechanisms are not readily available. Historical evidence indicates, however, that credentialing has been a positive factor in the implementation of change. Arising in response to unscrupulous training schemes and the proliferation of unqualified practitioners, credentialing has been instrumental in promoting higher standards in nursing education and service. Recent trends toward advanced preparation and practice have introduced new ramifications in the appraisal and certification of competence. Similar to beginning practice, legal sanction is obviously the most appropriate credential for the expanding scope of nursing, but attempts to garner external support for this proposal have not been widely successful. What has emerged instead is a multitude of varying credentialing processes. The final outcome of this unsupportable situation remains to be seen. It is evident, however, that the multiplication of credentialing mechanisms has neither achieved uniformity in nursing education nor diminished confusion for the public.

References

1. Acts and Joint Resolutions Passed by the General Assembly of the State of Virginia During the Extra Session of 1902-3-4, c. 191, secs. 1–12, 1903

2. American Nurses' Association: Facts About Nursing, 80-81. New York, American Journal of Nursing Co., 1981, p. 9

3. American Nurses' Association, Committee on Education: American Nurses' Association's first position on education for nursing. Am J Nurs 65:106–111, 1965

4. Committee for the Study of Credentialing in Nursing: The Study of Credentialing in Nursing: A New Approach, Vol. I. Kansas City, Missouri, American Nurses' Association, 1979

5. Committee on Publication: Third International Congress of Nurses, Buffalo, Pan-American Exposition, 1901, p. 344

6. Dock LL: A national association for nurses and its legal organization. Nursing World 3:175–178 (pt. 1); 3:204–208 (pt. 2), 1896

7. Dunwiddie M: A History of the Illinois State Nurses' Association 1901–1935. Chicago, Illinois State Nurses' Association, 1937, pp. 3–14

8. Editor's table. Trained Nurses 9:103, 1893

9. Fallon IT: Letter to Sophie A. Bruckner, 1903

10. Fitzpatrick ML: The National Organization for Public Health Nursing, 1912–1952: Development of a Practice Field. New York, National League for Nursing, 1975, pp. 7–80

11. History Files. Archives of the Virginia Nurses' Association, James Branch Cabell Library, Virginia Commonwealth University, Richmond

12. Joint Commission on Accredition of Hospitals: Accreditation Manual for Hospitals. Chicago, Joint Commission on Accreditation of Hospitals, 1980, pp. 116–121

13. Journal of the Senate of the State of New York—126th Session, Vol. I, Albany, 1903

14. MacDonald G: Development of Standards and Accreditation in Collegiate Nursing Education. New York, Teachers College Press, 1965, pp. 59–73

15. McIsaac I: Report of the Interstate Secretary. Am J Nurs 12:875–884, 1912

16. McIver P: Public health nursing legislation. Public Health Nurse 22:372–376, 1930

17. Miller J: The philosophy of professional licensure. JAMA 102:1088–1089, 1934

18. National League for Nursing: Criteria and Standards Manual for NLN/APHA Accreditation of Home Health Agencies and Community Nursing Services. New York, The League, 1980

19. National League for Nursing: Policies and Procedures of Accreditation for Programs in Nursing Education. New York, The League, 1979, pp. 10–25

20. New Jersey State Nurses' Association: New Jersey Nurse, Fiftieth Anniversary Issue. Newark, The Association, 1952, p. 6

21. New York: Laws of the State of New York Passed at the 126th Session of the Legislature, c. 293, art. 12, secs. 206–209, 1903

22. New York State Education Law, art. 139, sec. 6092 (1972)

23. North Carolina: Public Laws and Resolutions of the State of North Carolina, c. 359, secs. 1-11, 1903

24. Picciano J: Personal communication, 1981

25. Proceedings, Maryland State Association of Graduate Nurses, 1903–1904. Baltimore, J. H. Furst Co., 1905, pp. 15–49

26. Report of the New York State Nurses' Association 1901–1906. New York, The Irving Press, 1907, p. 11

27. Report of the Proceedings of the New Jersey State Nurses' Association for the Year 1902–1903. Montclair, The Association, 1904, p. 15

28. Roberts MM: American Nursing. New York, Macmillan, 1959, p. 187

29. Rogers ME: Nursing: To be or not to be. Nurs Outlook 20:42–46, 1972

30. Schmidt MS: Why a separate organization for state boards? Am J Nurs 80:725–726, 1980

31. Shannon ML: The origin and development of professional licensure examinations in nursing: From a state-constructed examination to the State Board Test Pool Examination. Doctoral dissertation, Teachers College, Columbia University, 1972, Ch. III

32. Statutes of New Jersey, Vol. III. Newark, Soney and Sage, 1911, pp. 3337–3338

33. Stewart IM: The reminiscences of Isabel M. Stewart. Unpublished typewritten transcript of tape-recorded interviews, Oral History Research Office, Columbia University, 1961, pp. 47–50

34. Stewart IM, Austin AL: A History of Nursing From Ancient to Modern Times. New York, G. P. Putnam's Sons, 1962, pp. 208–224

35. Vaughn JC: Educational Preparation for Nursing—1979. New York, National League for Nursing, 1980, p. 2

36. Wyche ML: In Heinzerling EL(ed): The History of Nursing in North Carolina. Chapel Hill, University of North Carolina Press, 1938, pp. 66–99

4

Nursing Organizations—
Instruments of Progress

The history of American nursing during the twentieth century is the history of its organizations. No other single force has shaped the course of events more or contributed as much to the attainment of professionalism. Organizations have served as mechanisms for effecting progressive changes in nursing practice, education, and service and have provided standards so vital to the improvement of patient care. They have provided channels of communication among nurses and between nursing and the consumers of health care. Our organizations have been the forum for exchange of ideas and collectives for action relative to issues confronting the individual nurse and the professional group as a whole. Nursing organizations have encouraged and fostered the development of nursing research and have assisted in securing a distinct and significant identity for nursing within the health care arena.

Over the years, sociopolitical and environmental forces affecting both the delivery of care and the situation of the individual nurse have stimulated formation of organizations. Each association that resulted was a response to a major concern confronting the profession or a particular group within it. At various points in our history, organizations have multiplied in number, later to merge or dissolve as the needs of special groups were met and priorities were identified as common to all in the field.

Today we are again experiencing a rapid proliferation of nursing organizations, each addressing itself to the needs of a special group or practice field within the profession. The dilution of the profession's strength and diffusion of its leadership as a result of numerous interest groups are potential hazards. Unity on major issues is an imperative if nurses are to determine the future of the profession. On the other hand, the development of today's newer organizations reflects the complexities of the sophisticated, technically advanced, and rapidly changing age in which we live. The phenomenon speaks to the pluralism that exists within nursing, and the diversity and specialization so characteristic of a mature profession.

Perhaps it is time to evaluate the results of the two-organization plan for American nursing that was implemented in 1952. The past thirty years have been fraught with change, and the emergence of large numbers of new organizations mandates the careful and deliberate consideration of alternatives for the future. How can diversity within the profession be positively utilized to unite us on major questions? What are the mechanisms that will assist us in achieving that end? What plan of organization is best for nursing?

The American Nurses' Association (ANA) and the National League for Nursing (NLN) of 1952 were outgrowths of many groups and social forces that have laid the foundation for the present. As we consider future directions, it is useful to reflect on our past. Awareness of the evolution of organized nursing may assist us in understanding our present condition better and may provide perspective and a valuable frame of reference for decisions that will be important determinants of the future.

American Nursing Before the Establishment of Organizations

The establishment of the first nursing organizations in America was stimulated by serious issues and conditions that jeopardized both the recipients and the providers of nursing care. Without endowments and, therefore, financial independence, training schools for nurses fell under the control of medicine and hospital management. Located within the institutions, the training schools served as departments of nursing service for the hospitals and were a major economic asset in the provision of patient care (15).

Large numbers of pupils were admitted to the programs several times a year; even the smallest hospitals opened schools to ensure a ready supply of cheap labor for the institution; and the education that students received was incidental to their responsibilities as workers in the hospital (15). The apprenticeship system of nursing education served neither to improve the quality of patient care nor to encourage the sound development of education for nurses. As scientific advances in medicine occurred, an even greater burden was placed on nursing students to provide care and assume the management of hospital units. In addition, many hospitals engaged in the practice of sending inexperienced, unsupervised pupils into the community to provide care for patients at home.

The exploitation and manipulation of graduate nurses was a further consequence of the inequities experienced by students and a clear reflection of social conditions in America that oppressed all women. Hospitals, relying on the inexpensive student labor force, employed relatively few graduate nurses. Those few usually served in the capacity of superintendents, being responsible for both the service and the training schools, which, in essence, were the same. On completion of the training program, the graduate nurse was forced to practice in private duty situations, largely outside the hospital. In addition, she had to compete for these positions with pupil nurses (12) and untrained lay workers, who were frequently placed by private registries operated by physicians.

In addition to the obvious exploitation of nurses, several related problems existed. Without standards or controls, inferior training schools were allowed to proliferate and the qualifications of pupils admitted to them differed greatly from place to place. As a graduate nurse, competition with the untrained for positions in private duty was commonplace. Nurses who were fortunate enough to find employment were victims of isolation, which prevented continued learning and growth (51). They worked long hours for low pay and received no benefits related to their personal well-being or future security. Most important, no standards of practice and no means of assuring safe nursing care for the public existed.

By the end of the nineteenth century, conditions had reached a critical point and several superintendents of large, well-established training schools were voicing concern for the future. It was believed that improvements could result only from a mechanism that would break the pattern of isolation among nurses and unite their efforts toward attainment of common goals. Improvement in the education of nurses was seen as a first step in upgrading nursing practice and improving the conditions of the graduate nurse. These circumstances and beliefs gave rise to the inception of organized nursing in the United States.

The Early Organizations

American Society of Superintendents of Training Schools and the National League of Nursing Education

The first nursing organization established in America was the Society of Superintendents of Training Schools (which changed its name of the National League of Nursing Education [NLNE] in 1912). Formed in 1893, it was a response by the nursing leaders of that era to conditions that resulted in poor educational programs for the preparation of nurses and low quality performance in nursing practice. For some time, visionary superintendents had voiced concern about the proliferation of programs and the exploitation of pupil nurses, which created inadequate training programs and diluted efforts to provide the best possible care to hospitalized individuals.

In England, Mrs. Bedford Fenwick, a former superintendent at St. Bartholomew's, had been instrumental in the successful establishment of an association for the registration of trained nurses. On her first visit to America in 1893, enroute to the Chicago World's Fair, Mrs. Fenwick stopped in Baltimore and met with Isabel Adams Hampton, a Bellevue graduate, who was superintendent of the fledgling training school at Johns Hopkins. The International Congress of Charities, Corrections and Philanthropy was to be held at the Exposition, and included in the plan was a conference of hospitals and dispensaries under the direction of Dr. John S. Billings, formerly of Hopkins. At Mrs. Fenwick's suggestion, Billings agreed that a subsection on nursing should be planned and recommended that Isabel Hampton be asked to organize the meeting (11).

The meeting was held, attended by both American and Canadian nurses, and papers that reflected the major issues and concerns facing nurses and nursing were read. Many believed that an association that would link nurses in a common cause was a necessity, and it therefore was postulated that alumnae associations of schools of nursing might provide the basis for organizing nurses. However, such a proposal was contingent upon a mechanism that would facilitate communication among superintendents, since they were in the best positions to stimulate the formation of alumnae associations and promote the interests of nursing through development of standards of training. The decision was to establish an association of superintendents as a first step.

Following the meeting of the nursing subsection on June 15, superintendents were asked to remain for a special conference, which was held at St. Luke's Hospital. Eighteen superintendents attended that historic meeting and agreed to form a temporary organization until an official meeting could be held the following year. In the interim, a committee was to work on outlining the purpose of the organization and the membership qualifications. The committee members were Isabel Hampton, Johns Hopkins; Mary Davis, University Hospital, Philadelphia; Louise Darche, New York City Training School, Blackwell's Island; Sophia Palmer, Garfield Hospital, Washington, DC; Irene Sutliffe, New York Hospital; Mary McKechnie, City Hospital, St. Louis; and Anna Alston, Mt. Sinai, New York. The group decided to convene on January 10, 1894 in New York City.

Over forty superintendents attended the New York meeting, at which the objectives of the association were articulated:

1. To promote fellowship of members
2. To establish and maintain a universal standard of training
3. To further the best interests of the nursing profession (11)

The primary goal of the Society was the improvement of education for nursing, and the group was intended to represent an elite, admitting to full membership only those superintendents whose schools met approved standards. However, the problems that confronted graduate nurses continued to be a parallel concern.

The Society realized that a national association of nurses required strengthening the existing alumnae associations and developing new ones. This, they believed, would provide a network and foundation for the proposed organization of graduate nurses, and it was this interest in developing a national association of nurses that occupied the time and attention of the Society during the next two years.

With this goal in mind, Lavinia Dock undertook a study of professional organizations and the laws governing their operation. Using her findings and Miss Hampton's ideas as a basis, Miss Dock presented a paper at the third meeting of the Society in 1896 in which she proposed a plan for an association. Her paper, "A National Association for Nurses and Its Legal Organization," proposed alumnae associations as the mode of entrance in a national organization, with the eventual development of local and state units that would elect delegates (12). Through her preliminary investigation, Miss Dock determined that incorporation was a problem to be addressed. A charter taken out in one state for the national association would be recognized by all, but headquarters would have to be located in the state issuing the charter. She also recognized that inclusion of Canadian nurses would be impossible at the time of incorporation (12).

Following a discussion of Miss Dock's paper, a committee of the Society was appointed and charged with preparation of a constitution for a national nurses organization and asked to meet with delegates of well-established and prominent alumnae associations prior to the next convention of the Society. This group met in New York in September 1896. The next year, the work of the committee was accepted and the Nurses' Associated Alumnae of the United States and Canada was called into existence at the fourth annual meeting of the Society, held at Johns Hopkins in February 1897.

With the launching of the Associated Alumnae, the Society was able to turn its attention to matters of major interest to its members in their positions as administrative officers of schools of nursing. Concern for educational standards and improvement in programs led logically to considerations of the preparation of teachers (supervisors) of nursing. It was generally agreed that those who taught pupils required more education than their own experience or a training program had provided.

With Isabel Hampton Robb as the chairperson, an education committee of the Society took up the question of teacher preparation. Among its members were Linda Richards, Adelaide Nutting, Mary Agnes Snively, and Lucy Dram. The result of the committee's deliberations was a decision to approach Dean James Earl Russell of Teachers College, Columbia University in an attempt to interest him in the problem. The committee was successful.

Eventually a plan to open a course in hospital economics at the college was developed. Teaching staff were initially members of the Society who contributed their time, and the Society took responsibility for financially underwriting the course and selecting applicants for admission (19). This project was considered so vital to the struggle to improve standards in schools of nursing that several members of the Society contributed their personal funds in order to provide a salary for Anna Alline, the first full-time instructor in the program.

Supporting the course at Teachers College was a constant drain on the treasury of the Superintendents' Society. Even after 1906, when Adelaide Nutting assumed the position of professor of nursing and a department was developed, the major financial burden for the program fell to the Society. The program for graduate nurses became the Society's major project, and it is possible to conclude that many of the advances made in nursing education over the years would have been severely retarded without the continuing interest and help of the Society in the Teachers College program.

In 1907 the Society was incorporated, and by 1909, local branches were operant in Chicago and St. Paul. Other areas were urged to do the same. Since there was considerable interest in developing these local and state branches, the Society and Associated Alumnae shared the salary of an interstate secretary, whose major activity was the provision of consultation and field service. Isabel McIsaac was the first person to be appointed (1911) and was followed by Adda Eldredge (1913). Neither organization was able to afford the headquarters staff needed to carry on its work, especially work related to legislation—specifically, licensing laws. The amount of volunteer effort during those early years was phenomenal. Many of the organizations' activities emanated from the institutions in which their leaders were employed. Hence, much of the work of the Society, which changed its name to the National League of Nursing Education (NLNE) in 1912, was based at Teachers College. No official headquarters was established until 1920.

During the formative years of both the Society and the Associated Alumnae, relationships were close, communications were good, and activities of one organization were designed to complement the other. The differences in purpose and emphasis were clear and deliberate, but the unity of thought and action on major issues confronting nursing and nursing education was an outstanding characteristic. The strength that evolved through the different activities of each group, which were directed to common aims, was a significant factor in improving nursing practice, creating an identity and voice for the nurse in American society, and moving nursing toward professionalism.

The first joint meeting of the Society and Associated Alumnae was held in 1910. In 1912, the Society, renamed the NLNE, became an affiliate member of the American Nurses' Association (ANA) (the Associated Alumnae was renamed in 1911). This arrangement eventually led to legal difficulties, and in 1918 the NLNE reincorporated under the District of Columbia. However, a pattern of cooperation had been developed, and for many years the organizations convened together and had headquarters in the same location. In 1932 the NLNE was officially designated the Education Department of the ANA. The arrangement was explained in the *American Journal of Nursing* (23):

> . . . the Executive Secretary of the League also bears the title of and serves as education secretary of the A.N.A. This means that if a problem dealing with the education of nurses, either undergraduate or post graduate, arises in the A.N.A. office, the matter is referred to Miss Wheeler or she is called into conference.

The importance of the NLNE during the many years of its existence cannot be minimized. It addressed every phase of nursing education and undertook studies that both directly and indirectly influenced the quality of education. It assisted some programs to improve and brought pressure to bear on those that did not meet standards. As a result of NLNE activities, many inferior programs closed.

The most active committee of the NLNE was its education committee. As early as 1911, Adelaide Nutting suggested the need for a comprehensive study of nursing education for which she unsuccessfully solicited funding from the Carnegie Foundation. In 1918, a subcommittee began collecting data on nursing schools, and following publication of the Goldmark Report, the organization interested Frances Payne Bolton in funding the initial work of a joint, independent committee on the grading of nursing schools (30). The project, under the direction of May Ayres Burgess, embarked on three major studies: (1) a study of supply and demand for nursing service; (2) a job analysis related to nurses' functions; (3) the grading of nursing schools.

Throughout the years, the NLNE participated in numerous joint ventures with the ANA and National Organization for Public Health Nursing (NOPHN) and engaged in studies and published materials on schools of nursing and faculty qualifications. It set standards for staff education in nursing service, rendered consultation and advisory services to schools, and provided vocational counseling for prospective students. In addition, it established scholarship and loan funds, set standards for nursing service in hospitals, providing clinical placements for students, and attempted to coordinate activities of nursing education and service.

Perhaps the most outstanding contribution of the NLNE to the profession was its efforts in the field of curriculum development. It produced three curriculum guides that had a major impact on the preparation of nurses in the United States. Adelaide Nutting chaired the committee that developed the first two guides (1917, 1927), and was assisted by Isabel Stewart, who took primary responsibility for development of the third (1937). The majority of work in preparation of the guides was done at Teachers College, where both women were employed and where space for the project had been donated (48). The publication of the guides firmly established the NLNE as the authoritative source on curriculum and instruction in nursing. Each revision suggested higher standards, such as better prepared faculty and more exacting selection of students. Breadth of content, including preventive aspects of nursing care, was eventually added. The NLNE was the primary resource for superintendents of schools as well as supervisors and instructors, to whom membership was extended in 1912.

In 1938, the association began surveying schools and placing them on an accreditation list. The same year, under the leadership of Isabel Stewart, a joint committee of the NLNE, Association of Collegiate Schools of Nursing (ACSN), and Teachers College considered "the possibility of developing objective techniques of measuring nursing on a cooperative basis; to take steps to initiate such a cooperative project and to seek funds for its support" (33). Early efforts to establish a nursing unit of the Testing Service of the American Council on Education were unsuccessful. But in 1940, R. Louise McManus, who succeeded Miss Stewart as chairperson of the committee, forged ahead with the plan and secured support to launch the NLNE Pre-nursing and Guidance Test Service. The project was begun at Teachers College and after five years was transferred to NLNE headquarters. By 1950, all boards of nurse examiners in the country had joined the State Board Test Pool.

The tremendous influence and accomplishments of the NLNE on American nursing education are best reflected in the annual reports that chronicle its life. Its success as a progressive force was largely due to the diligence of its leaders. Although confronted with the formidable task of changing an apprenticeship system of nursing education, they were unwavering in their efforts to professionalize preparation for nursing practice.

Nurses' Associated Alumnae of the United States and Canada and the American Nurses' Association

When Lavinia Dock addressed the third meeting of the Superintendents' Society in 1896 to report on her investigation relative to developing a national nurses' association, she expressed the role she envisioned for such an organization in the country and the necessity for nursing to chart its own course, manage its own affairs, deal with its own problems, and practice self-government (21). She believed that such an organization could meet the challenge of the problems arising from inadequate training programs and exploitation of graduate nurses and could address itself to the welfare of the individual nurse.

Miss Dock chaired the meeting of the committee of the Society and representatives of alumnae associations that convened to approve the constitution for the new organization in September 1896 at the Manhattan Beach Hotel. Alumnae representatives from ten training schools attended. Having approved the constitution for the association, which was named the Nurses' Associated Alumnae of the United States and Canada, preparation was made for ratification by the alumnae associations, committees were appointed, and bylaws were drafted.

At the second delegates meeting held in conjunction with the superintendents' convention in Baltimore the following year, the original constitution was amended to include concern for the financial problems of nurses and to raise eligibility criteria for membership to graduates of hospitals having 100 beds or more (13). Membership was to be through the alumnae associations of training schools, and the bylaws were developed to cover both Canadians and Americans. Isabel Hampton Robb was elected the first president of the association.

Eligibility for membership was a continual problem during the early years as a result of membership in the organization through the affiliated membership of alumnae associations. Frequently, alumnae associations of training schools deemed substandard were denied membership. As a consequence, many nurses who might have benefited the most were excluded. Eventually, criteria had to be modified because it was necessary to organize and gain the support of large numbers of nurses in order to promote legislation dealing with the registration of nurses. In addition, incorporation laws required the elimination of Canadians from the membership. Canadian nurses continued to be invited guests at meetings and close ties were maintained, but in 1900 the organization became the Nurses' Associated Alumnae of the United States and the following year was incorporated in New York.

The method chosen by the association to effect improvements in the condition of graduate nurses was through the promotion of registration bills in the States. Sarah Sly served as interstate secretary and directed her energies to collecting and disseminating legislative information. Major campaigns for registration laws required the stimulation of state and local associations. By 1903, five states had state associations and four of the five—North Carolina, Virginia, New Jersey, and New York—had secured state registration for nurses. As the movement toward state registration grew, membership increased. By 1909 there were 15,000 individual members, representing over 100 alumnae associations; twenty-eight state associations; and a smaller number of city and county associations (16). Passage of licensure laws was a direct result of the association's efforts and established minimum standards for nursing practice to protect the public and to protect nurses from competition with the untrained.

In order to provide a link between members and to unite them to win state registration, it was recognized that a means of communications between the organization and members was essential. There had to be a means by which nurses could become informed on general issues and the organization's response to situations that affected the welfare of nurses. It was also necessary for nurses to be made aware of new and better approaches to patient care as they developed. It must be remembered that the majority of nurses remained in private duty due to the economic reliance on students for service in hospitals. So it was even more crucial that a bridge be built among individual nurses who by virtue of their employment situation suffered from isolation and a lack of colleague relationships. From the beginning, leaders viewed establishment of a publication as a necessity. The association required an official organ, which could also report on important business of the Superintendents' Society.

In 1900 the Publications Committee of the Associated Alumnae reported that a stock corporation had been formed (financed through the personal contributions of leaders), and in October of 1900 the first issue of the *American Journal of Nursing* was published. Publication emanated from Rochester, New York for many years, and the first editor, Sophia Palmer, held that post for the next twenty-five years. It was hoped that the organization would eventually be in a position to hold the controlling interest in the stock. That goal was realized in 1912, when ninety-nine of the one hundred shares were owned by the association.

By 1911, the organization had experienced exceptional growth and was well established and recognized as the official spokesperson for nursing in the United States. But confusion regarding structure and eligibility for membership continued. There were numerous proposals for change in structure and a general belief that the time had come for constituent membership in the association through the states. Although the name of the organization was changed in 1911 to the ANA, it remained a federation of alumnae associations until 1916. However, the federation of state, local, and alumnae associations continued until 1916. At the convention of 1916 it was decided to establish membership through state associations, and in 1918, affiliated alumnae associations were asked to resign and come in through state associations.

Between 1912 and 1919, the NLNE and NOPHN were affiliate members of the ANA. The three organizations convened together annually until 1918 and then biennially until 1952. When the ANA was reincorporated in 1917 in the District of Columbia, the other two organizations resigned as affiliates (1919), but relationships remained close. Although the change of membership in the ANA through constituent state associations was, in most respects, advantageous and practical, it also gave visibility to a problem that plagued the ANA until 1948—the membership of the black nurse.

The ANA never specifically barred black nurses from its membership; the organization's structure from 1916 onward acted to exclude large numbers. With membership achieved through state associations and members of the delegate body elected through them, black nurses, particularly those in the South, were eliminated from participation. In the early 1920s, an ANA committee to study the status of black nurses was established and representatives met with Adah Thomas of the NACGN to determine the qualifications of the NACGN for some kind of affiliation with the ANA (5). No progress was made and limited data concerning the committee's efforts can be found. Although there is no evidence of ANA attempts to address the membership problem of black nurses until late in its history, it must be viewed in the context of the racism and discrimination that pervaded all facets of American life. In 1946 the ANA House of Delegates recommended that state associations eliminate racial bars to membership, and in 1948 an individual membership plan for black nurses was developed to allow direct membership in the na- tional body if state membership was exclusionary (8). Also in 1948, the first black nurse was appointed to the ANA headquarters staff and another was elected to the ANA Board of Directors. By 1954, following the dissolution of the NACGN, the establishment of the ANA Inter-Group Relations Program, and the reorganization of the nursing organizations, only one state nurses' association and three district associations in two southern states continued to bar blacks from membership (8).

Throughout the years, the ANA's contributions to the welfare of nurses, to professionalism in nursing, and to the development of standards paralleled advances in the profession as a whole. As one problem was eliminated, a new one replaced it. In the early years, major overriding concern was for state registration and the stand- ards of registries that placed private duty nurses. In time, the organi- zation provided relief funds for ill and disabled nurses, investigated insurance and pension plans for nurses, and developed scholarship programs. It was always concerned with conditions of nurse's work—the length of the work day, the just wage, and equity in the job market.

During World War I, the ANA in cooperation with the American Red Cross and the military secured relative rank for nurses. Follow- ing World War II, the ANA obtained permanent rank for nurses in all branches of the armed forces. It was responsible for the reclassifica- tion of civil service positions of graduate registered nurses in the category of professional and scientific service. It also provided valua- ble field consultation to states and served as a clearing house for nursing affairs.

The ANA served as a central bureau for state boards of nurse ex- aminers, developed a professional counseling and placement center for nurses, developed a code of ethical practice, developed the De- partment of Research (1946), and cooperated with the other nursing associations in developing standards and qualifications for nursing practice. Collaborative activities with the other organizations was facilitated during the middle years by location of headquarters in the same place. With each year, participation in joint studies and com- mittee work with the other groups increased. Particularly in war- time, cooperative efforts were intensified, and the ANA was especially significant in gathering data concerning the nursing needs and resources of the country. As time passed, the ANA continued to grow and build strength.

Early in its history, the ANA recognized the need for special interest groups in the organization so that nurses could identify and grow professionally in a specialty area, yet still participate and be involved in issues relevant to all nurses through the larger body. The first two special interest groups, the private duty section and the section on mental hygiene, were formed in 1923.

In the years up to and during the restructuring of the nursing organizations, the ANA made formidable gains. As the spokesman for nursing, it gave the field visibility: it represented the United States in the International Council of Nurses, it was instrumental in securing federal funding for nursing education, and it accomplished much in improving the status and welfare of the individual nurse. Most important, the ANA defined and promoted the implementation of functions, standards, and qualifications for nursing practice.

National Association of Colored Graduate Nurses

While the Society of Superintendents of Training Schools and the Associated Alumnae were laying the foundation for their futures, a new organization was being formed. It was an association of and for black nurses. Racial discrimination and inequities experienced by black Americans for so many years were not unknown among those who selected nursing was a career. The struggle for equal opportunity and professional advancement had to be waged in the North as well as in the South, for exclusionary practices, although more subtle in the North, did exist.

In its early years the Associated Alumnae admitted members through the alumnae associations of their training schools. Hence, Mary Eliza Mahoney, considered America's first black graduate nurse (New England Hospital for Women and Children, 1879), would have been eligible for membership by virtue of her membership in her alumnae association (49). But the patterns of discrimination were such that no early efforts were geared toward inclusion of black nurses.

The idea and impetus for establishing an organization of black graduate nurses came from Martha Franklin, a graduate of the Training School of Woman's Hospital in Philadelphia. In late August 1908, under the sponsorship of the alumnae of New York's Lincoln School for Nurses and its president, Adah Thomas, a meeting was held at St. Mark's Methodist Church in New York City (50). It was believed that black nurses could best improve their own condition if they had a collective voice and vehicle for action.

By the end of the first meeting, an association called the National Association of Colored Graduate Nurses (NACGN) had been formed. Martha Franklin became its first president. The objectives of the association were to achieve higher professional standards, to break down the discriminatory practices facing Negroes in schools of nursing, jobs, and nursing organization activities, and to develop leadership among Negro nurses (31). The NACGN, through the determination of its leaders and untiring support and persistence of its members, believed that it had met all of its objectives at the time of its dissolution in 1951.

Like the other nursing organizations, for many years the NACGN relied on volunteers in order to carry out its programs. Membership in the association was open to all who held state registration, and one of its earliest efforts was the fight to break down barriers that prohibited black nurses from becoming registered in certain states.

An on-going theme and thrust of the NACGN was equality for black nurses and treatment on the same basis as others. In order to accomplish these goals, the leadership realized that equality for black nurses could be accomplished only within the broader context of equality for all people, and throughout its history, ties between the NACGN, the Urban League, and the National Association for the Advancement of Colored People (NAACP) were a source of strength.

During the formative years, Adah Thomas was a driving force. It was she who led the campaign for acceptance of black nurses in the Red Cross for service with the Army Nurse Corps in World War I. She established a registry for black nurses in New York in 1918 and later authored the first book on black nursing history.

The struggle for acceptance of qualified black nurses continued on all fronts throughout several decades, and the NACGN, which incorporated in New York in 1920, was chiefly responsible for any progress made. The NACGN provided consultation and field service to black schools of nursing and made a concerted effort to assist schools to raise education standards. In the early 1920s, it led a campaign to urge black nurses to register to vote as citizens of the United States. In the later 1920s, an official organ, the *National News Bulletin*, established a channel of communication among the nurses and between them and the organization.

By that time, interest in black nurses was beginning to grow and efforts were made to establish some liaison between the NACGN, the NLNE, and the NOPHN. The two latter groups were concerned with standards and practice in education and the NOPHN, in particular, was involved in problems affecting public health nurses and health care of blacks in the rural South. Some dialogue occurred, but discriminatory practices within certain state branches of the NLNE created problems. The NOPHN was more successful in its efforts to include blacks. As a progressive and liberally oriented organization, having relationships with non-nursing groups such as the Julius Rosenwald Fund, the NOPHN was increasingly able to work closely with the NACGN. Direct membership in the NOPHN rather than membership contingent on state membership was also a factor that worked positively in building the relationship.

An outstanding characteristic of the NACGN was its emphasis on the development of young leaders who would continue to work toward its objectives in the future. Advanced education to prepare the leadership group was a priority, and in 1929 a scholarship fund was established. The first recipient of the NACGN award was Estelle Massey (Osborne), who later became president of the organization and eventually became the first black nurse to serve on the ANA Board of Directors. Estelle Massey used her scholarship to study at Teachers College, where she was the first black nurse to earn a masters degree with a major in nursing from that institution.

As the activities of the NACGN increased, it was imperative to employ permanent staff. In 1929, Belle Davis, of the National Health Circle for Colored People, gave part-time assistance, and in 1934, through the generosity of the Rosenwald Fund, space was provided for headquarters and a permanent executive officer was hired. That person was Mabel K. Staupers, who served from 1934 to 1949, at which time she resigned and was subsequently elected the last president of NACGN. Mrs. Staupers later chronicled the history of the organization in her book, *No Time for Prejudice* (49).

With a headquarters and staff, the NACGN was in a position to take more systematic and aggressive action and become the principal information service for all groups and the government of data concerning black nurses. Through the period of the New Deal, the NACGN seized every opportunity to improve the status of the individual nurse, elevate standards of education and practice, and promote racial integration.

In order to encourage the integration of black nurses, the NACGN program was organized on a regional basis. This local approach was considered the best way to accomplish goals relative to admission of blacks to schools of nursing, equality in jobs, and integration of state nurses' associations and leagues of nursing education. In 1936, through the efforts of the NACGN and the influence of Rev. John LaFarge of the Catholic Interracial Council, the Catholic University of America began to admit black graduates to its programs (49). This event was considered a major breakthrough in the District of Columbia and the South.

As was the case with other nursing organizations, World War II stimulated cooperative efforts among the NACGN and other groups. The National Council for War Services planted the seeds of change within organized nursing in America. During the war years, the organization monitored the participation of black students in the Cadet Corps and actively exposed discriminatory practices in the military. As a result of the war and participation on the National Council, integration was approached. Increasingly, schools of nursing once closed to blacks accepted them. Acceptance of blacks in all branches of the military was achieved by the end of the war, and gradually, some state nurses' associations opened their membership.

The NACGN became involved in the Committee on Structure of the National Nursing Organizations, and in 1948 the ANA House of Delegates voted to permit direct membership in the organization for those individuals still barred from state membership. The same year, Estelle Massey Osborne was elected to the ANA Board of Directors. At its convention in Louisville, Kentucky, in 1949, the NACGN, believing that its objectives had been met, voted dissolution, although it phased out its program gradually over the next two years. In 1950 the platform adopted by the ANA House of Delegates supported "full participation of minority groups in association activities . . . and the elimination of discrimination in job opportunities, salaries, and other working conditions . . ." (6). In this way, the ANA committed itself to assume responsibility for the functions of the NACGN.

On January 21, 1951 at St. Mark's Methodist Church, site of the first NACGN conference, the last meeting of the association was held. Through its efforts, black nurses had achieved visibility and recognition, standards of nursing practice and education had been improved and maintained, and the concerns of blacks in American life had come to the attention of nurses and the public. The NACGN was dauntless in its determination and had a profound impact on nursing in the United States.

Perhaps the comments of Mabel Staupers best describe the role the NACGN played in the history of American nursing: "By organizing, these women proclaimed to the entire nursing profession that they had created an instrument through which they could oppose discrimination in the nursing field on all fronts" (50). The bestowing of the ANA's Mary Mahoney Award, first instituted by the NACGN in 1936, is a constant reminder of that organization and the contributions of its members.

The National Organization for Public Health Nursing

The zeal of nurses in a specialty group and the accomplishments that can be made when nursing talents are combined with the interests of the public is the story of the National Organization for Public Health Nursing (NOPHN). Throughout its forty years' existence, it promoted professional nursing in the community, successfully elevated standards of practice and education in public health nursing, and conducted studies and programs that helped move nursing toward professionalism.

The NOPHN, like the field of practice it addressed, was an outgrowth of the humanitarian movement that gave rise to the establishment of settlements and voluntary organizations concerned with conditions of the poor. It was directly related to the social response of America during the late nineteenth and early twentieth centuries. Since the development of visiting nurse agencies was made possible through the efforts of laypersons, it is not surprising that the genesis of the NOPHN was inextricably linked to the former. The results of the public health movement reflected the value of nursing service in the community and the potential gains that could be realized if nursing care and health teaching were provided in the home. Quite logically, the formation of visiting nurse associations increased rapidly. By 1910, over 1900 agencies employed visiting nurses and demands for the service continued to mount (22).

Many nursing leaders, especially Mary S. Gardner of the Providence District Nursing Association and Lillian D. Wald of the Henry Street Nurses' Settlement, were worried about the lack of preparation most nurses had for work in the community. In addition, no standards for the practice or management of the service existed. No definite educational qualifications were imposed, there was a lack of adequate supervision, and most leaders agreed that the typical hospital school training was not sufficient for the work. In 1910, a postgraduate course to prepare nurses for work in public health was begun at Teachers College, but relatively few nurses had the opportunity for this additional education. It was also recognized that well-intentioned lay board members were interested in employing nurses to provide a service but were not equipped to monitor quality or develop standards. A notable exception was the board of the Cleveland Visiting Nurse Association. Through their publication, *Visiting Nurse Quarterly*, laypersons made a plea for the development of guidelines for public health nurses, who were expected to function with a high degree of judgment, skill, and initiative.

Mary Gardner was convinced that the best way to attack the three-dimensional problems of public health nursing—education, practice, and agency management—was to form a new nursing organization. There was little desire for still another association, but there was also a realization that the existing groups were not in a position to give the time and attention to public health nursing issues.

At the annual convention of the ANA and the Superintendents' Society in 1911, the ANA Committee on Visiting Nursing requested that a joint committee of both groups be appointed to study the feasibility of a third organization directed toward public health nursing (7). The committee, chaired by Lillian Wald, with Mary Gardner as its secretary, met four times during the next year and sent letters to all known visiting nurse agencies to solicit opinions about the formation of a special association. They also asked agencies to send representatives to the annual meeting of the ANA and Superintendents' Society, to be held in Chicago in June 1912. Sixty-nine agency delegates representing all parts of the country attended and an equal number of nurses involved in public health attended as members of the two established nursing organizations (4).

The joint committee recommended a national visiting nurse association, which as an organization would become an affiliate of the ANA. The group would develop and implement standards of visiting nursing to include qualifications and preparation of nurses, techniques of agency management, and nursing practice. It was further suggested that the association be a cooperative effort of nurses and non-nurse members so as to include board members who employed nurses in voluntary agencies (4).

Jane Delano, president of the ANA, was the most prominent opponent to the plan and preferred that the proposed work be done as a section of the ANA. After considerable discussion and the influential arguments of Lillian Wald, who pointed out the necessity to consider resources for funding that lay members could provide, Miss Delano was persuaded to support the idea of a new organization. Named the National Organization for Public Health Nursing (NOPHN), it became an affiliate of the ANA and elected Lillian Wald its first president. The purpose of the organization, as expressed in its constitution, served as a guide for NOPHN activities during the next four decades:

> The object of this organization shall be to stimulate responsibility for the health of the community by the establishment of visiting nursing and all other forms of public health nursing; to facilitate efficient cooperation between nurses, physicians, boards of trustees and other persons interested in public health measures; to develop standards of ethics and tech-

niques of public health service; to establish and maintain a
central bureau for information, referral and assistance in mat-
ters pertaining to such service and to publish periodicals and
issue bulletins from time to time to aid in the general accom-
plishment of the organization.

Unlike the other organizations, the NOPHN began its operations
without the usual obstacles, limitations, or financial problems. The
Cleveland Visiting Nurse Association publication, *Visiting Nurse*
Quarterly, was given to the new association as its official organ and
the cost of publication was assumed by laypersons in Cleveland for
many years. Through gifts from affluent visiting nurse association
board members, it was possible to rent space in New York, establish
headquarters and salary a part-time executive and secretary at once.
Ella Phillips Crandall, the instructor in the public health nursing
course at Teachers College, was named the executive secretary, initially dividing her time between teaching and the organization, and
after a year devoted full time to the directorship of the NOPHN.

A major difference between the NOPHN and other groups was its
membership. Three categories were established: corporate membership for agencies, membership for nurses who met the stringent eligibility requirements and associate membership for non-nurses.
Because the NOPHN was an affiliate of the ANA, voting privileges
and full membership were not extended to non-nurses until 1919,
when the ANA was reincorporated and the NLNE and NOPHN became truly autonomous bodies. However, like the NLNE, the
NOPHN's president served ex-officio on the ANA Board of Directors and eventually located headquarters at the same address.

From the outset, the idea was to centralize NOPHN activities at
the national level and to place on-going projects within specific
committees. Eventually, some state and local organizations for public health nursing evolved, but they were never systematically developed nationally and were more incidental than deliberate outgrowths of the NOPHN program.

Within the first few years, the NOPHN formed standing committees that addressed every phase of visiting nursing. The issue of specialized versus general practice in public health nursing was a peren-
nial question throughout the years, but as early as 1912, specialties
already existed. Therefore, specialty sections were formed to meet
the needs of rural nurses, tuberculosis nurses, infant welfare nurses,
mental hygiene nurses, and industrial nurses, all of whom were considered, with the generalist, under the broad umbrella of public
health nursing. Over the years, the organization attempted to meet
the needs of special interest groups as they emerged. As a result, a
school nursing section and midwifery section eventually were
added.

Efforts were directed at developing standards of practice and criteria that could be used by agencies in managing services and hiring and paying the nurses. Consultation and field service were believed to be the best ways to influence standards of care, and the executive secretary and, later, special field staff spent a great deal of time making on-site visits to agencies to offer advice.

Another major area of NOPHN activity centered around education for public health nursing. As an organization it stimulated and guided the establishment of many postgraduate courses in public health nursing in universities throughout the country. An education secretary provided schools with consultation on curriculum, and in 1920, the NOPHN took on the responsibility for formal accreditation of postgraduate programs in public health nursing. Thus it became the first nursing association to involve itself in accreditation of any type of educational program in nursing (29).

The NOPHN assumed responsibility for educational matters in postgraduate and staff education programs in public health nursing and collaborated with the NLNE on matters involving public health nursing in the basic curriculum. It also developed a nursing library and loan packages for nurses who wished to engage in independent study. Always interested in staff education, it produced in-service education materials and slides for loan to public health nursing agencies. A significant contribution to the education of the public health nurse was the organization's periodical, which included numerous articles designed to help the practitioner improve her practice. In addition to these services, the NOPHN, which was highly influenced by the Metropolitan Life Insurance Company, became a clearinghouse for statistics and a variety of data regarding public health, legislation, and community nursing resources.

It has been said that the NOPHN was resented by the other nursing organizations and that its members frequently considered themselves superior. In fact, most NOPHN members were members of the ANA and, sometimes, the NLNE as well. It is possible that the alleged rift between the ANA and the NOPHN during the early years was a result of the composition of the ANA. Originally, the ANA was largely made up of private duty nurses. On the other hand, the NLNE represented an educational elite and the NOPHN was a financially strong organization that encouraged preparation of public health nurses in university-based programs and a certain degree of elitism.

The resources of the NOPHN benefited all groups, however, and were vital to the Red Cross and the Council of National Defense during World War I. Through the influence of its lay members and its association with significant individuals attached to foundations, financial assistance made many studies and projects in nursing possible. The Rockefeller Foundation grant, which financed the study of nursing and nursing education in the United States conducted by Josephine Goldmark, and the generosity of Frances Payne Bolton in funding the initial work of the Committee on Grading of Nursing Schools are but two examples of the NOPHN's influence in securing funds for the good of the profession as well as itself (25).

Although the NOPHN coexisted peacefully with the other two organizations, they did not work as closely as they might have until the social forces of the 1930s, followed by World War II, brought them into closer contact and numerous joint committees were formed. Quite unlike the other associations, the NOPHN established itself as an important member of the National Health Council and enjoyed the status with which it was regarded by non-nursing groups. For many years, most of its collaborative activities were in the broad field of public health, and it became nursing's voice in the American Public Health Association (APHA), the National Tuberculosis Association, the American Child Health Association, and a host of other national voluntary organizations. It also served as a valuable resource of information for the federal government. Through the efforts of the NOPHN, a nursing section was formed in the APHA in 1923.

Through these relationships, it was possible for the NOPHN to obtain funding for numerous studies, research projects, and advisory services on all aspects of public health nursing. In contrast to the ANA and NLNE, which were first able to establish headquarters in 1920, the NOPHN was well established and in the same year had an annual operating budget of $100,000 (34). Even when difficult times came and the NOPHN was forced to close two of its four regional offices, benefactors, especially Mrs. Bolton, came to the rescue and encouraged the leadership to not retrench the NOPHN's programs.

The contributions of non-nurse members were not just financial. The inclusion of persons associated with business, finance, and insurance companies provided valuable input in assisting local agencies to improve their management techniques. In addition, professionals of the stature of C.E.A. Winslow added to the strength and visibility of the organization and the advancement of public health nursing.

In addition to its concentration on matters concerning standards for public health nursing education, practice, and service, the NOPHN was quite successful in addressing itself to the needs of individual nurses. It sponsored a vocational counseling and placement center and never lost sight of its responsibility to "educate" the practicing nurse through the pages of its magazine.

With the period of the Depression, recovery, and the beginning of Social Security, the NOPHN served as a resource on public health nursing for the government and contributed a great deal to the expansion of official (tax-supported) public health programs. Closer relationships began to develop with the ANA and NLNE and climaxed during World War II.

During the years of the structure study, the NOPHN was the most aggressive advocate of a two-organization plan and non-nurse membership in nursing organizations.

If the history of the association is considered, the position of the NOPHN during the structure study can be better understood. Through the combined efforts of nurses and laypersons, much had been accomplished and it was feared that reorganization would alter the cooperative activities that had been so well established over the years.

When the decision was made to restructure the nursing organizations, the NOPHN voted dissolution and agreed to have its programs absorbed by the new National League for Nursing (NLN). It was also in 1952 that its periodical ceased publication, but the organ of the new organization, called *Nursing Outlook*, "would continue in the tradition of *Public Health Nursing* serving the public health nurse and all those interested in public health nursing service in their communities. . ." "In effect, *Nursing Outlook* will be the successor to *Public Health Nursing*" (46).

The NOPHN, perhaps the most progressive and socially aware group within organized nursing, was responsible for many innovations and advances in nursing and public health. Its contributions to practice, education, and service were significant to the evolution of professional nursing in America.

Association of Collegiate Schools of Nursing

Increased emphasis on collegiate preparation for professional nursing and the development of basic nursing programs in collegiate institutions during the late 1920s were reflected in the activities of the NLNE Committee on Nursing Education in Colleges and Universities. Nursing educators, who were desirous of fostering this development, called a conference under the aegis of the NLNE in 1928 for the purpose of discussing common problems and goals in establishing nursing programs within institutions of higher learning. At the 1932 NLNE convention in San Antonio, they met again and decided to plan a special conference of representatives of collegiate schools in order to consider development of a formal mechanism for exchange and mutual assistance.

The following January, with the cooperation of Isabel M. Stewart and Dean William Russell of Teachers College, the meeting was held at that institution and was chaired by Dean Russell. Representatives of over twenty collegiate institutions and the leaders of the national nursing organizations attended (17). Discussion at the conference centered around methods to develop interrelationships between schools of nursing and collegiate institutions and the best ways to assist colleges in establishing basic nursing programs. The result was the formation of an association of collegiate schools, which would be able to devote its full attention to those particular matters. By the end of the meeting, the new organization, the Association of Collegiate Schools of Nursing (ACSN), had become a reality and Annie Goodrich, dean of the nursing program at Yale, became the first president.

The intention was not to duplicate activities of any existing group or to take on school inspection or accreditation activities. The purpose was promotion of the sound development of collegiate nursing programs through mutual assistance and self-help activities of member institutions. As an organization of generally homogeneous institutions, membership was extended to schools who met the eligibility criteria (17):

Colleges, schools, departments or divisions of nursing which are constituent parts of an accredited college or university, which offer a basic professional or combined academic and professional course in nursing leading to a baccalaureate degree, or which offer an advanced course in nursing leading to a baccalaureate or higher degree.

Specific membership criteria for full membership included (1) control of the nursing program by the nursing department (to the extent that other departments in the institution controlled their programs), (2) control of the nursing curriculum by the nursing department, (3) organization of nursing faculty on the same basis as the rest of the college faculty, (4) adequate library and laboratory facilities for students, and (5) administrative control of the nursing program lodged in the university (rather than a service agency). Associate membership was offered to those schools that were in the process of meeting the criteria and could be assisted through representation in the organization. The major objective was to improve existing programs, but the ACSN also attempted to discourage the development of programs when there seemed to be a paucity of resources or when it deemed a particular institution an unsuitable place for establishment of a nursing program.

At the first annual meeting, held at Yale in 1934, nineteen schools qualified for membership. The number gradually increased in the years that followed. Chief among the concerns discussed at the ACSN meetings were the length of nursing courses and problems related to planning field and laboratory experiences for students. A primary area of interest was the development of clinical laboratory experiences, which clearly departed from the traditional apprenticeship model of the diploma school. The organization had no provision for consultation services to schools, but a system of peer assistance developed. When a particular program required expert advice, the ACSN frequently asked a representative of a member school in the same vicinity to visit and provide the help needed. In addition, close relationships between the ACSN and well-known educators such as Earl J. McGrath, Robert Hutchins, and Ralph Tyler provided valuable input.

Each year, member schools sent reports to ACSN detailing developments in their respective programs, reporting on innovations, and identifying problems that they wished the ACSN to consider at its next meeting. The majority of member schools were those with basic nursing programs, but the association also encouraged advanced programs in nursing, such as those developed through funds from the Kellogg Foundation. It also encouraged certain universities to develop programs for the preparation of curriculum specialists and educational consultants in nursing education. An outstanding characteristic was the emphasis the association placed on development of student-centered approaches in teaching and student involvement in all aspects of the nursing curriculum.

By the 1940s, the thrust of the ACSN was directed toward stimulating member schools to experiment with different patterns of basic education and to hire faculty who met the prescribed qualifications of faculty in the rest of the university in which they were employed. This second interest led the organization to consider issues related to development of masters degree programs in nursing, particularly those that would prepare individuals in a functional area for teaching and administration in collegiate programs. Basic undergraduate education in nursing, it believed, should prepare and qualify a student for graduate study.

The identification of the ACSN with higher education and the desire of member schools to have nursing qualify on an equal basis with other departments in colleges and universities naturally evoked attention to the need for research in nursing and the preparation of nurse researchers. In line with this interest, a special ACSN conference on research in nursing was held in 1948 at the University of Chicago. Member schools were encouraged to require projects with a research focus as term projects from students in their programs, and abstracts of completed projects were sent to the ACSN. It thus became a kind of clearinghouse and resource for information on studies related to nursing and nursing education. A review of project titles and abstracts reveals that early research efforts reflected a degree of sophistication that can be regarded as quite remarkable, given the times and newness of nursing within the university. A wide variety of investigations were pursued by students—clinical field studies, empirical studies related to nursing service and nursing education, and historical investigations.

In its later years, the ACSN debated the question of an internship for baccalaureate graduates and analyzed the problems of the "patchwork" education received by nurses who obtained their basic preparation in diploma schools and later studied for a baccalaureate degree. The organization worked closely with the American Council on Education and the joint committee of the NLNE and NOPHN on postgraduate education in nursing. It collaborated with the NLNE and the Department of Nursing Education at Teachers College to develop the cooperative Testing Bureau in an attempt to measure the objectives of nursing education.

Among the most active representatives of member schools during the later period were women who played a significant role in the collegiate programs of the time. In addition to Annie Goodrich and Isabel Stewart, notable representatives were Marion Howell, Shirley Titus, Elizabeth Burgess, Elizabeth Bixler, R. Louise McManus, Agnes Gelinas, and Sr. Olivia Gowan. By 1945, the number of schools offering baccalaureate degrees in nursing numbered 138 (3), but in 1952 only 37 schools qualified as bonafide collegiate schools as defined by the ACSN.

The on-going interest of the ACSN in research in nursing intensified with each year. In 1950, the association's Committee on Research, which was chaired by Helen Bunge, recommended that the American Journal of Nursing Company be approached to undertake publication of a special periodical covering research in nursing (18). That recommendation eventually resulted in the publication of *Nursing Research.*

When the plan for a new structure and organization of national nursing associations was finalized, it was decided that most of the traditional responsibilities of the ACSN would be assumed by the Department of Baccalaureate and Higher Degrees of the new NLN. During its relatively short period of existence, the ACSN accomplished much: it served to advance nursing education in colleges and universities, stimulated interest in graduate education and research in nursing, gave visibility to standards considered desirable for collegiate nursing programs, and, most of all, provided a means by which collegiate schools and representative faculty could exchange ideas and attempt to solve common problems.

Change in the Structure of Organized Nursing

In 1940, the country was preparing for its inevitable involvement in the war, and it was determined that the number of nurses would have to be increased to meet the war effort. Although there were several nursing organizations in the United States, no one association was truly in a position to speak or act on behalf of all nurses; nor did any single group have the data required to determine the existing nursing resources of the country.

It was believed that a commission representing all nursing interests would facilitate activities concerning nursing and the national defense. Originally called the Nursing Council on National Defense, the commission's formation was considered to be a temporary measure to unify nursing activities directly and indirectly related to defense and to act as a coordinating body and clearinghouse for information. This "temporary" council had a profound effect on the futures of the nursing organizations that comprised its membership and became the catalyst for change in the structure of organized nursing. Voting members of the Council included the ANA, NLNE, NOPHN, ACSN, NACGN, and the Red Cross Nursing Service. The American Association of Industrial Nurses (AAIN), established in 1942, joined shortly after its formation. Ex-officio members were representatives of the Army and Navy Nurse Corps, United States Public Health Service (USPHS), Veterans Administration, Childrens Bureau, Office of Indian Affairs, American Hospital Association, and the Canadian Nurses' Association.

Among the Council's priorities were the determination of the nation's nursing resources and recruitment of larger numbers of students into nursing programs. A subcommittee on nursing of the Federal Security Agency maintained close liaison with the Council. The subcommittee's administrative officers were prominent members of the profession who were on loan to the government from their respective employment situations and were active members of one or more of the national nursing organizations. In this way, the subcommittee and Council maintained open channels of communication and freely shared information, facilities, and resources.

In late 1940, the Council was reorganized and renamed the National Nursing Council for War Service. A program grant from the Kellogg Foundation and assistance from the Milbank Memorial

Fund made it possible to hire an executive secretary and develop a more active program. A committee on procurement and assignment was set up to aid the Red Cross and subcommittees in enrolling nurses for the military and to keep a check on the number of nurses needed at home.

The common cause that united the efforts of the nursing groups during the war brought about the realization that they could work together, toss vested interests aside, and speak for nursing with a strong and single voice. But significant as this was, it was viewed as incidental to the accomplishment of immediate, war-related goals and Council programs, which were accelerated after the attack on Pearl Harbor. With the passage of legislation (June 1943) that created the Cadet Corps Nursing Program, the Council focused its attention on recruitment of nursing students and preparation for an anticipated draft of nurses into the military.

At the close of the war, the Council, having engaged in postwar planning, decided not to dissolve but to continue functioning until another coordinating body replaced it, or until the joint committee of the nursing organizations recommended methods for continued coordination among the nursing associations. Eventually, the National Nursing Council engaged Esther Lucile Brown to direct a study concerned with the organization, administration, and financial support of professional and practical nursing as a basis for influencing the quality of nursing for the public. It also appointed a committee to plan for a single accrediting agency for nursing education. The Council terminated existence in 1948, and the National Nursing Accrediting Service was established the same year.

The experience gained during the war persuaded the associations' leaders that cooperative efforts could increase the efficacy and efficiency of organized nursing and that a permanent measure to ensure collaboration should be seriously pursued. Participation on the Council pointed out the potential that could be exploited through united nursing efforts. As early as 1939, an idea for closer working relationships among the national organizations had been proposed and the passage of Social Security had stimulated many joint committees of the groups. At that time, the ANA, in response to a recommendation made by a state nurses' association, had voted to appoint a special committee to consider consolidation of the ANA, NLNE, and NOPHN, and the next year it voted to conduct a study to determine how the organizations might function in a more uniform manner (9). But the war intervened, and, consequently, the study was never conducted.

However, the continued existence of the Council (renamed the National Nursing Council) after the war encouraged on-going coop-

erative endeavors among the organizations. The war had made in-
roads into the staff and resources of all the associations. This,
coupled with the pattern of cooperation developed through
participation on the Council, set the stage for events that followed.
Flexibility and openness to change became increasingly important
as the organizations realized that new trends in health care mandated unified planning by nursing.

Joint committees concerned with auxiliary nursing services,
health insurance, and integration of social and health aspects of
nursing in the basic curriculum consumed a large portion of time
and resources of the organizations. Practically and economically, a
consolidation of the organizations was a reasonable proposal, but
the ANA had gained in strength and some of the associations were
threatened. They believed that the ANA was interested in annexa-
tion, not merely cooperation. Collaboration was valued, but initially, the autonomy of the individual groups was valued far more.

The NOPHN, in particular, resisted the idea of consolidation and
believed that more than one nursing organization was necessary to
meet the increasingly diverse and specialized needs of the profession. Influenced by its long history of involvement with laypersons
and non-nursing organizations, it considered a proposal for consolidation to be regressive and narrow in its rationale (35). If a study was
to be conducted for the purpose of finding ways for the organizations
to move together on questions of common concern, the NOPHN
insisted that it be done under the auspices of a special committee
acting for organization but not drawn from the boards or staff of the
associations (35). The other groups capitulated, and Amelia Grant, a
former NOPHN president, was asked to develop a plan for the study
of the six organizations, which included the ANA, NLNE, NACGN,
NOPHN, ACSN, and AAIN.

Simultaneously, a joint advisory committee to give attention to a
joint study of national professional nursing organizations recommended the formation of a national planning committee to project a
five-year program of the participating organizations. It was thought
that a joint study of interrelationships had to be based on comprehensive studies of the individual associations and their respective
programs. To this end, the staff of each association worked dili-
gently to identify common activities of the various groups and, in
several instances, made suggestions for facilitating cooperative activities and preventing overlap and duplication of programs. These
data were compiled and sent to the joint committee to aid in designing the actual study.

In April 1945, a committee called the Promoting Committee for
the Structure of National Professional Nursing Organizations (composed of three members and the executive officers of the six associa-

tions) selected the firm of Raymond Rich Associates to conduct the study. The prospectus developed by Amelia Grant, having received the endorsement of all groups except the AAIN, was placed at the disposal of the firm.

A report of the study, "Report on the Structure of Organized Nursing," was delivered at the biennial convention of 1946. The study found that the six organizations were divided on three main points: non-nurse membership (the NOPHN and NLNE permitted this), special interests (the NOPHN and AAIN in particular), and program emphasis. These having been taken into consideration, the report by Rich Associates proposed two alternative plans for organized nursing.

The first plan (Plan I) suggested a single organization, the ANA, with five classes of membership within it: professional nurses, public members, allied professionals, nursing schools and service agencies, and non-nursing organizations. All members would have the same rights and privileges, but only nurse members would hold membership of the International Council of Nurses (ICN), be eligible for the proposed National Academy of Nurses, be involved in collective bargaining units within state and district organizations, and have final authority in matters of a strictly professional nature (47).

This single organization would be composed of sections representing various clinical specialties. Members would join a section of choice and vote in election of a directing council for the section. The council would, in turn, appoint specialty boards drawn from the professional membership of the section. Each section would elect two representatives to the House of Delegates and have a vote on the nominating committee for the ANA Board of Directors.

The Academy of Nurses was envisioned as a body composed of professional nurses who qualified as fellows after passing specialty board examinations. It was to be governed by an elected council of regents, empowered to grant certification to fellows and diplomates, to accredit schools, and to appoint boards of review for the purpose of evaluating the quality of schools and candidates proposed for admission to the Academy. In addition, the plan suggested a series of commissions to study general problems in nursing and establishment of a national nursing center wherein the activities of American nursing could be centralized (47).

The other plan suggested by Rich Associates (Plan II) called for a two-organization system. One organization, the ANA, would admit only nurses, and its suggested structure was identical to that described in the single-organization plan. The second association was to be a national organization for nursing service, which would include nurses, laypersons, allied professionals, and agency members.

It would consist of local councils with governing power vested in a national convention of members who would elect a board of directors representative of the various categories of membership. In this plan, cooperation between the two organizations would be achieved through a joint commission to work on common concerns and through a national nursing center, which would have representatives from both organizations on its board (28).

Reactions to the Rich Report were mixed. The ANA favored Plan I, but the other groups were less than positive about any plan that would give the ANA increased status and control. Regardless of the differences in opinions and preferences expressed, one point was patently clear: the question was no longer how the organizations' work could be coordinated but how to best develop a new system and structure for accomplishing that earlier objective. It would appear that the executives and officers of the various associations were more disposed to making concrete plans for change than their respective memberships. The Rich Report brought about some friction and misunderstandings among the six bodies, but it is probable that political factors within the leadership group played a significant role in continuing the planning for change. Emotions within the organizations ran high and the time for effecting change had not yet arrived, but the seed had been planted.

Following the Rich Report, a new committee on structure was formed, with five of the six organizations agreeing to participate. Later in the year, the ANA decided to continue its participation and financial support. It was composed of fifty-two members representing the organizations, with the presidents and executives of each serving in an ex-officio capacity. Hortense Hilbert was its chairperson. The years between 1947 and 1952 were filled with activity, most of which was directly related to planning for restructuring and organizations. However, each group continued to carry out its individual program responsibilities.

As deliberations continued, the positions of individual associations became clear. For example, in January 1947, the NOPHN Board of Directors unanimously passed a resolution reiterating that it would only support a structure plan that made provisions for non-nurse membership. By April of 1947, the structure study committee of the six nursing organizations had exhausted its funds and the ANA had still not voted to contribute continued financial support for the project. In September, the first special delegates' meeting in the history of the ANA was held and full participation in the on-going study was approved. However, the ANA again expressed its belief in limited membership of laypersons and viewed their appropriate participation as advisory in nature.

In January 1948, the committee on structure recommended that still a new committee be formed to develop a new comprehensive structure plan. This was done immediately with financing from all involved associations. The following April, one month before the convention in Chicago, representatives of the six boards of the nursing organizations met at the ANA's request to discuss a "Tentative Plan for One National Nursing Organization," which had been developed by the committee.

The "Tentative Plan" was a compromise, designed to please and appease all groups. Membership was to include nurses, non-nurses, and agency members, but sections were to be developed for only the nurse group, each having its own constitution, authority, and eligibility rules. In many other respects, the plan resembled Plan I, proposed by Rich Associates. At the convention in Chicago, discussion centered on how such a plan would be received by the ICN, whose constitution defined constituents as national associations or federations of nurses. The question was whether an American constituent that included non-nurses could retain membership in the ICN. Only the Grand Council of ICN, which was scheduled to meet the following year, was in a position to decide. None of the six groups wanted to jeopardize ICN membership; on the other hand, some groups, particularly the NOPHN, continued to be unwilling to agree to a one-organization plan unless it permitted non-nurse and agency membership. It was decided that if inclusion of non-nurses in a single association was judged untenable for continued ICN membership, a two-organization plan would be implemented (36). This being the case, the structure committee proceeded to develop an alternate plan.

Within the individual organizations, differences of opinion persisted. In the NOPHN, the battle was waged through the pages of its magazine. Some believed that the need for the consumer voice and their participation in planning for nursing and health care was vital and that involvement in a nursing association was one way to facilitate this. Elizabeth Fox, a former NOPHN president, wrote in support of "two independent organizations in full control of their own affairs but working together on projects and sharing facilities. Two great but unlike tasks need two unlike organizations" (26). On the other side, Margaret Arnestein said: "It seems to me, that if we cannot compromise at this point but insist upon setting up a second organization, we will start down a path that never ends. For then each time some group does not agree with another group, they will set up a separate organization and will end up with six or more . . . ." (14).

When the question of non-nurse membership in a single American nursing organization was referred to the ICN at its board meeting in September, no action was taken. Instead, the matter was referred to its membership committee. Lack of a formal response by the ICN was interpreted to mean that the Council considered it unwise to change its eligibility criteria for membership, but no official statement has been found to document this. Having no word from the ICN, the structure committee focused on development of the two-organization plan, which it presented to the board of the six organizations in combination with a revised single-organization plan.

The single-organization plan was not unlike the "Tentative Plan" proposed earlier, but it included an attached forum of non-voting agencies and laypersons. The second design, a two-organization plan, called for an ANA developed along the lines of the "Tentative Plan" and another association, the Nursing League of America, which included nurse, agency, and non-nurse members. Coordination of the two groups was to be achieved through a joint board of directors (20). The ANA continued to support a single-organization plan but the others preferred the proposal for two associations. By that time, most were eager to have a final decision made and hoped it could be finalized by 1950. With this in mind, the structure committee planned to terminate at the end of 1949.

During 1949, the NACGN, meeting in Louisville, voted its dissolution, effective in 1951. At the January 1950 meeting of the joint boards of the associations, the two-organization plan was passed and steps begun for ratification by the membership of each association. At the 1950 Biennial Convention in San Francisco, the ANA House of Delegates cast a majority vote for a two-organization plan; the NOPHN membership adopted the same plan, while the NLNE awaited the mail votes of its membership.

Following the convention, a structure steering committee, chaired by Pearl McIver, was appointed to implement the two-organization plan. It was determined that the ANA would require bylaw changes and that the NLNE structure would be used as a framework for developing bylaws for the new association. This decision was primarily based on legal considerations related to the incorporation laws governing the existing groups.

The new structure made provisions for two distinct organizations. The American Nurses' Association (ANA), a professional organization for nursing whose membership would be comprised of only nurses, would have the responsibility for developing standards of nursing practice, would define qualifications for the profession, promote legislation for nursing, collect data on nursing resources, promote and protect the general welfare of nurses, and be the official voice for American nursing in dealing with the government, allied professions, the public, and the ICN. There were to be three classes of membership—active, associate, and student—and seven practice groups, including a special council for students.

The new organization, the National League of America (NLA), would be an association concerned with furthering the development of nursing for the welfare of people. It was to focus on the ways by which organized nursing services were provided and ways of providing nurses with the educational preparation necessary for practice on graduation. Its goals would be to foster the development of nursing service and education through the combined efforts of nurses, citizens, community agencies, schools of nursing, and allied professional groups. It would be charged with the responsibility for defining standards for nursing services and education, would carry on accreditation activities, and would provide consultation services to individuals, schools, and agencies (32). There were to be two membership categories—individual and agency—and two major divisions—Nursing Service and Nursing Education.

The time between 1950 and the spring of 1952 was a period of transition. Staff for the new organization were committed and bylaws were revised and developed. Anna K. Fillmore, NOPHN general director, was chosen to be the first general director of the new NLA, and at the January 1952 meeting of the joint boards, dissatisfaction with the name "National League of America" prompted a name change to the National League for Nursing (NLN) (27). At the same meeting, plans were made to terminate publication of *Public Health Nursing* to give way to *Nursing Outlook*, which would be the official organ of the NLN. Changes were made rather smoothly, but in April 1952, the AAIN voted not to disband and join the NLN but to remain an autonomous organization. The controversial question of student members in the ANA also became in issue, and it was decided not to include them at the time.

The new structure for organized nursing became a reality at the Biennial Convention held in Atlantic City, June 15–20, 1952. That historic meeting, the theme of which was "Nursing United Promotes New Health Goals," was attended by over 9000 individuals. From years of discussion and planning, a two-organization plan had emerged. The ANA and the NLN had inherited a rich past and held the future in their hands.

Recent Perspectives

The period following restructuring was not without its problems. Adjustments for the ANA were minor but the NLN experienced the difficult situation of being a new organization, with a new structure, but incorporating the major programs once carried on by the NLNE, ACSN, and NOPHN. Several staff members of the earlier associations were employed by the NLN. In some respects this was a great asset; in others it can be viewed as problematic, for a new organization required new approaches and perspectives.

During the time of the structure study, Hortense Hilbert had said: "Reorganization or adoption of a new structure is not merely a reshuffling . . . it is something new, bigger and better, which will provide for the whole of nursing greater unity and strength of purpose" (37). The NLN took this idea seriously and made remarkable progress in developing its programs over the next several years. But Anna Fillmore reflecting on those years at NLN's fifth anniversary said: "That unification doesn't necessarily lead to simplification certainly has been illustrated. . . ." (24). Change brought with it advantages and disadvantages for both organizations.

The achievements and contributions of the ANA and the NLN over the past thirty years are too many to enumerate, too far-reaching to evaluate. Each organization, in its own way, has done much to improve and promote the nurse's condition, nursing practice, service, education, and research. Each has attempted to keep pace with societal changes and has helped to set trends and formulate future directions for American nursing. The testing and accrediting services of the NLN, its research activities relative to emerging educational patterns in nursing, and its inclusion of the consumer voice for the betterment of health care through nursing are but a few of the benefits derived. The ANA, with its progressive programs on economic and general welfare, its development of standards for practice, the certification of practitioners, and its 1965 Position Paper on education, has done much to advance the profession as a whole. Needless to say, the support of the organizations for federal funding for nursing education benefited many. The other nursing organizations, including the many that have recently been established, meet contemporary needs. Of particular note are the National Student Nurses' Association, the American Association of Colleges of Nursing, the Federation of Specialty Nursing Organizations, and the American Association of Critical Care Nurses.

The National Student Nurses' Association

History in the making was evidenced in 1952 by nurses and students of nursing alike: the American Nurses' Association was reorganized; the National League for Nursing came into being; the National Association of Colored Graduate Nurses, the Association of

Collegiate Schools of Nursing, and the National Organization for Public Health Nursing were dissolved; and the National Council of Student Nurses, the forerunner of the National Student Nurses' Association, was formed.

Prior to 1952, schools of nursing or alumnae associations sent students to the ANA and NLNE conventions. These conventions provided students the opportunity to interact with one another and to meet the leaders in nursing. The *American Journal of Nursing* began a student page in 1922. Articles by students were published, and by 1940 regular news of student activities was carried. In 1952 the new bylaw for the ANA that provided an ANA student council was not adopted; therefore, an independent national student organization was a logical movement (44, 45).

The National Student Nurses' Association (NSNA), established in 1953, is the national organization for nursing students in the United States and its territories. It is the largest independent student organization in the country and the only one for nursing students. Its decision-making body is the House of Delegates, made up of representatives from state and school constituent associations. Each year the House elects a board of directors to carry out the work of the organization between meetings of the House. The NSNA's purposes, as stated in their bylaws, are (42):

a. To assume responsibility for contributing to nursing education in order to provide for the highest quality health care

b. To provide programs representative of fundamental and current professional interests and concerns

c. To aid in the development of the whole person, his/her responsibility for the health care of people in all walks of life

The functions of the NSNA include the following (40):

a. To have direct input into standards of nursing education and influence the educational process

b. To influence health care, nursing education, and practice through legislative activities as appropriate

c. To promote and encourage participation in community affairs and activities toward improved health care and the resolution of related social issues

d. To represent nursing students to the consumer, to institutions, and to other organizations

e. To promote and encourage students' participation in interdisciplinary activities

f. To promote and encourage recruitment efforts, participation in student activities, and educational opportunities regardless of person's race, color, creed, sex, age, lifestyle, national origin, or economic status

g. To promote and encourage collaborative relationships with the American Nurses' Association, the National League for Nursing, the International Council of Nurses, as well as the other nursing and related health organizations

The NSNA represents the interests of students at the ANA, NLN, the National Federation of Specialty Nursing Organizations, Coalition for Health Funding, N-CAP, ANA Commission on Human Rights, ANA/NSNA Common Interests and Goals Committee, and the NLN Long-Term Care Committee.

The major programs of the NSNA include the following:

Project Tomorrow. This professional and career planning program helps students make important career decisions.

A Voice in Washington. NSNA monitors all legislation relevant to nursing and nursing education and testifies when necessary before congressional committees on matters affecting nursing students. NSNA's position on various pieces of legislation is based on policies adopted by the House of Delegates and Board of Directors. On new issues that arise between meetings, the board member responsible for legislation decides the initial response of the association based on association policies.

Because the legislative arena is such a large one, NSNA maintains close working relationships with the legislative staff of the ANA, the NLN, the Coalition for Health Funding, and other organizations. Since legislative strength lies in the number of people being represented, cooperative efforts are undertaken whenever possible.

Community Health Activities. NSNA members are encouraged to participate in community health projects that provide some kind of service to the community plus a chance for nursing students to utilize or gain knowledge and skills.

Minority Recruitment Project. NSNA members have ongoing recruitment programs in their state and local associations. During the past 15 years, NSNA has sponsored a national recruitment project, "Breakthrough to Nursing," in which nursing students provide prospective recruits with tutorial help, seek financial assistance and scholarships, and give personal support to nursing candidates (39).

Financial Assistance. NSNA's scholarship program is made possible through the contributions of corporations, organizations, and individuals. It helps members pay for their education.

Convention. The NSNA Convention provides the opportunity for students from various programs throughout the country to meet together to share ideas and discuss mutual concerns. Participation in the House of Delegates familiarizes students with parliamentary procedure and the operation of a democratic organization. Exciting sessions with dynamic leaders of nursing are always part of the annual meeting.

Publications. Imprint, the official magazine of the NSNA, portrays the student's perspective of the nursing profession and is written for and principally by students. An up-to-date commentary on public issues and legislation affecting health care and the nursing profession is included (43). *Imprint* educates students on health care issues and legislation and, by clarifying their effects on the profession and on the student, encourages active student advocacy.

The annual *Imprint Career Planning Guide,* published exclusively for nursing students, contains information on career options, self-assessment, decision-making, job availability, and career opportunity profiles.

The Dean's List, published five times a year, is intended for faculty of nursing programs. It provides a concise, informative communications vehicle for undergraduate nursing educators (38).

Other publications include guidelines on areas such as legislation and community health, which are prepared periodically to meet student needs (41).

National Federation of Specialty Nursing Organizations and ANA

The 1950s and the turbulent 1960s brought about the formation of a variety of specialty nursing organizations. As the number of nursing associations increased, the communications gap among them grew wider. There was a desire for unity among leaders of a number of specialty groups. However, their memberships did not believe the ANA to be concerned with the needs of their specialty, and anger and distrust directed toward the ANA prevailed.

In 1972, the Board of Directors of ANA saw the need "to explore how the organizations can work toward more coordination on areas of mutual interest" (23). Consequently, they decided to invite the presidents and staff of nursing organizations to a meeting at ANA headquarters in Kansas City. Continuing education and relationships with physician's assistants were among the areas of mutual interest identified at this exploratory meeting.

The First National Congress in Nursing, organized for the purpose of seeking mutual support and cooperation among nursing specialty groups and the ANA, was called by the American Association of Critical Care Nurses (AACN) (40). This historic event was held in San Clemente, California, January 23-25, 1973.

During this meeting, the group agreed in principle to the following concepts:

  a. Support for individual continuing education and individual accountability in maintaining competence in practice

  b. No support for mandatory continuing education for relicensure to practice until the ANA completes its study of the issue

  c. Essential that ANA seek participation of all specialty nursing groups in their deliberations and ultimate decisions regarding continuing education as a basis for standardizing those continuing education units for all nursing organizations (23)

The "CEU" was adopted as the basis for standardizing continuing education units for all nursing organizations. The group unanimously agreed "that a universal and cooperative effort be made to recruit all professional nurses into at least one of the professional nursing groups in order that understanding be fostered and solidarity be enhanced" (23).

In June of the same year a third meeting was held in Denver. At this meeting of seventeen organizations the group was named the Federation of Specialty Nursing Organizations and ANA. The following criteria for membership was established (23):

  1. A national organization of registered nurses governed by an elected body with bylaws defining purpose and functions for improvement of health care and a body of knowledge and skill in a defined area of clinical practice.

  2. The composition of this group is limited to include two members per organization.

  3. Any organization not meeting the criteria may have one representative audit meetings by written request and approval of the host organizations.

The seventeen organizations attending the meeting became a thirteen-member federation with four auditors. Operating rules were adopted and a decision to invite the nursing press to attend future meetings of the Federation in their entirety was reached. The organization has grown and now numbers more than 25 specialty groups. There is a formal structure provided for in bylaws with policies and operating rules. In 1981, the name of the Federation was officially changed to the National Federation for Specialty Nursing Organizations.

American Association of Critical Care Nurses (AACN)

A cardiac nursing symposium held in October 1968, at Baptist Hospital in Nashville, Tennessee, set the stage for a national association. On September 22, 1969, at the Second Cardiac Symposium, the American Association of Cardiovascular Nurses was formed.

The goals and priorities of the founding organization included:

1. Setting standards of education and practice
2. Disseminating knowledge through educational programs
3. Establishing a central information bureau
4. Publishing a periodical
5. Facilitating communication and cooperation with other health care groups (4)

Local chapters, which numbered 26 by 1971, had been formed and were actively sponsoring educational opportunities for a national membership, which totaled 2800. That year a special malpractice insurance program was added to the already lengthy list of member benefits.

The Association's newsletter began branching into other aspects of critical care as well as cardiovascular nursing. It became apparent that the core knowledge needed for cardiac intensive care was applicable to other areas of critical care. In January 1972, the founding group reincorporated as the American Association of Critical Care Nurses (4).

Heart and Lung, The Journal of Critical Care is the official publication of the Association and is designed to help critical care practitioners stay abreast of current scientific information.

National headquarters were established in 1972 in southern California and membership swelled to 6000. In 1974, annual chapter leadership forums were introduced, as well as the first National Teaching Institute, which drew over 3000 participants. In 1975 *Focus*, AACN's official newsletter, was introduced to facilitate communication among a membership of more than 20,000 nurses and 123 local chapters. Membership continued to grow and the association's leadership sought to unify nursing specialty groups and the ANA.

The AACN continues to provide a coalition of nurses, which can identify and study common issues, problems, and solutions that face professional nursing (2). The organization is an excellent example of a specialty group which is meeting the needs of nurses with special clinical practice interests.

American Association of Colleges of Nursing

The American Association of Colleges of Nursing was established in 1969 to answer the need for a national organization exclusively devoted to furthering the goals of baccalaureate and graduate education in nursing. In many ways it is reminiscent of the former Association of Collegiate Schools of Nursing.

The AACN provides baccalaureate and higher degree programs in nursing with a framework through which issues critical to nursing can be considered and acted on expeditiously. Membership is extended to baccalaureate and higher degree programs.

In serving the public interest, the AACN exists to improve the practice of professional nursing through advancing the quality of baccalaureate and graduate programs, promoting research, and developing academic leaders (1).

A unified voice for nursing's needs has been achieved through close working relationships with the ANA and the NLN.

The activities of the organization are numerous. The Data Bank Project, now in its fourth year, conducts an annual survey of institutional data, including salaries of nursing faculty, nursing deans, and other administrative faculty. The data are analyzed and disseminated so as to be available to membership within a six-month period. Institutional data include enrollment and graduations, preparation of faculty, and other characteristics of baccalaureate and graduate education in nursing that are important in determining trends. Salary data serve as a factual resource in budget-making. Recently, the AACN also enlarged its institutional Data Service by providing member schools with printouts showing their ranking with peer groups on certain variables.

The AACN, on a continuing basis, provides information to congressional committees and governmental agencies on the needs of baccalaureate and higher degree programs and the types of legislation that will increase the quality and quantity of professional nursing in all health care settings.

AACN's publication series, with approximately three issues annually, addresses vital issues in nursing, and a newsletter published approximately monthly informs the members of AACN's activities.

Workshops and conferences have been sponsored on grant writing, faculty clinical practice, and graduate education. Since 1976, the AACN has sponsored jointly with the NLN a summer seminar for deans, with subjects relevant to deans in schools of nursing.

To think, to investigate, to act in the interest of higher education for nursing remains the hallmark of the AACN. It has become an important forum for deans of collegiate nursing programs to share ideas and deliberate issues.

Sigma Theta Tau

Sigma Theta Tau is the national honor society of nursing, which has as its major goals the promotion of research and leadership in nursing. Founded in 1922 at the University of Indiana, it has established chapters in approximately 166 collegiate schools of nursing. Selection for membership in Sigma Theta Tau is based on scholarly achievement and professional leadership. Those eligible for nomination are baccalaureate degree students and graduate students in nursing programs and community nursing leaders who are invited to membership through chapters in their local universities.

Through its conferences, official publications, and research fund, Sigma Theta Tau makes significant contributions to advancing scholarship in nursing, and promoting nursing education within senior colleges and universities.

American Academy of Nursing

The American Academy of Nursing was established in 1973 under the aegis of the American Nurses' Association. Its objectives are:

- To advance new concepts in nursing and health care.
- To identify and explore issues in health, in the professions, and in society as they affect and are affected by nurses and nursing.
- To examine the dynamics within nursing, and examine the interaction among nurses as all these affect the development of the nursing profession.
- To identify and propose resolutions to issues and problems confronting nursing and health, including alternative plans for implementation.

Membership in the academy is considered a special honor and is reserved for those graduate nurses who are members of the ANA, have provided evidence of outstanding contributions to nursing, and evidence of the potential to continue these contributions. Individuals are nominated for membership and those selected for inclusion on a ballot must be elected by current academy members. Those who become Fellows in the Academy (FAAN) represent a select leadership group within the profession.

Comment

Differences in emphasis and opinion are essential to the development of futuristic ideas and progressive action, but unity and collaboration on the major issues confronting the whole of American nursing are essential for the survival of the profession and, ultimately, the improvement of health care. Today, more than ever, cooperative efforts among all nursing associations, large and small, are crucial. There must be flexibility and room for diverse interests, but there must also be a workable means to accomplish desirable ends for the entire profession. The path to professionalism in nursing and the development of nursing's professional associations share a common history and continue to focus on a common goal.

References

1. American Association of Colleges of Nursing: Washington, DC, AACN, 1981

2. American Association of Critical Care Nurses: AACN Entering the Eighties. Irvine, 1980

3. American Nurses Association: Facts about Nursing. New York, ANA, 1946, p. 39

4. American Nurses Association: Federation of Specialty Nursing Organizations and ANA—A History. Kansas City, ANA, 1980

5. American Nurses Association: Proceedings, Twenty-fifth Convention, 1922

6. American Nurses Association: Proceedings of Convention, 1950

7. American Nurses Association: Report of Committee on District Nursing, Proceedings of Fifteenth Convention, 1912

8. American Nurses Association: Report of Program in Inter-Group Relations in Nursing, May 27, 1954

9. American Nurses Association: Report of Special Committee to Consider Consolidation of the Three National Nursing Organizations, Proceedings of Thirty-second Convention, 1940.

10. The ANA in the proposed structure. Am J Nurs 51:594–597, 1951

11. American Society of Superintendents of Training Schools: Proceedings of the First and Second Annual Conventions, 1894–1895

12. American Society of Superintendents of Training Schools: Proceedings, 1896, pp. 42–66

13. American Society of Superintendents of Training Schools: Proceedings, 1897

14. Arnstein M: Sometimes compromise is needed. Public Health Nurs 40:427–428, 1948

15. Ashely J: Hospital Sponsorship of Nursing Schools: Influence of Apprenticeship and Paternalism on Nursing Education in America, 1893–1948. Doctoral dissertation, Teachers College, Columbia University, 1972, p. 66

16. Associated Nursing Alumnae of the United States and Canada: Minutes of Executive Committee, October 1908

17. Association of Collegiate Schools of Nursing: Report of Conference on Collegiate Schools held at Teachers College, January 1933

18. Association of Collegiate Schools of Nursing: Report and Minutes, Committee on Research, April 21, 1950

19. Christy TE: Cornerstone for Nursing Education. New York, Teachers College Press, 1970

20. Committee on Structure of National Nursing Associations: Handbook on the Structure of Organized Nursing, 1949, pp. 10–36

21. Dock LL: A National Association for Nurses and its Legal Organization, Annual Report of the American Superintendents of Training Schools, 1896, p. 60

22. Dock LL: The history of public health. Public Health Nurs 14:524, 1922

23. Editorial. Am J Nurs 32:672, 1932

24. Fillmore AK: Our first five years. Nurs Outlook 6:14, 1958

25. Fitzpatrick ML: The National Organization for Public Health Nursing, 1912–1952: Development of a Practice Field. New York, National League for Nursing, 1975, pp. 72–77, 87

26. Fox EG: I vote no. Public Health Nurs 40:427–428, 1948

27. Joint Board of Directors of the Six National Nursing Associations. Minutes, January 1950

28. Joint Committee on the Structure of National Nursing Organizations. Report, August, 1947, pp. 6–9

29. MacDonald G: Development of Standards and Accreditation in Collegiate Nursing Education. New York, Teachers College Press, 1965, p. 67

30. Munson HW: The Story of the N.L.N.E. Philadelphia, W. B. Saunders, 1934, pp. 36–39

31. National Association of Colored Graduate Nurses. Objectives of the Association, typewritten materials, ME Carnegie Collection, New York

32. The NLA in the proposed structure. Am J Nurs 51:647–653, 1951

33. National League of Nursing Education. Forty-fifth Annual Report, 1939, p. 209

34. National Organization for Public Health Nursing. Minutes, Board of Directors, April 19, 1921

35. National Organization for Public Health Nursing. Minutes, Board of Directors, January 21, 1941

36. National Organization for Public Health Nursing: Proceedings of Twenty-first Convention, June 1948

37. National Organization for Public Health Nursing: Minutes, Business Meeting, June 1950

38. National Student Nurses' Association: Annual Report, 1981

39. National Student Nurses' Association: Breakthrough to Nursing, 1973

40. National Student Nurses' Association: Bylaws, 1981

41. National Student Nurses' Association: Twelve Reasons Why You Need the National Student Nurses' Association, 1982

42. National Student Nurses' Association: Getting the Pieces to Fit, VI, 1981

43. National Student Nurses' Association: Legislative Handbook, 1980

44. National Student Nurses' Association: NSNA's Ten Tall Years, 1963

45. National Student Nurses' Association: NSNA '77—Twenty-Five Years Young and Still Growing, 1977

46. Nursing Outlook, editorial. Public Health Nurs 44:483, 1952

47. Rich RT: The Structure Study. Report delivered at the Biennial Convention of Nursing Organizations, Atlantic City, September 24, 1946

48. Roberts ME: American Nursing—History and Interpretation. New York, Macmillan, 1954, p. 282

49. Staupers MK: No Time for Prejudice. New York, Macmillan, 1961, pp. 1–3, 36

50. Staupers MK: The story of N.A.C.G.N.. Am J Nurs 51:222, 1951

51. Swort A: The ANA: The Formative Years, 1875–1922. Doctoral dissertation, Teachers College, Columbia University, 1973, pp. 59–79

5

Nurse Influentials—Ideas and Innovations

Professional nursing in the United States has evolved in the way it serves the health needs of the nation. Many ideas and events influence the way a profession evolves. There is no single causative factor. The people who chose to be nurses at different stages of history were critical to the development of nursing in their times. The great body of individual nurses are quickly forgotten. It is the exceptional nurse, frequently a leader and innovator in a particular facet of the profession's development, that history remembers.

Ralph Waldo Emerson believed that all history is biography. One individual and the record of his or her life can be a meaningful lens through which we can examine some of the major innovations in American nursing. All change begins with an idea. Frequently a leader becomes identified with an idea and is able to mobilize resources to actually bring about a meaningful change. Professional nursing has its share of individuals who contributed to its growth and development in a variety of ways. Some of the earlier leaders were identified with more than one major innovation. The following biographical portraits of selected late leaders reflect the significance of individuals in shaping the development of American nursing. They are but a few of the leaders who shaped American nursing.

Isabel Adams Hampton Robb (1859–1910): Architect of American Nursing Organizations

Isabel Hampton was born in Welland, Ontario, the fourth child in a family of eight. Her parents, Samuel and Sarah Lay Hampton, were of Scotish and English heritage. Mr. Hampton was self-employed with a successful tailoring business. It was a comfortable home but not luxurious, and young "Addie" grew up an avid reader. She attended the public schools and was quite a good student. She earned a teaching certificate and taught in a nearby county school for several

189

years. At that time, teaching was about the only respectable occupation for middle-class women.

Even in the early years, there was a restlessness and ambition in the young, intelligent Miss Hampton. She confided to her sister Carolyn, "if I were a man, I wouldn't stop at anything; I would be Premier of Canada" (15). Teaching school children no longer interested her, and she entered the nine-year-old Bellevue Hospital Training School for Nurses in New York City in 1881. As a pupil nurse, she was hungry for knowledge. She was more interested in ideas than in the never-ending practical work expected of the pupils during their twelve-hour day. She graduated in 1883 and for a brief period of time served as a relief supervisor at Women's Hospital in New York. Subsequently, Isabel Hampton spent two years as a staff nurse at St. Paul's Hospice in Rome, Italy. St. Paul's was under Episcopal auspices and each year a few American nurses were selected to nurse at St. Paul's. These years increased her awareness of the necessity of a liberal education for the professional nurse and she augmented her earlier classical education while in Rome.

Isabel Adams Hampton had the soul of an educator. Her major concern in nursing was to develop and raise the standards of nursing education. This was an overwhelming challenge in the years before the turn of the century. Each training school was a law unto itself. Training schools proliferated as it became increasingly obvious that this was the best and most inexpensive way of providing nursing care for patients. Miss Hampton developed a strong political sense for survival while she accomplished important educational reforms at the Illinois Training School in the 1880s. She saw the lack of standards, the dearth of unity regarding professional goals, and the absence of control over who were qualified nurses and who were not as major widespread problems by the time she was established as Superintendent of Nurses and Principal of the Johns Hopkins Training School of Nurses in Baltimore, Maryland. In 1880 she wrote to Margaret Lawrence (10):

> *This question of what to do with unqualified nurses . . . Like you I have lain awake nights trying to see some way out of it . . . it seems to me that the best and only right solution to the problem is to organize an American Nurses' Association . . . The managers and superintendents of nurses' schools ought to meet at some central point to discuss the question carefully and then decide on the best action to take . . . Carefully study out and formulate the rules and regulations for the association. . .*

Several years would pass before the vision expressed in this letter would become reality. Writers of the nursing literature of the time, primarily in *The Trained Nurse and Hospital Review*, also discussed these problems. Finally an opportunity presented itself and Isabel Hampton planned a national forum at which nurses could examine these issues. Lavinia Dock, M. Adelaide Nutting, and Ethel Bedford Fenwick met at Hopkins and worked with Miss Hampton in planning the program for the International Congress of Charities, Correction and Philanthropy held in Chicago in 1893. As chairman of the subsection on nursing, Isabel Hampton carefully designed the program. It was no accident that individuals like Edith Draper were invited to read papers such as "The Necessity of an American Nurses' Association."

At the close of the meeting, after all twenty-eight papers had been read and discussed, Miss Hampton invited the superintendents of training schools to meet with her for the purpose of forming an organization. The group called itself the American Society of Superintendents of Training Schools for Nurses. Isabel Hampton chaired the meeting that brought the organization into being and subsequently served on the executive committee. Perhaps she refused to be an officer because she knew she would soon be married. The first convention of the Superintendents' Society was held in January 1894. Isabel Hampton Robb wrote to the new organization while completing her European wedding trip.

Although nursing colleagues were dismayed by her marriage (they believed marriage would preempt her interest in nursing) Mrs. Robb made her most important contribution to American nursing after her marriage. The role of Victorian wife and mother must have seemed very different for this charismatic former superintendent of nurses and principal of a training school.

Isabel Robb's interest in nursing and her vision for its future remained unchanged. Her practical work for the profession and its goals forced her to be extraordinarily well organized. Letters from her to colleagues tell of her balance between maintaining a home in Cleveland and the important work she was doing in nursing organization. She had a nurturant, almost motherly leadership style and made herself available for consultation, comfort, and conversation. Because she was no longer employed in nursing she was not competing for any particular position, which made her advice even more trusted. As the former teacher of many, she enjoyed a special relationship with the other leaders in American nursing at that time.

Mrs. Robb and others were proud of the Superintendents' Society but believed that staff nurses in hospitals, private duty, and the public sector needed their own organizations. The needs and perspectives of the superintendents were, after all, very different. The Associated Alumnae of Trained Nurses of the United States and Canada was formally organized in 1897. Isabel Hampton Robb, who had recently delivered her first son, was elected as the organization's first president. In her inaugural address she outlined the goals she believed were crucial for professional development. Goals that today remain only partially achieved. She served the organization as president until 1901.

Mrs. Robb was the prototype of the professional woman. She accomplished much before her premature death in a traffic accident in 1910. All that she did for nursing was due to her beliefs and zeal as an educator. Isabel Hampton Robb wanted better standards for nursing and nursing education. Her books included *Nursing: Its Principles and Practice* (1894), *Nursing Ethics* (1900), and *Educational Standards for Nurses* (1907). Her writings were one other avenue through which she influenced the emerging profession.

Lillian Wald, who graduated several years later from New York Hospital School of Nursing, was a contemporary and colleague of Mrs. Robb. As chairman of the education committee, Mrs. Robb had created "the cause" at Teachers College, and together with Lillian Wald, she garnered the financial support that brought the Department of Nursing Education at Teachers College, Columbia University, into being. These two very different nurse leaders convinced the philanthropist Helen Hartley Jenkins to underwrite the first nursing program in an institution of higher learning. Isabel Hampton Robb was an influential nurse who had a great impact on the young profession, and who believed that professionalism depended on the ability of nurses to organize.

Lillian Wald (1867–1940) and the Development of Public Health Nursing Practice

Lillian D. Wald was born in Cincinnati, Ohio, the third of four children born to Max and Minnie Schwarz Wald. Mr. Wald, a dealer in optical goods, brought up his family in Rochester, New York. The family was of German-Jewish heritage but not particularly religious. Lillian attended Miss Crittenden's School, along with other comfortable middle-class children. An intelligent young woman, she applied to enter Vassar College but was rejected because she was only sixteen years old. Several years later she graduated from the New York Hospital School for Nurses. Her first position was as a nurse in an orphan asylum. After a year of working with orphaned children Miss Wald attended the New York Women's Medical College, and while a student, she gave some classes to immigrant women on New York's lower east side. It was an experience that revolutionized her life. Lillian Wald had already chosen to practice nursing outside the hospital walls. Her unplanned visit to a sick, untended woman in a tenement was a challenge that committed her to develop a new area for nursing practice that revolutionized the field.

The economic depression of the 1890s coupled with the high immigration rate and a high incidence of communicable disease, made New York's lower east side an extremely unhealthy environment in which to live. Lillian Wald and another New York Hospital graduate, Mary Brewster, moved to this neighborhood.

The young nurses were careful to avoid being connected with any sponsoring organizations because they wanted to live among the people and be available when they were needed. This lack of any affiliation made them acceptable to everyone. Other settlement work had already begun, but Wald's ideas, including the use of nursing skills, were unique. The people called on them and they were phenomenally successful as health care providers. When a case warranted it, the young nurses would refer a particular patient to a physician at one of the free dispensaries. Mary Brewster's health forced her to give up the work, but Miss Wald continued. The first decade of Lillian Wald's life on the lower east side was filled with the challenge of an interesting and full practice. The care of patients in their homes went far beyond the physical. Miss Wald was their health educator, sanitary engineer, family counselor, friend, and, in some cases, provider.

To facilitate her work, Lillian Wald became an accomplished fund raiser. Philanthropists, such as Jacob Schiff and Mrs. Solomon Loeb, became important sources of support. Miss Wald recorded details of her practice in letters to the philanthropists (14):

> I took Hattie Isaacs, the consumptive, a big big bunch of flowers and while she slept I cleaned out the window of medicine bottles. Then I bathed her, and the poor girl had been so long without this attention that it took me nearly two hours to get her skin clean. She was carried to a couch and I made the bed, cooked a light breakfast of eggs and milk which I had brought with me, fed her, and assisted the mother to straighten up then left. In this case the mother has more than the tenement intelligence, the girl is American born and the family would have been willing to attend the invalid, but she is so ill and emaciated that it required some skill to give her a bath in bed without causing suffering. . . .

Clearly, Miss Wald epitomized what would become the role of the public health nurse. Her thorough and creative mind led her to attend to social and other conditions that made people sick. This quite naturally brought her into political awareness and galvanized her into action.

As a leader she expressed herself most effectively in social situations, but she was also skillful in oral presentation. Lillian Wald was not as militant as Lavinia Dock in her approach to change. She was interested in the election of officials who would assist in resolution of problems that she, as a nurse, perceived. She supported Seth Low for a second term as mayor of New York because, in her opinion, during his term the Health Department was run effectively and he had been supportive of the idea and the subsequent introduction of school nurses into the educational system.

Miss Wald had creative ideas about how nurses would effectively keep people well. The Metropolitan Life Insurance Company's nursing service for policyholders and the Red Cross' Town and Country Nursing Service were credited to her. It was Lillian Wald who organized the first public health nursing service. To accomplish these goals she had to give up her own personal practice and assume the role of an administrator.

On excellent terms with nursing colleagues at Teachers College and elsewhere, Lillian Wald also had a very broad acquaintance with people in many walks of life. She had a genius for motivating people to get things done. Lillian Wald was responsible for opening another practice area for nurses in school nursing. She offered the free services of a Henry Street nurse for a one-month demonstration. The results were tangible: fewer children were out of school due to illness. Soon school nurses were employed throughout New York City.

Miss Wald is also credited for the concept of a federal bureau to promote child health and welfare. She had first-hand experience with lower east side children who lost their health and their spirit as members of factory labor forces. Congress finally established the United States Children's Bureau.

A creative practitioner and an administrator par excellence, Miss Wald was also a gifted educator. She saw the necessity for additional specialized education for those nurses who wished to practice in public health. She and Adelaide Nutting of Teachers College, Columbia University, established an educational opportunity for nurses wherein they could take their theoretical coursework at Teacher's College and utilize the Henry Street Settlement as their clinical laboratory. This arrangement lasted for many years.

Lillian Wald was clearly a literate woman. In addition to the letters she wrote to educate and raise funds, she wrote many articles. Her books include *The House on Henry Street* (1915) and *Windows on Henry Street* (1934).

Miss Wald was active in a variety of organizations—the Pushcart Commission and the State Commission to Report on Conditions and Industrial Opportunities for Aliens in the State of New York, which led to the State Board of Industries and Immigration. Lillian

Wald also had a broad perspective. When the National Organization for Public Health Nursing was formally established, the lay members and nurse members elected Miss Wald as their first president.

Like Lavinia Dock, Lillian Wald was a pacifist. She was active in the American Union Against Militarism. When the United States entered World War I, Miss Wald was active in nursing work and became a member of a subcommittee of the Council of National Defense. She remained at home caring for the civilian population while individuals like Jane Delano and Julia Stimson found new challenges for nurses in military service. Above all, Lillian Wald was an innovator and charismatic leader who used the political system within and outside nursing to further her ideas and deliver health and social services to the poor.

Julia Catherine Stimson (1881–1948) and the Army Nurse Corps

Julia Stimson was the second child of seven born to the Reverend Henry Albert and Alice Bartlett Stimson. The Stimsons were an old New England family with a tradition of service to the community. Education was also an important value. All of the Stimson children had significant careers. Miss Stimson's maternal grandfather, Reverend Samuel Bartlett, had served as president of Dartmouth College for many years.

A graduate of the public school in St. Louis, Miss Stimson earned a B.A. from Vassar in 1901. She continued her studies in biology at Columbia University during 1901 to 1903. A meeting with Annie Goodrich (then superintendent of the New York Hospital Training School for Nurses) is said to be the impetus Miss Stimson needed to commit herself to a career in nursing. She graduated from the New York Hospital Training School in 1908 and earned an M.A. in sociology, biology, and education at Washington University, St. Louis, in 1917.

Well educated as a woman, and particularly well educated as a nurse, Miss Stimson's first position was as superintendent of nurses at the Harlem Hospital. While in this position she became keenly aware of the unusual needs of her predominantly underprivileged patients. She and a nurse colleague developed a social service department at the hospital.

Moving to St. Louis, Julia Stimson set up a similar social service department at Barnes and Children's Hospitals, affiliated with Washington University. She served as superintendent of nurses from 1913 to 1917.

Although an administrator, an educator, and a contributor to nursing literature, Julia Stimson is best remembered for her role in the Army Nurse Corps. Miss Stimson had been a Red Cross nurse since 1909 and had become a member of the National Committee on Red Cross Nursing. After several abortive efforts, the enrolled nurses of the American National Red Cross Nursing Service finally became the reserve of the Army Nurse Corps in a plan almost identical to what had been envisioned by Isabel Hampton Robb. These Red Cross nurses could, with their consent, be assigned to active duty if necessary.

The Red Cross began to organize these hospital units at American hospitals so that they would be ready for mobilization when necessary. Miss Stimson was the chief nurse of Base Hospital No. 21 at Washington University.

Miss Stimson became an Army Nurse in 1917 and was sent to France to work with the English Expeditionary Forces. The archives at New York Hospital hold the Julia Stimson Collection. In the diaries she kept almost all of her life and the letters she wrote to her family during these years of war service, a poignant picture of her experience emerges. It is clear how the tall, clear-eyed, rather lovely young woman develops the look of a disciplined and somewhat stern leader. She tells her family that she must not weep, for others need her to lean on as they weep at the injuries inflicted on the young soldiers from poison gas and other war-related injuries.

Miss Stimson was an excellent organizer and administrator and became the chief Red Cross nurse in France. Later she became the army's director of nursing service for the American Expeditionary Forces. She had tremendous responsibility, limited resources, and no real military rank. Her work was not easy.

It should be remembered that frequently things could be accomplished under the auspices of the Red Cross that would be impossible for the military to do for a variety of reasons. For example, when the French had promised to care for the American wounded but did not have the necessary facilities, it would have been a diplomatic disaster for the Americans to send in a military base hospital. They could, however, come in as an American Red Cross hospital. Julia Stimson's position and role gave her the ability to be an impacting force on the administration of nursing in the acute emergency of war. There had been political difficulties surrounding Miss Stimson's appointment, but fortunately they were resolved.

Miss Stimson's letters reveal her thorough knowledge of what was going on, as well as her sincere pride in the work of the American nurses (5). Often there were problems when Americans arrived to take over the French hospitals. Supplies were inadequate or nonexistent, incoming and outgoing staff could not speak the same language, and Red Cross nurses may have specialized in tuberculosis, child welfare, or social service work when surgical skills were what was necessary. These and many other problems were solved by Miss Stimson and those she appointed.

Julia Stimson was a compassionate woman and felt deeply about nurses who became ill or were injured while on active duty. Obviously this side of this formidable woman was not readily perceived.

After the Armistice, while still in Europe, Julia Stimson received a letter from Annie Goodrich. Miss Goodrich, then Dean of the Army Training School, asked Miss Stimson not to make any plans until they had a chance to talk together. Julia Stimson became the next Dean of the Army Training School and remained in that position until the school closed in 1933. A few months after becoming the Dean, she also became Superintendent of the Army Nurse Corps.

Her administration of military nursing and nursing education was said to be brilliant. She was particularly interested in improving personnel policies as well as professionalizing the military nurses. The nurses were encouraged to participate in their professional organizations, and opportunities for postgraduate studies were developed. In 1920 Congress granted nurses relative rank, which gave them authority in military hospitals but not the privileges and salaries of commissioned officers. The latter did not come until World War II. All of these developments, the excellent image of the nurse during war service, and the shortage of nurses, partially due to the great influenza epidemic, made nursing an attractive career.

Julia Stimson was the first woman in the army to become a major. Major Stimson played an important role in recruiting women, particularly college-educated women, into the Army Nurse Corps. She was recalled to active duty at the beginning of the United States' involvement in World War II because she was a successful recruiter. She believed in military nursing as a meaningful way to serve society as well as to live a fulfilling personal life.

Active all her professional life in national nursing organizations, after her retirement from the military, Major Stimson devoted more time to association work. She served on the board of directors of the National League of Nursing Education (NLNE), and served as president of the American Nurses' Association (ANA) during the difficult days of World War II.

Major Stimson wrote well, and her letters to her family are excellent examples. In addition to letters, she kept detailed daily diaries as early as her days at Vassar. She wrote many articles and a nursing text *Nurses' Handbook of Drugs and Solutions* (1910). A series of letters from her to the family illuminating her war experiences were published under the title *Finding Themselves* (1918).

She received the Distinguished Service Medal, awarded by General Pershing, and a citation from the Allied Expeditionary Forces. Mount Holyoke College conferred an honorary degree on Major Stimson in 1921, and she received the Florence Nightingale Medal of the American Red Cross in 1929.

Major Stimson was a formidable woman with the necessary skills required of a leader in wartime. She had vision, power, and sensitivity so critical to nursing in the military.

Isabel Maitland Stewart (1878–1963) and Nursing Education

Isabel Stewart was the fourth child in the family of nine born to Francis and Elizabeth Farquharson Stewart. Isabel Stewart's parents had emigrated from Scotland, and her father was self-employed as a farmer and sawmill owner until his business failed. The family then moved to western Canada. Isabel Stewart's early background is, in many ways, reminiscent of Isabel Hampton's early origins.

Miss Stewart attended public schools in Pilot Mound and Winnipeg, Manitoba, and Chatham, Ontario. She taught for a while in the local schools. A graduate of the Winnipeg General Hospital Training School in 1903, Isabel Stewart practiced as a private nurse, did district nursing briefly, and then joined the staff of the Winnipeg General Hospital as a nursing supervisor. She earned a B.S. (1911) and M.A. (1913) at Teachers' College, Columbia University. She was the first nurse in the department to receive a master's degree.

Isabel Stewart's greatest contribution to nursing was as an educator. She was known to many as "Miss Curriculum." After a trip to Great Britain she entered Teachers College in 1908 on a small scholarship from the Superintendents' Society. This was one year after M. Adelaide Nutting, her mentor, teacher, and friend had been appointed professor. Miss Stewart was one of nursing's most indefatigable leaders. It is difficult to pinpoint an advance in nursing education during Miss Stewart's tenure in which she did not play a part.

Before 1910, Teachers College offered graduate nurses educational opportunities primarily in nursing administration. With the Helen Hartley Jenkins endowment, the Department (later a division) of Nursing Education was created. Opportunities and programs in public health and the teaching of nursing became available. The program to train teachers was Isabel Stewart's idea, and Miss Nutting gave her full reign and responsibility. Miss Stewart designed and taught the first courses as well as planning, facilitating, and evaluating the practice teaching component. In short, she became a fine teacher and curriculum specialist.

While at Teachers College, she became an assistant, an instructor, assistant professor, and, in 1925, succeeded her beloved Miss Nutting as the Helen Hartley Foundation Professor of Nursing Education and director of the department. She directed the department for twenty-two important years, years of rapid development for professional nursing.

Her leadership style was distinctly her own. Isabel Stewart was a quiet worker. Frequently she would begin as the secretary of an organization or a committee and when colleagues and peers recognized her abilities she would become the chairperson. For example, she served as secretary for the National League for Nursing Education (NLNE) (name changed from Society of Superintendents in 1912) in 1915 and became a second vice-president in 1920. She rarely seemed to want to hold the primary office of an organization. Isabel Stewart worked long and hard behind the scenes.

Stella Goostray credits Isabel Stewart with the idea of an Association of Collegiate Schools of Nursing (ACSN). A series of conferences at Teachers College were the beginning of the organization. When the ACSN was founded, Miss Stewart sat on its board, was its first secretary, chaired committees, and, in an unusual move for her, served as president from 1937 to 1941 (9).

At Teachers College, Miss Stewart was in a good position to be aware of developments in all facets of education. She sought new ideas and constantly tried to utilize and adapt the better ideas to nursing education. She was profoundly influenced by her colleagues in higher education, like Dewey and Thorndike, who were also members of the Teachers College faculty at the time. As chairman of the International Council of Nurses committee on education, Isabel Stewart was able to disseminate those new educational ideas widely. She profoundly affected the development of nursing education around the world.

Miss Stewart's concern for a standard curriculum for nursing was expressed through her activities on the NLNE's education committee (later named the Curriculum Committee). Characteristically serving as secretary (1914–1919) and chairman (1920–1937), she did much of the work that resulted in the *Curriculum Guide* first published by the NLNE in 1917 and later revised in 1927 and 1937. These guides were developed by a volunteer committee with members from all parts of the country. It was an incredible accomplishment, particularly when you consider the problems of transportation and finances during those times. The first guide (1917) was invaluable in the United States World War I effort to provide for the nation's nursing needs. The timely *Curriculum Guide* was used to develop the federally supported Army Training School for Nurses. This was the first time federal money had been used to subsidize nursing education.

Miss Stewart was an active, productive organization member. She spearheaded an NLNE ways and means committee, which resulted in a plan for grading and classifying schools of nursing. Appointees to committees on which Miss Stewart served learned while they worked with Miss Stewart, and they worked very hard. Isabel Stewart saw committee work as a way of educating and socializing potential young leaders. Much of the early work of the NLNE was carried out in the form of projects conducted by her students at Teachers College.

Miss Stewart helped to alleviate the nursing shortages of both world wars. She wrote many of the recruiting materials during the first war and also chaired the curriculum committee of the Vassar Training Camp. This innovative program brought college graduates into a preclinical course and then sent them to various hospital training schools for an accelerated clinical program. Many subsequent leaders in American nursing were graduates of the Vassar Training Camp. It is interesting to note that "History of Nursing" was an important component of the preclinical course. Miss Stewart believed the professional needed a knowledge of the past.

During World War II, Isabel Stewart chaired important committees of the National Nursing Council for War Service (1940–1942). The Council itself had been an idea of Miss Stewart's. This quiet but forceful nursing leader was also instrumental in bringing the Cadet Nursing Corps into being and served on its advisory board. The Cadet Nursing Corps was another federally funded effort to develop adequate nursing resources for World War II.

Her enthusiasm for the history of the nursing profession was expressed in a variety of ways. The Mary Adelaide Nutting Historical Collection and the Nursing Education Department Archives at Teachers College are one example. Miss Stewart was largely responsible for this rich resource for scholars of nursing history. Isabel Stewart was a fine scholar and historiographer. She co-authored *A Short History of Nursing* (1920) with Lavinia Dock and later wrote *A History of Nursing From Ancient to Modern Times: A World View* (1962) with Ann L. Austin. Miss Stewart wrote *The Education of Nurses* (1943), which is an excellent history of nursing education, and many articles that frequently focused on education. She edited the *American Journal of Nursing's* Department of Nursing Education for years.

Isabel Stewart was well recognized for her accomplishments. She received the Adelaide Nutting Award from the NLN, an L.L.D. degree from Western Reserve University, a medal from the government of Finland, and honorary membership in the McGill University History of Nursing Society. She was a member of a variety of honorary societies. She would have been proud to know that the Isabel Stewart Professional Chair in Nursing Research had been established to honor her in the Department of Nursing Education at Teachers' College. She was a scholar, an educator, and an early advocate of nursing research. Most important, she was an "idea person" who influenced all of nursing education for the better.

Mary May Roberts (1877–1959) and Nursing Journalism

Mary Roberts was the oldest child in a family of four born to Henry and Elizabeth Scott Roberts. Her parents were of Scotish-English heritage and had settled in Cheboygan, Michigan. Henry Roberts was employed at the local sawmill, which was the most important industry in the community.

The young Mary enjoyed winter sports as she grew up in the small lumber town. She was educated in the public schools. An excellent student, she graduated as valedictorian of her four-member high school class.

Mary Roberts' desire for a college education was financially impossible. She applied to become a student in a well-known Detroit school of nursing and was rejected without being told the reason. It was devastating to her at the time. She later learned she was rejected because she was too young.

Mr. Roberts was bitterly opposed to nursing, seeing it as hard work with very little status. A summer guest persuaded Mr. and Mrs. Roberts that nursing was an acceptable career option. Mary Roberts attended the Jewish Hospital Training School for Nurses in Cincinnati and graduated in 1899. Her father, not completely won over, offered her a return ticket. She credits him and that incident with giving her the determination to see her nursing education through. Later, she received a B.S. and diploma in nursing school administration from Teachers College, Columbia University.

In her own mind, Miss Roberts divided her professional life into two almost equal periods. The first was devoted to nursing in a variety of positions: she had been a clinic nurse, an assistant superintendent, a superintendent, and, like most other nurses, had some "private duty" experience. She remembered people who thought she was an excellent nurse, although she sometimes felt inept herself. Her contribution to the nursing effort of World War I was to join the American Red Cross and recruit nurses for that organization. She later served as chief nurse and director of the Army School of Nursing Unit at Camp Sherman, Ohio.

Mary Roberts was forty-two when she went back to school. Her twenty-year nursing career had been varied, but certainly not exceptional. She emerged from her adult educational experience with new skills, new perspectives, and, most important, new opportunities. She took a variety of courses, many that helped prepare her directly or indirectly for the important work she would do in nursing literature. The second half of her professional life was devoted to "help oncoming generations of nurses secure a better education" (11). She participated in this effort through the power of the press.

In 1921 Mary Roberts was appointed co-editor, with Katherine DeWitt, of the *American Journal of Nursing*. Eventually, Miss DeWitt became the managing editor and business manager, and in 1923 Mary Roberts was named editor, a position she held until her retirement in 1949.

Mary Roberts was an intellectual. She had an enormous sense of responsibility and was respectful of the power she had as the editor of the *American Journal of Nursing*. She served as editor during the difficult years of the Depression, as well as the challenging years of World War II. From 1920 to 1950 the *Journal's* circulation grew from 20,000 to 100,000.

Mary Roberts took the time to assess her readers and their needs. Her primary interest was in nurses who nursed at the bedside. She went to them to find out what their problems were and what they were thinking. She wanted nurses to be better nurses, because according to her "the world needs good nurses."

Her editorial policy was to satisfy the multifaceted needs of a growing profession with a highly literate magazine (journal). Mary Roberts believed that as an editor she had a practical opportunity to promote goodwill in addition to promoting good health.

Although Miss Roberts is remembered for her contribution to literature, one who writes is essentially an educator. Miss Roberts had an encompassing concept of what nurses needed for their continuing education. Beyond clinical interests, Mary Roberts wanted nurses to be prepared to think and act responsibly regarding the critical issues facing the profession. She believed that a knowledge of their history was important in understanding the present and the future.

She was an editor par excellence who sensed unexpressed needs. According to those who knew her, Mary Roberts could help people see things more clearly—she listened to people. People would stop in her office to discuss a decision or problem and after talking it over would leave satisfied that they were making the best decision.

An innovative journalist, Mary Roberts appointed a field representative to travel constantly, assessing the reader, as well as promoting the *Journal*. She would also poll her readers by letter or telegram. She used the pages of the *Journal* to further professionalize nurses by supporting changes called for by the Goldmark Report (1923).

The prototype of a professional herself, Mary Roberts was a hardworking committee member in nursing affairs. In addition to her organizational work and her journal work, she was an administrator and had to have business acumen. After World War II the morale of the nursing profession and the financial condition of the American Journal of Nursing Company were both in serious trouble. Fortunately, the difficulties were resolved.

Although popularly remembered as a journalist and editor, Mary Roberts conceived other nursing innovations. Several years after joining the *Journal* staff, Mary Roberts began to talk about a nursing information bureau. This agency would provide financial and intellectual services from a central location. Nurses and others used the Nursing Information Bureau (NIB) as a source of information about nursing from 1934 to 1948. It was, in fact, a badly needed public relations arm of the profession. The NIB had the responsibility of answering inquiries about nursing; it produced interpretive pamphlets, sent out bulletins to key nurses around the country, worked with state information bureaus, and began publication of *Facts About Nursing*. Unfortunately, maintaining the Nurses Information Bureau was expensive and when the Journal Company had financial difficulties after World War II, the NIB had to be dissolved. It had served an excellent purpose—a central clearinghouse for information about nursing to keep the public informed. The lack of public understanding about nursing has been a problem at various times throughout the profession's history. Mary Roberts was always concerned about the nursing profession's image.

The *Journal* supported a variety of other projects while Miss Roberts was the editor. She of course continued to write her excellent timely editorials predicting what would become the issues and helping to shape the response of her nurses.

Mary Roberts' retirement in 1949 gave her time to make another contribution to improving the nurses' image. In 1954 she wrote *American Nursing: History and Interpretation*, a classic history of nursing that is extremely accurate and well written. She also was very involved as a charter member of the History of Nursing Source Committee.

A warm, wise, discreet, intense woman, Mary Roberts was very influential as a leader of nurses. She used the pages of the *Journal*, the Nurses Information Bureau, and her book *American Nursing: History and Interpretation* to educate nurses and the public about nursing. She recognized the enormous power of the written word and judiciously used her influence to further the goals of professional nursing.

Miss Roberts received numerous awards throughout her career. Among them were The International Red Cross Florence Nightingale Medal (1949) and the Mary Adelaide Nutting Award for Leadership in Nursing (1949). She was particularly pleased when the American Journal of Nursing Company established a fellowship in journalism and named it after her (1950).

Stella Goostray (1886–1969) and Nursing Administration

Stella Goostray was the first child born to Job Goostray and Jane Wyllie Goostray. A younger brother and three older children from Mr. Goostray's previous marriage completed the family. Family heritage was Scotish and English and they were Episcopalians. Mr. Goostray was actively involved in the iron industry and made nationally recognized contributions to the improvement of foundry practice; he also was interested in history. The young Stella Goostray was educated in the Boston public schools.

Stella Goostray's work as a young adult was as an assistant editor for an Episcopal Church magazine. World War I seemed imminent and Miss Goostray decided to enter nursing school. When the United States became involved, she wanted to be able to serve, hopefully in Europe. She entered the Boston Children's Hospital Training School in 1915 and immediately contracted typhoid fever. Re-entering in 1917 after her convalescence, she graduated in 1920. During these student years she became increasingly aware of the inadequacies of nursing administration from both service and educational points of view. Student nurses from the Children's Hospital affiliated with the Massachusetts General Hospital, the Manhattan Maternity Center, and the Henry Street Settlement. They took their formal academic work at Simmons College in Boston, which was considered a good program for that time.

Miss Goostray entered Teachers College, Columbia University when Adelaide Nutting was teaching the nursing administration component. Stella Goostray and Mary Roberts were both students in administration at the same time. Her first teaching position was as instructor and later that same year as educational director at the Philadelphia General Hospital School of Nursing. Her years at Philadelphia General were busy and productive; she earned a fine reputation as a teacher and administrator. During her spare time she took courses at the University of Pennsylvania. Teachers College awarded her a B.S. in 1926 after she had spent a semester commuting from Philadelphia on Saturday mornings to satisfy the degree requirements. Miss Goostray earned her M.Ed. from Boston University in 1933.

In 1926 Stella Goostray was invited to return to Children's Hospital School of Nursing in Boston as an instructor for a year and then to assume the directorship of both the school and nursing service. This dual directorship has been the general pattern for most of nursing's recorded history. Miss Goostray officially became the superintendent of nurses and principal of the School of Nursing in 1927. Her tenure lasted until 1946. She made many major changes in administration policies while at Children's Hospital.

Some of the problems Stella Goostray grappled with were common to other nurse administrators:

1. No voice or membership on standing hospital committees

2. Not being invited to participate in ad hoc meetings at which important decisions or policy-making occurred

3. Fragmented authority when private wards had nursing superintendents who were responsible directly to hospital administrators rather than the director of nursing

4. Hospital administration that was not supportive to the professionalization of nursing. Miss Goostray was able to garner support for Rockefeller Foundation-funded nurse students to study at Children's Hospital.

5. Unreasonable bureaucratic demands from others regarding nursing education: for example, requiring students to spend a certain number of hours in the operating room regardless of the kind of learning experience it was

6. Maintaining quality nursing care with insufficient nursing staff (in this case World War II pulled many nurses into active duty, depleting the numbers available for the civilian population)

Stella Goostray's style was direct. She was decisive and knew how to be an administrator. She did not accept a challenging position until she had been educated for it. Miss Goostray also developed young leaders to carry on while she was attending to other important nursing work.

Concrete examples of Miss Goostray's contributions as an administrator of both nursing service and nursing education included improving the quality of nursing service and nursing education by increasing the number of auxiliary workers (this was before World War II, which is usually credited with bringing auxiliary workers into hospitals in force); more staff nurses were hired; and Miss Goostray worked with faculty to have them more involved in decision-making affecting students and evaluating student progress.

Stella Goostray encouraged professionalism among her staff and eliminated the past practice of docking the wages of those who were absent from the clinical area while attending a professional meeting. She fought to keep control of students' educational experience when demands were made for more student clinical hours by physicians and hospital administrators.

Stella Goostray was extremely active at the national level in nursing affairs. She was one of those who made the significant studies in the 1930s and 1940s possible. Her own institution was not neglected. She had developed support personnel and saw to it that nursing care and nursing education at the Children's Hospital continued to be of high quality.

Although remembered particularly as a fine administrator, Stella Goostray made many other important contributions. At the national level, she was on the NLNE's Committee on Education. She chaired the Subcommittee on Nursing at the White House Conference on Child Health and Protection (1930). A member of the Board of Directors of the *American Journal of Nursing,* she served as secretary and became president (1931–1938). She served as secretary and later president of the National League for Nursing Education (1940–44) and was also a charter member of the NLNE's Committee on Early Nursing Source Materials (a committee to preserve history of nursing materials).

Miss Goostray's interest and role as an educator were expressed in the classroom as well as in her work with Dr. May Ayres Burgess and the Committee on the Grading of Nursing Schools. She took leave from Children's Hospital to work as a consultant on this important project. Her master's thesis, which partially fulfilled the degree requirement for Boston University, was titled "The Significance of Accreditation for Nursing Schools."

As chairman of the National Nursing Council for War Service from 1942 until 1946, Stella Goostray played an extremely significant role. She was said to have complete recall, an ability well utilized in the emergency situation as they planned for nursing service during a world war (7). The sound knowledge base of an administrator also facilitated her leadership role in this extremely important committee.

More locally, Stella Goostray was probably the major consultant and a member of the advisory committee as the Boston University School of Nursing began to evolve. Initially, several nurse educators guest lectured in a course called "Trends in Nursing"; 200 nurses enrolled. The Division of Nursing Education developed in the School of Nursing and became an autonomous School of Nursing in 1946–1947. Stella Goostray taught nursing administration in that initial "Trends in Nursing" course. She later helped develop New England's first associate degree program. Also at the local level, Stella Goostray served as a member and then chairman of the Massachusetts Board of Registration in Nursing.

Retiring at the age of sixty, Miss Goostray was also involved in other pursuits. A firm believer in layperson participation in NLN activities (the League started accepting layperson memberships while she was president), she also believed nurses belonged on boards of directors of various community services. Stella Goostray served on the Board of the United Community Services (1949–1951). She was also very active in the Massachusetts Nurses' Association during her retirement.

A woman who wrote well, Stella Goostray contributed to the literature of the profession. She wrote on a variety of subjects. In addition to numerous articles, she wrote *Drugs and Solutions* (1924), revised as Introduction to *Materia Medica* (1939) and as *Mathematics and Measurement in Nursing Practice* (1963); *Applied Chemistry for Nurses*, co-authored ninth edition (1924); *A Textbook in Chemistry* (1966); *Fifty Years of the School of Nursing, The Children's Hospital, Boston* (1941); and *Memories of Half a Century of Nursing* (1969).

Although Miss Goostray had several serious illnesses, she lived a long and full life. Honors came to her toward the end of her life: the Mary Adelaide Nutting Award for Leadership in Nursing (1955) from the NLN, the R. Louise McManus Medal for distinguished service to nursing (1967), and an honorary Doctor of Science from Boston University in 1967. Stella Goostray was invited by Dean Russell and Miss Stewart of Teachers College to succeed Isabel Stewart as director of the Division of Nursing Education at Teachers College, Columbia University, in 1945. She refused, partly because she felt she was too old. In her words: ". . . the invitation to succeed such great leaders as Mary Adelaide Nutting and Isabel Maitland Stewart was the greatest honor of my professional career" (8).

Lydia Williams Hall (1906–1969) and the Development of a Conceptual Model for Nursing Practice

Little is known about the early life of Lydia Williams Hall. The first child born to Anna Ketterman Williams and Louis U. Williams, she had a younger brother who died in childhood. Although born in New York City, Lydia Williams grew up in York, Pennsylvania and probably attended public school. Her father is believed to have been a physician (1).

Lydia Williams graduated from the York Hospital School of Nursing in York, Pennsylvania in the 1920s. She earned a B.S. in public health nursing, an M.A. in teaching natural sciences from Teachers College, Columbia University, and an additional fifty-nine credits in curriculum and teaching post masters at the same institution.

Her early professional experiences were at York Hospital as an instructor in the School of Nursing and as the supervisor of pediatrics nursing. Moving to New York City, she worked as a head nurse at St. Mark's Hospital before working as a staff nurse, assistant supervisor, and supervisor at the Visiting Nurse Service of New York.

Lydia Williams married Reginald Hall, a salesman for Hallmark cards, but she continued to be a very active professional. Her interest in chronic disease began very early in her career and she was particularly involved in the care of coronary invalids.

Although an administrator and an educator, Lydia Williams Hall is remembered as one of the earliest of the nurse theorists. She had an idea, and through the use of a variety of resources was able to implement her idea at the Loeb Center for Nursing and Rehabilitation at Montefiore Hospital, Bronx, New York, thereby implementing a conceptual system of nursing practice.

Lydia Williams Hall believed that nursing practice should be based in a theoretical framework. She further believed that it was essential for nursing service administration to be theoretically based. Nursing theory and theory of nursing administration were inseparable in Mrs. Hall's mind (13). Her focus was nursing practice, and she believed that nursing administration should facilitate practice.

Inherent in her framework are important concepts, which include borrowing from growth and development theory, Carl Roger's interviewing theory, principles of teaching/learning, and a careful analysis of motivation. Interestingly, Mrs. Hall was concerned about nurses' satisfaction and autonomy, in addition to her concern for the patients' care and cure. Mrs. Hall believed professional nurses belonged at the bedside, where they could plan with patients the type of care that was needed. At this time nurses prepared at the baccalaureate level were generally encouraged to take "leadership positions" away from the bedside.

The nurses who practiced at the Loeb Center were the primary caregivers at the patients' bedside. They planned with the patient how his or her care was to be implemented. Patients at the Loeb

Center were primarily people who were chronically ill or needed a long convalescence or rehabilitation. Physicians were used as resources, while the only other staff in addition to the nurses already mentioned were those whose clerical and other duties kept the unit operating.

Lydia Williams Hall was a consummate educator and excellent public speaker. She used every modality to garner attention and support for her theoretically based nursing practice model. One of the most lucid discussions of her nursing model was in a paper she presented at Catholic University in 1965, "Another View of Nursing Care and Quality."

A creative, vivacious woman, Lydia Hall was also warm and responsive. Her ideas arose out of her desire to have a conceptual framework for nursing practice. She could communicate well and influenced many to adopt her way of thinking. Her flamboyance and nonconformity drew attention to her ideas, and she was successful in drawing many to her way of thinking. She believed that professional practice had to be based in theory and attempted to articulate and apply theoretical constructs in developing a system of delivering nursing care.

Lydia Williams Hall is remembered for her innovative model of patient care. She received the Nursing Education Alumni Association's (Teachers College, Columbia University) Achievement in Nursing Practice Award in the mid-1960s. Her greatest satisfaction would probably be in the knowledge that the Loeb Center and many other hospitals continue to utilize her framework as the basis for nursing practice and primary nursing care.

Helen Lathrop Bunge (1906–1970) and the Development of Nursing Research

Helen Bunge was born in La Crosse, Wisconsin. She had three brothers and a sister. Both of her parents were college graduates, and her father and two of her brothers practiced law.

An excellent student, Helen Bunge was the salutatorian of her high school graduating class in La Crosse. She then attended the Connecticut College for Women for two years. Returning to Wisconsin, Helen Bunge earned a B.A. with a major in sociology (1928). She continued to study at the University of Wisconsin in Madison and in 1930 received the Graduate Nurse Certificate.

Her first nursing position was as head nurse at Wisconsin General Hospital (now University Hospitals). She soon became involved with the School of Nursing at the University of Wisconsin in Madison and taught nursing arts and ward management. Later, she became the assistant to the director of the School of Nursing. She later received an M.A. (1936) and an Ed.D. (1949) from Teachers College, Columbia University.

When Helen Bunge was in New York studying at Teachers College, she was one of the students Isabel Stewart recommended to board with Adelaide Nutting, who was retired from her position as director of the Nursing Program at Teachers College. This must have been an important experience for Miss Bunge. What conversations about nursing they must have had. Correspondence indicates a warm relationship and that they kept in touch until Miss Nutting died in 1948.

World War II interfered with the formal education of many. Helen Bunge contributed to the war effort by deferring the completion of her doctoral dissertation and becoming an assistant professor of nursing at the Frances Payne Bolton School of Nursing at Western Reserve in 1942. The pressure of providing nursing service for World War II had reached a crisis level in the civilian sector. As coordinator of the basic program, Miss Bunge was involved in the meetings that resulted in another nursing education program, a hospital school of nursing, which was federally funded. The old program had required graduation from an accredited college as an entrance requirement since 1934 (6). It must have seemed like a step backward to Helen Bunge and other faculty members.

War has often been the impetus for others to attempt to either control nursing or to lower standards to increase the number of nurses. Miss Bunge was dean when the abbreviated nursing course was voted out of existence at the end of the war.

Although Helen Bunge was an excellent educator and an educational administrator, she is particularly remembered as a leader in developing nursing research. A frank, honest, frequently critical woman, Miss Bunge was effective in fostering the development of nursing research.

During the late 1940s and early 1950s Miss Bunge's interest and focus changed from undergraduate nursing education to nursing research. She resigned as dean at Western Reserve in 1953 to become the executive officer of the Institute of Research and Service for Nursing Education. This institute, which was funded by the Rockefeller Foundation, was located at Teachers College, Columbia University and was the first research institute for nursing in the country.

During the six years Helen Bunge was director, thirteen projects were completed. Some related to nursing education and the others to nursing service. The Institute was designed for a threefold purpose: research, consultation, and teaching. Two formal research courses were developed for advanced students as part of the Institute. Miss Bunge was often critical of students' research. She was, in many ways, a perfectionist where nursing research was concerned (12).

As a pioneer in the field at nursing research, she met many difficulties. The development of nursing research in the 1950s was rudimentary and most studies were descriptive in nature.

Dr. Bunge believed that research was the business of every professional nurse (4). She believed that some nurses would prepare themselves to identify problems and design large research projects, while others would conduct small clinical studies; but all nurses had the responsibility to use research findings to improve their practice. She believed that the knowledge and use of research finding was essential to the continued professionalization of nurses and the improvement of patient care. Nurses had to, in Miss Bunge's opinion, move toward experimentation rather than continue to depend on tradition and authority if they wanted more independence and autonomy in their roles as health care providers.

Another expression of Helen Bunge's interest in nursing research was her committee work. The Association of Collegiate Schools of Nursing had established the Nursing Research Committee in 1947 and Helen Bunge served as its chairperson. A clear problem identified by the Committee was the lack of awareness about nursing research. Research was developing, but most nurses were ignorant of the findings. There was no vehicle through which researchers could learn what other researchers were studying. The Association of Collegiate Schools of Nursing assumed responsibility to report nursing studies and delegated the task to the Research Committee (3). The journal *Nursing Research* was an outgrowth of this effort.

Helen Bunge, the first voluntary editor, expressed the goal of the new journal (2):

"To inform members of the nursing profession and allied professions of the result of scientific studies in nursing, and to stimulate research in nursing."

There was a twenty-member editorial board, but a great deal of the work was done by Miss Bunge. The American Journal of Nursing Company helped in many ways and served as the publisher.

The new journal was partially financed by a contribution of $500.00 from nurses around the country; voluntary staffing by Miss Bunge (the editor), the executive committee, and the editorial board; and by the sale of an incredibly large number (8500) of subscriptions. It was a good beginning.

Lack of knowledge about publishing, scarcity of good research reports, and lack of time and money were early problems. The journal survived and continues to be an important part of nursing literature. Helen Bunge served as voluntary editor between 1952 and 1957, and it was one of her most significant contributions to nursing.

Helen Bunge also worked with other organizations. She was an advisory board member for the American Red Cross, the Veterans Administration, and Defense Committee on Women in the Service. She served on various committees for the ANA and the NLN and was president for the Wisconsin League for Nursing in the 1930s. At the international level, Dr. Bunge was vice-chairman of the Council and Executive Committee of the Florence Nightingale International Foundation. One other expression of her interest in nursing research was her work as a member of the United States Public Health Service's first Nursing Research Study Section.

Helen Bunge's major contribution to nursing literature was quite naturally in the area of research. As the first editor of *Nursing Research*, she laid the foundation for a prestigious journal. Her own publications include articles and editorials about research. She is more remembered as one who facilitiated and encouraged research in nursing then as a nurse researcher herself, but her influence had tremendous impact on the maturing profession. She recognized research and the preparation of nurse researchers as an imperative for American nursing, and was the most significant person in moving the cause forward during the post World War II era..

Helen Bunge was a member of Phi Beta Kappa, received the Achievement Award in Research and Scholarship from the Nursing Education Alumni Association, Teachers College, Columbia University, 1967; the Distinguished Service Award from the University of Wisconsin Alumni Association, 1969; and the Mary Adelaide Nutting Award from the National League for Nursing in 1969. Helen Bunge's hopes have been realized with the growing emphasis on nursing research that exists in contemporary nursing and the growing numbers of well prepared nurse researchers in the field.

Summary

The women discussed here represent a few selected innovators in nursing. They each had ideas that were timely and were able to mobilize resources to effect the called-for changes and activities.

There are similarities among these leaders as well as important differences. Many were well educated, were from comfortable economic backgrounds, and had known professional fulfillment in another field before they came into nursing. All were invested in their careers. Most of them had an interest in the history of nursing as well as its future. This interest is easily documented in the lives of Stewart, Roberts, and Goostray. It can also be documented in the lives of Isabel Hampton Robb and Helen Bunge. Miss Wald wrote at least two documents about the history of the Henry Street Settlement. Most of these leaders were somehow affiliated with Teachers College, Columbia University, and had strong networks within the profession.

The differences are embodied in the ideas, particular interests, and subsequent innovations that they created and developed. They are outstanding role models for nursing and represent a variety of leadership styles. Most important, they were comfortable with change and knew how to influence nursing through their ideas, vision, and energies.

References

1. Alfano G: Personal communication, February 27, 1982

2. Bunge HL: A cooperative venture (editorial). Nurs Res 11:1, 1952

3. Bunge HL: The first decade of nursing research. Nurs Res 11:4, 1962

4. Bunge HL: Research is every professional nurse's business. Nurs Res 7:816, 1958

5. Dock LL: History of American Red Cross Nursing. New York, Macmillan, 1922, pp. 565-567

6. Faddis M: A School of Nursing Comes of Age—A History of the Frances Payne Bolton School of Nursing Case Western Reserve University. Cleveland, Alumni Association of the Frances Payne Bolton School of Nursing, 1973, p. 203

7. Goostray M: Personal communication, February 22, 1982

8. Goostray S: Memoirs of Half a Century of Nursing. Boston, Nursing Archives of Murgar Memorial Library, 1969, pp. 45–50

9. Goostray S: Isabel Maitland Stewart. Am J Nurs 54:303, 1954

10. Hampton I: Copy of Letter to Mrs. Lawrence, July 13, 1880. Baltimore, Johns Hopkins Nursing Archives

11. Roberts M: Letter to Betty Cianelli, February 28, 1950. Boston, Nursing Archives of Murgar Memorial Library

12. Smith LC: Helen L. Bunge—Nurse, Teacher, Scholar. Madison, Wisconsin, School of Nursing, University of Wisconsin, 1979

13. Tubridy A: Lydia Hall's Contributions to Administrative Thought, unpublished undated paper. Boston, Nursing Archives of Murgar Memorial Library

14. Wald LD: Letter to Jacob Schiff, July 25, 1893. New York City Public Library, Manuscript Division

15. Ware E: Transcript of interview by C. Schofield, November 1939. Baltimore, Johns Hopkins Nursing Archives

6

Landmark Studies—Stimuli for Change in Nursing

Nursing has always been willing to seek and to take advice from others, to look at itself critically as well as to open itself to in-depth analysis, public scrutiny, and objective evaluation for the benefit of furthering its growth and development as a profession. Probably no other organized group has submitted so readily and so frequently to such internal and external investigation in order to improve the education and practice of its members.

During the first three-quarters of the twentieth century, the nation experienced major social, political, and economic changes that significantly affected the lifestyle, attitudes, beliefs, and values of the American people. In the face of new technology, advances in the sciences, rapid growth of hospitals, and increased needs and demands for health care, nursing emerged as an integral and essential element of the society.

Because nursing has evolved over the years as an important component of the American health care delivery system, the primary focus of interest and concern to both the profession and the public has been the adequate preparation of nurses for practice. Thus, in addition to self-examination by the profession, other groups, such as allied health organizations, government agencies at all levels, sociologists, and various private foundations, have been and continue to be involved in studying nurses and nursing. The extent of their involvement has ranged from identifying problems and issues in nursing to providing financial support for an investigation, conducting a specific study, and suggesting solutions and helping to put those recommendations into effect.

There have been many efforts to examine and plan for nursing and nursing education, but only a relative few have attracted national attention or had profound influence and widespread impact on the profession's development to warrant recognition as historical milestones.

Herein is a review of those landmark studies in the course of nursing history that have provided insight, direction, and guidance to the profession in a way that has significantly contributed to its progress. A brief description and analysis of the studies included in this chapter will reveal the purposes of each study, in what historical context they were undertaken, and how their results, conclusions, and recommendations influenced the outcome of nursing education and practice.

Nursing and Nursing Education in the United States (The Goldmark Report, 1923)

Generally considered by authorities to be the initial major landmark study of American nursing and nursing education, this report (26) was a result of a three-year investigation begun immediately following World War I. With the war terminating in 1918 and the devastating influenza epidemic subsiding toward the end of 1919, the country at peace was now able to assess its strengths, renew its hope, and turn its attention to unsolved problems. Likewise, as nursing emerged from the scourges of war and disease, its sights were focused on taking stock of the present situation and planning for the future. The indispensable role nursing played during the preceding years of peril served to highlight the importance of the work of nursing in the minds of both the profession and the public. A restored sense of faith in itself provided nursing with the necessary energy and enthusiasm to face the tasks that lay ahead.

Prior to the war, nursing had been openly criticized by various medical groups who either believed nurses were overtrained or that the standards of nursing education were too low and the profession was failing to supply the country with enough nurses who were highly trained (49). Many nursing leaders were convinced of the need for sounder, broader educational programs to prepare nurses for expanded roles, but their requests for nationwide reforms in many of the nursing schools went unheeded. As early as 1911, the profession appealed in vain to the Carnegie Foundation to conduct an impartial, scientific study of the system of nursing education similar to their epochal study of medical education (The Flexner Report) completed the year before (53). In 1912 Adelaide Nutting's report, *The Educational Status of Nursing*, revealed the appalling educational practices and the substandard living and working conditions of the students in nursing schools throughout the country. Although this study had little direct or immediate influence on changing nursing education, its findings did highlight the need for major reforms and set the precedent for further investigations into the education and practice of nurses (31).

In 1918 Miss Nutting was responsible for bringing public attention to the pressing need for more and better prepared nurses. This time she approached officials of the Rockefeller Foundation about the lack of enough well-qualified nurses for public health service. Her initial meeting with them resulted in the appointment, in January 1919, of the Committee for the Study of Nursing Education (30). Financed under the auspices of the Rockefeller Foundation, the Committee was initially charged with investigating "the proper training of public health nurses" (26).

It soon became evident, however, that the original intent of the study was too narrow and would have to be broadened to encompass the subject of nursing and nursing education as a whole if valid conclusions were to be reached. A year later, in February 1920, the Committee expanded its scope of inquiry to include a study of nursing education in general. The Committee's mission, therefore, was ". . .to survey the entire field occupied by the nurse and other workers of related type; to form a conception of the tasks to be performed and the qualifications necessary for their execution; and on the basis of such a study of function to establish sound minimum educational standards for each type of nursing service for which there appears to be a vital social need" (26).

The Committee of nineteen, chaired by Dr. C. E. A. Winslow, who was professor of public health at Yale University, was composed of a diverse group of independent-minded professional and lay representatives, including six well-known nurses (M. Adelaide Nutting, Lillian Wald, Annie Goodrich, S. Lillian Clayton, Mary Beard, and Helen Wood) and ten physicians (two of whom were hospital superintendents) (26). The Committee was most fortunate to have as its secretary and chief investigator Josephine Goldmark, a social worker and author who was nationally renowned for her previous field research. She was handed the task of carrying out the purpose of the Committee, namely, to conduct an impartial, scientific study of nursing education and practice in the United States. Thus began a period of critical, unbiased, in-depth analysis of the nursing profession.

Given the limitations of time and financial resources, it was impossible for the Committee to undertake an extensive survey of the conditions in all training schools and nursing services. Instead, under Miss Goldmark's expert direction, field investigators gathered and synthesized the opinions of leading nurse educators as well as surveyed twenty-three representative schools of nursing and forty-nine public health agencies in various sections of the country. The public health nursing organizations were reflective of general and specialty types of service rendered in publicly and privately controlled agencies in both rural and urban settings. Although the schools chosen also represented large and small, public and private, general and special hospitals, a disproportionate number of them were above average in their educational standards. Surprisingly, the enrollment in this relatively small sample of schools (from a total of over 1800 institutions) covered the records of more than 2400 students (26).

After approximately three years of intensive investigation to collect and analyze the facts gleaned from the schools, public health organizations, and selected individuals, a preliminary report of the Committee was released in 1922. This was followed by the publication in 1923 of an exhaustive, comprehensive but remarkably interesting 585-page volume entitled *Nursing and Nursing Education in the United States* (26), which detailed the results of the questionnaire survey of Josephine Goldmark.

This final Report, more commonly known as the Goldmark Report and sometimes also referred to as the Rockefeller Study, was divided into two main parts. Part A examined the functions of the nurse in public health, in private duty, and in institutions; Part B considered the training of the nurse in hospital schools, university programs, and postgraduate courses. In the process, the Report dealt with the financing of various types of nursing education, the licensing of nurses and subsidiary workers, the preparation of nurse teachers and administrators, and the fundamental weaknesses of the hospital schools. Illuminating statistics, clearly labeled tables, well-documented sources, and excellently organized material woven into the context of the book lay bare the hard facts collected by the highly qualified field investigators, leaving little doubt as to the validity of their findings. In addition, the study's credibility was further enhanced by the fact that Miss Goldmark was not herself a nurse and was, therefore, more likely to be objective in her assessment.

While the study identified numerous problems and issues in nursing, it also fairly revealed the profession's success and progress along certain lines. Overall, though, it clearly pointed out that the traditional apprenticeship system of diploma education, so prevalent in the hospital schools across the nation, was not an adequate method for preparing nurses for professional practice. The conclusions of the Committee, which were based on the survey results, remarkably echoed similar sentiments expressed by many nursing leaders of the day. The conclusions issued by the Committee, and the recommendations contained therein, are noteworthy not only for their comprehensiveness but because unfortunately a number of them deal with issues that are yet to be resolved and, therefore, remain familiar in their relevance to contemporary nursing (26):

Conclusion I

That, since constructive health work and health teaching in families is best done by persons: (a) capable of giving general health instruction, as distinguished from instruction in any one speciality and (b) capable of rendering bedside care at need; the agent responsible for such constructive health work and health teaching in families should have completed the nurses' training. There will, of course, be need for the employment, in addition to the public health nurse, of other types of experts such as nutrition workers, social workers, occupational therapists, and the like. That as soon as may be practicable all agencies, public or private, employing public health nurses should require as a prerequisite for employment the basic hospital training, followed by a post-graduate course including both class work and field work, in public health nursing.

Conclusion II

That the career open to young women of high capacity, in public health nursing or in hospital supervision and nursing education, is one of the most attractive fields now open, in its promise of professional success and of rewarding public service; and that every effort should be made to attract such women into this field.

Conclusion III

That for the care of persons suffering from serious or acute disease the safety of the patient, the responsibility of the medical and nursing professions, demands the maintenance of the standards of educational attainment now generally accepted by the best sentiment of both professions and embodied in the legislation of the more progressive states, and that any attempt to lower these standards would be fraught with real danger to the public.

Conclusion IV

That steps should be taken through state legislation for the definition and licensure of a subsidiary grade of nursing service, the subsidiary type of worker to serve under practicing physicians in the care of mild chronic illness and convalescence, and possibly to assist under the direction of the trained nurse in certain phases of hospital and visiting nursing.

Conclusion V

That, while training schools for nurses have made remarkable progress, and while the best schools of today in many respects reach a high level of educational attainment, the average hospital training school is not organized on such a basis as to conform to the standards accepted in other educational fields; that the instruction in such schools is frequently casual and uncorrelated; that the educational needs and the health and strength of students are frequently sacrificed to practical hospital exigencies; that such shortcomings are primarily due to the lack of independent endowments for nursing education; that existing educational facilities are on the whole, in the majority of schools, inadequate for the preparation of the high grade of nurses required for the care of serious illness, and for service in the fields of public health nursing and nursing education; and that one of the chief reasons for the lack of sufficient recruits, of a high type, to meet such needs lies precisely in the fact that the average hospital training school does not offer a sufficiently attractive avenue of entrance to this field.

Conclusion VI

That, with the necessary financial support and under a separate board or training school committee, organized primarily for educational purposes, it is possible, with completion of a high school course or its equivalent as a prerequisite, to reduce the fundamental period of hospital training to 28 months, and at the same time, by eliminating unessential, non-educational routine, and adopting the principles laid down in Miss Goldmark's Report, to organize the course along intensive and coordinated lines with such modifications as may be necessary for practical application; and that courses of this standard would be reasonably certain to attract students of high quality in increasing number.

Conclusion VII

Superintendents, supervisors, instructors, and public health nurses should in all cases receive special additional training beyond the basic nursing course.

Conclusion VIII

That the development and strengthening of university schools of nursing of a high grade for the training of leaders is of fundamental importance in the furtherance of nursing education.

Conclusion IX

That when the licensure of a subsidiary grade of nursing service is provided for, the establishment of training courses

*in preparation for such service is highly desireable; that such
courses should be conducted in special hospitals, in small
unaffiliated general hospitals, or in separate sections of hospitals where nurses are also trained; and that the course should
be of 8 or 9 months' duration; provided the standards of such
schools be approved by the same educational board which
governs nursing training schools.*

Conclusion X

*That the development of nursing service adequate for the
care of the sick and for the conduct of the modern public
health campaign demands as an absolute prerequisite the securing of funds for the endowment of nursing education of all
types; and that it is of primary importance, in this connection,
to provide reasonably generous endowment for university
schools of nursing.*

The conclusions indicate that almost every conceivable aspect
and development of the nursing profession was carefully considered
and analyzed. Although the Report as a whole constructively criticized all phases of nursing, including public health service, which
was the original focus of study, it provided particular challenges to
the entire system of nursing education. Those recommendations
relating to the preparation of nurses strongly urged a reorganization
of the schools and major improvements in the training of students.
Most attention was given to the findings that emphasized the many
problems and weaknesses inherent in the apprenticeship system of
nursing education within the hospital schools.

Dr. Richard Olding Beard, President of the University of Minnesota and a friend and staunch supporter of nurses, carefully explored
the Committee's conclusions and offered a thorough review and critique of the Report. His interpretations were presented in a three-
part series published in consecutive issues of the *American Journal
of Nursing* (7). He applauded the Committee for its clear-cut, in-
sightful, and comprehensive investigation. He hailed the Report for
giving due recognition to the important role universities should play
in educating nurses, for suggesting higher educational standards and
admission requirements in the schools of nursing, and for highlight-
ing the need to secure adequate public financing to support nursing
education on an independent basis, free and separate from hospital
control. However, Dr. Beard soundly disagreed with the Committee's recommendation to use "subnurses" in the delivery of patient
care. He found it ironic, indeed, for the Committee to advocate the
concept of expanded roles for graduate nurses while, at the same
time, proposing the preparation of a less educated subsidiary worker
as a remedy for the maldistribution and shortage problem in nursing.

Nevertheless, Dr. Beard, along with leaders in nursing, medicine, and hospital administration, recognized this study as being the most significant, notable, and valuable contribution in the history of nursing up to that point in time. By the time this publication was released in 1923, nursing education in this country was celebrating its fiftieth anniversary. It was particularly fitting that this study not only marked a significant event in the half century of recorded history of American nursing, but it followed so closely on the heels of a comparable study, known as the Flexner Report, completed in 1910 by the Carnegie Foundation, which explored medical education in the United States.

Even though the Goldmark Report offered a sound basis for dealing with exceedingly complex problems, both manifest and latent, which faced the profession then and in the future, it unfortunately did not stimulate broad public interest or widespread professional action for reform. Because the Committee's findings were not extensively published in the news media, nor were the specific names of those schools in serious violation of acceptable educational norms disclosed, the public remained essentially unaware of the need for change. Just as nurses then were astonished by the realization that the Committee's conclusions revealed little that was new to them, nurses in these contemporary times are impressed more by the similarities than by the differences of today's issues compared with those of fifty years ago (51).

Despite its failure to create the same impact on nursing that the Flexner Report had on medicine a decade earlier, the investigation was an epoch-making event. One very important outcome and direct result of the study was the successful establishment of the Yale University School of Nursing—a great step forward in the collegiate nursing education movement. Credit must be given to the Rockefeller Foundation for initiating, directing, and supporting this highly informative, unbiased survey of the nursing profession.

Nurses, Patients, and Pocketbooks (1928)

This study was one of a series of three reports released by the Committee on the Grading of Nursing Schools, which was officially established in November 1925 for the purpose of grading and classifying schools of nursing.

Although the work of this committee followed closely in the shadows of the Goldmark Report, its origins can be traced as far back as 1911, when the idea of grading nursing schools was first given serious consideration by nursing leaders at the annual meeting of the National League of Nursing Education (NLNE). Plans were thwarted then by the refusal of the Carnegie Foundation to underwrite the financing of such an extensive project, which the nursing profession itself could not single handedly support.

The decision to create a grading mechanism to effect progressive improvement in nursing education nationwide received renewed attention in the mid-1920s with the efforts of other professional groups to standardize high schools, colleges, schools of law and dentistry, hospitals, and other types of institutions (50). In addition to the thrust of this general education reform movement, further impetus for the nursing profession to take deliberate action on the issue of grading was in immediate response to the American Medical Association's attempt to conduct its own study of the education and employment of nurses in order to improve the nursing service available to physicians (30).

Nursing's effort to take the lead in securing cooperation, endorsement, and necessary funding for a grading study from influential organizations and individuals resulted in the formation of the Committee on the Grading of Nursing Schools. Since the whole question of nursing education was seen as affecting not only nurses but hospitals, physicians, other allied professions, as well as the public, the representative associations of these self-interest groups agreed to join forces for the common goal of eventually improving the care of the sick. The Committee of twenty-one included two representatives each from the American Nurses' Association, the National League of Nursing Education, and the National Organization for Public Health Nursing; one representative and one alternate each from the American Medical Association, the American College of Surgeons, the American Hospital Association, and the American Public Health Association; four representatives from the field of university education; and three additional members at large (9). In April 1926, the Committee unanimously appointed May Ayres Burgess, Ph.D., a well-qualified statistician, as director of the program. She was highly regarded by nurses and others not only because she had past experience in the field of education but also because she had already demonstrated interest in nursing through her work on the study of private duty nursing (27).

In the fall of 1926, the Committee on Grading adopted a five-year program of study estimated to necessitate a budget in excess of $200,000. Accepting major responsibility for the cost of the study, nurses individually and collectively contributed over one-half the amount required to finance the program; the rest was donated by private foundations, member organizations, and interested laymen. One person in particular, Mrs. Frances Payne Bolton, a lay member of the Committee and a long-time friend and supporter of nurses, demonstrated her continued commitment to nursing by contributing funds totaling $93,000.

In formulating a plan of action to accomplish the task of grading, the Committee realized the magnitude and complexity of its assignment. It soon became apparent that extensive classification of schools could not begin until it had in hand preliminary background information about the profession. The original plan of grading, the term from which the Committee derived its official name, meant that certain minimum standards agreed to by the Committee had to be met by the schools if they were to be considered qualified to prepare graduates for the nursing profession. It was impossible to decide minimum standards until it was known what abilities graduate nurses should possess, and those abilities could not be determined until it was understood what the graduates would be called on to do in practice. Grading had to be based on and accompanied by a careful inquiry into the underlying facets of nursing education and employment (13). Facts were needed to clear up misconceptions about real or perceived problems in nursing and to unite the public and various interest groups on a common basis of logical action to ensure quality nursing service.

Thus, in November 1926, the Committee decided to divide its five-year program (which ultimately ran for eight years) into three separate projects: (1) a study of supply and demand for nursing service, which involved the problem of shortages of graduate nurses; (2) a job analysis of what nurses did and how they should be prepared for nursing service; and (3) the actual grading of nursing schools. The plan to concentrate on one project at a time, carry it to completion, and then publish the final results of each project in separate monograph reports was seen as the most economical, most effective, and most efficient way to handle such an ambitious program (13).

Two years after undertaking its first objective, the Committee published on schedule, in 1928, the results of its supply and demand study, with the 600-page report "Nurses, Patients, and Pocketbooks" (45). This book was appropriately and provocatively titled since it pointed out the profound economic problems in nursing related to supply and demand. Graphically illustrated facts and instructive data were presented in Part I of the book while Part II discussed the implications of the findings and possible remedies to cure the economic ills of the profession.

In the process of collecting statistics from nursing schools representative of all conditions and every section of the country, the Committee substantiated what many nurses suspected was true for some time. Specific findings indicated that, along with the phenomenal rate of growth of nursing schools since the turn of the century, educational requirements for entrance were minimal—only about fifteen percent required a high school diploma and fifty-four percent admitted students with one year of high school or less; student attrition rates were exceedingly high; most training schools were very small and were connected to hospitals, which were likewise too small or too specialized for adequate clinical experience; the average student work day was signficantly longer and the work week was much greater than for most other occupations (average fifty-five hours per week); a few schools employed more than one teacher for classroom instruction. Without doubt, most of the nursing schools as well as their affiliated hospitals were grossly ineffective as teaching institutions. It was evident that nursing schools existed merely to provide service to the hospitals, not for the primary purpose of educating students (9).

Generally, the study clearly demonstrated a serious overproduction of graduate nurses, which had led to chronic unemployment in the profession. Not only was there an oversupply of poorly prepared nurses, but they were geographically maldistributed, with most residing in large urban areas. The salaries and working conditions were poor, causing widespread dissatisfaction in the nursing ranks. And even though patients and physicians generally seemed pleased with the nursing services rendered, there was strong evidence of incompetence by a number of nurses. The constant complaint of shortages in nursing, thus, was not due to an inadequate quantity of nurses but to the lack of enough qualified nurses to meet public demands and expectations.

The study had four recommendations: (1) to reduce and improve the supply of nurses, (2) to replace students with graduate nurses, (3) to help hospitals meet costs of graduate services, and (4) to get public support for nursing education. It stressed the need for placing nursing schools on a sound educational and financial basis (45). Although these recommendations were not new to nursing, they carried the weight of fact and were not based on conjecture or opinion.

The Committee fully endorsed the Report and went on record as strictly adhering to two fundamental principles: that no hospital should be expected to finance the cost of nursing education, which was considered as much a public responsibility as the education of other professionals; and that the needs of the hospital for cheap labor did not justify its conducting a school of nursing (9).

The results of this report carried much weight with nursing, medicine, and the public not only because the work of the Committee was an example of true cooperative relations between representative interest groups, but also because the statistics were based on a large number of nursing schools nationwide, which gave authority to the findings. In addition, unlike the impact of the Goldmark Report, which dealt with but twenty-three cases, this study was more widely read, stimulated much more constructive thinking, and created active interest in the broader economic questions of the day.

An Activity Analysis of Nursing (1934)

This second monograph report, sponsored by the Committee on the Grading of Nursing Schools, was the result of a study done at the Committee's request by Ethel Johns, a nurse editor and consultant, and Blanche Pfefferkorn, also a nurse and the director of Studies at the National League of Nursing Education (29).

The question of job analysis, which was raised during the preliminary conferences on the grading of nursing schools, was given considerable attention by the Committee and became one of its three proposed projects. The Committee felt that an analysis of nursing functions was essential before a grading scheme could be formulated to judge the schools. The aim of nursing education and a thorough knowledge of the work of nurses had to be identified prior to satisfactorily determining what the training school should be like in order to adequately prepare graduates for nursing service (13).

The two nurse researchers conducted the investigation to document the exact functions of nurses in different occupational categories such as hospital, public health, and private duty nursing. They sought, through careful analysis, to discover not only what nurses actually did but also the kind of knowledge, skills, and training required for various types of nursing service. A combination of statistical and case study methods was used to deal with the problem of what good nursing is and what kind of education must be given to secure it (29).

The purpose of gathering such facts was to use them to standardize and improve the curricula in nursing schools across the country. It was realized that the content of nursing education must be based on actual duties and responsibilities that the average nurse was expected to assume in the practice of her profession. The objective was to more closely correlate nursing theory with practice or, in other words, to make nursing education relate more specifically to nursing service (31). Unfortunately, nursing tasks, rather than the processes used by nurses to acomplish the tasks, became a primary focus.

Nursing Schools Today and Tomorrow (1934)

This third and final report (21), conducted under the auspices of the Committee on the Grading of Nursing Schools, was a culmination of eight years of comprehensive study. It was the summary of an investigation for which the Committee was originally formed and named, and for which the results were most anxiously anticipated by nurses and the public.

To carry out the grading plan, the Committee first had to determine minimum standards for classifying schools based on factual knowledge about the underlying problems in nursing education and service and on an accurate understanding of the qualities the graduates needed to perform the activities required (as well as expected) of them. Thus, the actual grading of schools rested on the foundation of the two preceding projects on supply and demand and on the activity analysis of nurses sponsored by the Committee (21).

The standards of grading that were finally adopted for comparison purposes conformed not to some ideal standard but to conditions in the nursing schools as they actually existed around the nation. It was not enough to find out what a few leading schools were like, as did the Goldmark Report; the objective of the Committee was to obtain a clear picture of the whole in order to proceed with constructive thinking and to recommend appropriate action (10).

In all, three separate gradings by the Committee were done on the schools of nursing nationwide. Every school was invited to be included in the grading study, but participation was strictly voluntary. No school was graded except at its own request. What was believed desired was not so much a definite marking or rigorous grading of the schools but a scheme to stimulate their interest and understanding of nursing so that they would be moved to actively improve their system of education (13).

For this reason, the Committee conducted a series of gradings over several years so it was possible for the schools to upgrade themselves with time. Each study compared not only how individual schools measured up against one another per se, but also how the forty-eight states ranked in relation to one another. However, the Committee ultimately decided not to issue a list of the names of approved and unapproved schools since this was seen as unjust as well as unfeasible. Such a form of classification would, it was feared, retard the development of nursing education (14). Once certain essentials of a good school of nursing were agreed on, the schools were solicited for information concerning their educational programs and were then ranked by these items accordingly. No inspectors were used but each school filled out its own report on questionnaire forms. Based on statistical data, the process of grading was objective.

The final grade each school received was a composite number of the school's comparative standing on each item studied, indicating how near it stood to the top of the list. There was no percentage grade or arbitrary classification into, for example, A, B, or C categories (12).

The grading, a combination of statistical and case study methods, was carried through each year with increasing emphasis. At the end of the project, the entire experiment was described in a published monograph (21). No effort was made to purposefully discredit any school; in fact, every effort was made to help schools in every way possible to upgrade their programs. The objective was to reward the efforts of the good schools by giving them recognized standing and to support the poor schools by helping them see their defects and remedy them. The purpose was not to legislate out of existence those schools that did not meet generally acceptable standards but to assist them to achieve a higher status. In other words, the Committee's efforts were not judicial or punitive but educational—aiding schools to raise their standards for the improvement of nursing care to the public (23).

The Grading Committee had no enforcing power whatsoever; its singular policy as an appointed body was to study, gather facts, conclude, and offer recommendations. Its value was in supplying the profession with ammunition and allies, but any reforms in nursing education had to come from the actions of nurses themselves (11).

The first nationwide grading was completed in 1929, followed by the second survey in 1933, and the final report in 1934. Well over half of the schools in the country participated in the self-surveys (21). These follow-up surveys made it possible for schools to see the advancements they had made since the previous grading. Between the first and second surveys, the schools improved their standings in three-fourths of the almost 120 items studied by the Grading Committee (6). The third survey showed even further educational advancements. This was a truly remarkable record, considering the economic pressures during this time in American history.

The findings gathered over these successive years of grading offered unparalleled opportunity for diagnosing the serious weaknesses and deficiencies in nursing education. The 268-page report reiterated the distressful problem of oversupply and unemployment. It reinforced that the exploitation of student nurses existed under the apprenticeship system of education and painted a picture of what the average hospital school was like. It also brought to light the inadequate conditions in the schools and the essentials basic for professional education. While recommending specific improvements, the report also served as a source of information to prospective students, the public, and vocational advisors.

The Committee concluded that the most fundamental problem in nursing education was the lack of adequate financial support, which, if sufficiently provided by the public, would lift nursing education to the level of other respected professions (30). This final volume furnished the data and publicized the facts necessary to strengthen movements for reform and to mold public opinion in favor of nursing. Unmistakably, it demonstrated the benefits of honest and repeated evaluations to secure improvements in the schools.

A Curriculum Guide for Schools of Nursing (1917, 1927, and 1937)

Although this report (18) was the last of three separate curriculum studies carried out over a period of approximately twenty years under the leadership of the National League for Nursing Education (NLNE), it was the most extensive, most innovative, and most challenging of all the three publications.

Nursing leaders long recognized that standards of professional education correlated closely with standards of professional practice. The curricula of nursing schools were regarded as instruments for improving the quality of nursing practice as well as promoting growth of individual practitioners. Therefore, a primary target of focus to make nursing more flexible and more responsible to changing conditions and needs of a growing nation, was the educational structure of the school. However, since the curriculum was only a part of the educational program and total organization of a school, it was directly affected by the overall standards of any particular school. If a school lacked suitable personnel, resources, or equipment, then it was difficult, if not impossible, to put a predetermined curriculum into operation without considering its standards in relation to those of the entire school (62).

This was a dilemma faced by the Education Committee of the League in 1914, when it first undertook the task of devising the *Standard Curriculum for Schools of Nursing* (20), and general educational standards for all schools of nursing remained a problem during two successive efforts to revise this basic publication. The profession's constituency unanimously agreed that some kind of requirements had to be established, but it was not easy to decide what these standards should be, who should be responsible for their adoption, and how they should be enforced. There were those who believed that professional progress could best be achieved by having all schools conform to an approved pattern, while others favored flexibility for experimentation, creativity, and differentiation in programs and methods of teaching. These issues and problems in relation to curriculum standards reflected fundamental differences in philosophies and aims of nursing education (62).

The period during which the League's energies were directed toward curriculum revision, from 1914 to 1937, was characterized by a quest for reform, standard-setting, and stock-taking, not by the nursing profession alone but by the country as a whole. In 1914, the Education Committee of the NLNE under the direction of two notable nursing leaders, M. Adelaide Nutting, serving as chairman, and Isabel Stewart as secretary, began designing a curriculum plan for the schools of nursing. What they faced was a confusing, ineffective system of nursing education that was the disastrous result of the laissez-faire policy applied to the training of nurses since the turn of the century. The schools featured a variety of chaotic, carelessly selected, loosely connected subjects that, without any dominating purpose, handicapped the work of the best nursing instructors.

Constructing a basic curriculum that could be reasonably adapted to the conditions of each particular institution called for careful and thoughtful study. To provide for a systematic arrangement of recommended courses that would be an effective instrument for the training of nurses and yet not discourage innovation, progress, and individual initiative was a challenge of the first order. Certain educational standards and a degree of uniformity of subjects were especially important in light of the fact that similar demands were made on nurses regardless of where they practiced or from which schools they graduated (63).

The Education Committee, known as the backbone of the League because of its forward thinking, concrete objectives, and progressive ideals, took the initiative to formulate new policies. After more than two years of work, it released in 1917 the original *Standard Curriculum for Schools of Nursing* (20). This classic document marked a definite stage in the evolution of the profession. It was often referred to as a significant milestone in the development of nursing education. It was published at an opportune time, when the popular appeal for short courses (sometimes as few as six weeks in length) for nurses as a war measure was daily becoming more insistent. The publication was a crystallization of the beliefs of many who contributed so much to its development. It was an outstanding example of an attempt to elevate educational standards and, thus, raise the status of nursing schools throughout the country (28).

The stated purposes of the *Standard Curriculum* were (20):

> *. . . to arrive at some general agreement as to a desirable and workable standard whose main feature could be accepted by training schools of good standing throughout the country . . . to gradually overcome the wide diversity of standards at present existing in schools of nursing, and supply a basis for appraising the value of widely different systems of training.*

The publication was prepared with two objectives in mind: to serve as a guide for the nursing schools struggling to establish good standards of education and to represent to the public an idea of what the profession considered as acceptable training for nursing (20). It was not a model or even an example of minimum standards but a reasonable working guide to help schools achieve their potential in line with their own particular needs and conditions. The Committee never intended the *Standard Curriculum* to function as a compulsory requirement, although it was often humorously referred to as the nursing school Bible and was regarded by some as the "law and gospel" of the League (59).

Despite the disruption caused by World War I and the postwar period, a concerted effort was made by a number of schools to adopt the standards included in the new guide. State boards of nursing also attempted to conform to the League's general recommendations. It was recognized that if nursing schools were to attract intelligent recruits, they would have to more closely approach the types of educational standards found in colleges and universities of the day.

The guide proved most helpful to the directors and administrators responsible for managing the schools of nursing. It was reprinted five times and approximately 5000 copies were sold. Perhaps the most significant aspect of this new curriculum guide was that it stressed health and not disease. However, the ideals advocated in the *Standard Curriculum* were too exacting for the majority of schools to attain. Many were unable to conform to the curriculum in its entirety. Progress in achieving significant change was slow, especially in relation to such matters as decreasing the number of hours on duty in the hospital and increasing the time devoted to classroom instruction (59).

The first revision of this report, *A Curriculum For Schools of Nursing* (19), was published in 1927, exactly one decade after the printing of the original *Standard Curriculum*. Not coincidentally, work on the second curriculum began after the Rockefeller Committee's study on nursing and nursing education was completed in 1923. The movement for better curricula in schools of nursing was strengthened considerably by the findings of the Goldmark Report.

It prompted the Education Committee of the NLNE to push forward with a revision of the old curriculum guide. Valuable as the original had proved to be, there was evidence that a number of changes needed to be made to advance standards in line with newer developments and the improvements that had been achieved in the more progressive nursing schools (19). The fact that the first curriculum guide had been used so extensively made it all the more imperative to make this one accurate, up-to-date, and representative of the best ideas in the development of nursing education. The need for a richer curriculum paralleled the demands for a better prepared nurse to serve an increasingly more sophisticated world (41).

Prior to its appearance in published form, outlines of the new curriculum were issued through the *American Journal of Nursing* in an attempt to reach a wider audience and to get helpful criticisms and suggestions from the readers on the material that was to go into the book. The revised curriculum guide, it was anticipated, would further stimulate the schools to assume responsibility for upgrading their programs of classroom and clinical instruction if they were involved in the initial planning.

The word "standard" was purposefully dropped from the title in hopes of clarifying that the Committee did not advocate uniformity in all schools of nursing but instead wished to encourage schools to adopt the suggested outlines after considering their own particular needs and stages of advancement. The purpose of the curriculum was to stimulate thinking rather than to dictate certain requirements. It was intended that all schools would attempt to work toward achieving the recommendations but would not be seen as a failure if they did not fully meet the entire outline (40).

In actuality there was no drastic departure from the principles embodied in the original plan, but the basic subjects were rearranged for different emphasis to reflect the changing importance of each area of study. More stress was put on psychosocial aspects of care, on mental hygiene, and on public health nursing. Health protection, prevention, and promotion were more specifically addressed, and greater attention was given to the fundamental sciences as a foundation to the whole curriculum structure. It was realized, however, that the curriculum itself was relatively useless unless well-prepared teachers could be found in sufficient numbers to interpret and apply it (61).

This second curriculum volume appeared in print just as the Committee on Grading of Nursing Schools was initiating its fact-finding studies. The NLNE curriculum guide was the measure used by the Committee in its evaluation of nursing education programs offered in the schools under study. Significantly, the series of grading results showed that many of the schools that ranked in the upper quartile had achieved or gone beyond the recommendations put forth in the 1927 report. Thus, the standards of the League served as a pacesetter for the better schools (59).

In 1937, once again exactly a decade later, a second revision, *A Curriculum Guide for Schools of Nursing* (18), replaced the 1927 version. Work on it was started in 1934, just as the Committee on Grading had prepared the final results of its studies and while the country was in the midst of massive unemployment and still suffering in many other ways from the devastating effects of the Depression. During the national reconstruction period of the mid-1930s, nursing also was unmistakably in need of reform. The revelation of the Grading Committee plus the impact of economic conditions in the country as well as the new social legislation of the 1930s all pointed to the need for the nursing profession to rethink its aims and to advance its educational standards. Greater demands by the public for different types and increased amounts of nursing services required consideration of new objectives, new patterns of organization, and new means of support for nursing education.

Once again the NLNE became the pacesetter for nursing education and has as its chief professional responsibility determining what educational standards and programs were necessary for the proper selection and preparation of its prospective nurses. For many months the League's major project became the reconstruction of the curriculum, a fundamental step toward overall progress in nursing. Although not an ideal time financially to begin another curriculum revision, the League decided such a project would be a prime opportunity to reorient the profession about the need for rearranging nursing education programs. While the main purpose was to produce a curriculum guide that would be useful to nursing schools in the critical years ahead, an underlying objective was to get as many nurses as possible involved in cooperative planning for curriculum revision so that, in actuality, this project became a true democratic enterprise (60).

The Education Committee of the League had always taken the responsibility for curriculum projects, but it soon became evident that other League committees also had potentially important roles to play. Therefore, a Central Curriculum Committee was established to allow for active participation by representatives from many League committees as well as from other cooperating groups in nursing. Individual states were invited to form their own curriculum study groups to serve in an advisory capacity to the Central Committee as well as to review and critique its work. In addition, consultant groups composed of representatives from hospitals, medicine, public health, social welfare, education, and the lay public provided the Committee with expert advise on technical, social, and scientific matters. Input was sought and welcomed from literally thousands of nurses and interested groups throughout the country. The best ideas of all concerned contributed to the final curriculum revision (59).

The *Curriculum Guide* was far more than a patching up of the League's 1927 curriculum; the book represented a conservative approach to the progressive suggestions contained therein (73). As Isabel Stewart, chairman of the Curriculum Committee, explained:

> . . . . there is no change in its fundamental purpose. The Curriculum has always been intended as a guide to nursing schools in building their own curricula, not as a standard to be enforced, nor as a pattern to be slavishly copied. The purpose has been to encourage schools to look and plan ahead in their educational programs, to experiment with new materials and methods rather than to follow too closely the traditional curriculum, not to be satisfied with mediocrity but to aim at the best they can achieve, working toward that aim in a sane and reasonable fashion [18].

The *Curriculum Guide* was offered as an educational tool and guide, not as a mandate or recipe, to those nursing faculty, hospital administrators, and boards of trustees willing to use it in accordance with the professional goals and actual conditions of their own schools. The curriculum called for a two-and-one-half to three-year course of study to include regularly scheduled theoretical and practical instruction, not to exceed forty-four to forty-eight hours per week, with sufficient time for rest, study, and extracurricular activities and four weeks vacation per year. The first four months of the freshman year did not include any clinical practice, and the total nursing program contained more class time and less clinical work in comparison to earlier curriculum versions. More emphasis centered on integrating basic sciences into the art of nursing, on stressing the sociological and psychological aspects of care, and on incorporating the concept of health and wellness into all nursing courses rather than focusing primarily on the traditional concepts of sickness and disease.

Two underlying assumptions were made in relation to the proposed standards for nursing schools as a whole. The first was that the term "nursing school" as used specifically referred to an institution the primary function of which was to educate nurses; this definition represented a change from the earlier notion that the school existed first and foremost to provide nursing service to the hospital. The second assumption was that the curriculum should reflect an expanded scope of nursing responsibility by supplying a broad and sound foundation for professional practice in all settings and a basis for continued study and specialization. The nurse should be prepared to provide hospital as well as community services (30).

The impact of the League's three curriculum projects without doubt stimulated nursing schools to substantially improve their educational standards. They were invaluable sources of references, and even though the 1937 *Curriculum Guide* never underwent another revision, the schools continued to implement its recommendations for many years thereafter.

Nursing for the Future (1948)

This study (8), also referred to as the Brown Report or the School Study, fits into the historical sequence of analysis of nursing education in the country (69). It was considered to be the third major project about the status of nursing in America, the first being the Goldmark Report in 1923, which was stimulated by events surrounding World War I, followed by the Grading Study in the late 1920s and early 1930s.

This study, also in tune with the spirit of the times, was prompted by conditions inside and outside the profession that alarmingly had caused serious shortages of nurses across the nation. The social legislation of the 1930s and World War II gave added impetus to the public demands for health care services, while the nursing schools were finding it increasingly difficult to attract enough qualified recruits to meet the needs of society. Unable to fulfill either the quantitative or the qualitative demands for nursing service, the profession once again concluded that there was something not only drastically but chronically wrong with its system of nursing education (8).

In retrospect, some definite but inadequate gains were attributed to the two earlier studies. In general, the results fell far short of the expectations for improvements in nursing education and practice based on the extent and cost of the projects. Regretting that the findings of the earlier studies were not used more effectively, those interested in and concerned with nursing were inspired to make another determined and courageous effort to do a better job the third time around (46). Once more the decision was made to commission a study with the hope of understanding the changing needs of the nursing profession in order that efforts might be intelligently redirected for decisive action on the part of all those responsible for the adequate provision of nursing services.

In April of 1947, the Carnegie Corporation announced a grant of $28,000 to the National Nursing Council for an intensive study of nursing practice and the preparation required for it. Broadly stated, the purpose of this investigation was to answer the question: who should organize, administer, control, and financially support basic professional schools of nursing to adequately satisfy community needs (8).

Esther Lucile Brown, Ph.D., a social anthropologist of distinction and the director of the Department of Studies in the Professions at the Russell Sage Foundation, was appointed to carry out the study. She was amply suited for the task, as she had already conducted surveys on the role of education in other professions, which included social work, engineering, medicine, and law with respect to how this education could be adapted to meet the needs of society. In addition, she had authored *Nursing As A Profession*, first published in 1936 and revised in 1940. *Nursing For the Future* was to be the seventh in a series on the professions and, like the others, was oriented toward long-range social goals. Preliminarily, and most importantly, it was agreed that Dr. Brown would view nursing service and nursing education in terms of what was best for society, not what was best for the profession of nursing (8).

The study was launched under the aegis of the National Nursing Council, a cooperative group of representatives from nursing, medicine, hospitals, and voluntary and governmental agencies that coordinated activities planned to meet the needs of the war and postwar years. The Council enlisted the assistance of professional and lay persons to aid Dr. Brown in her work. The Professional Advisory Committee, composed of the leaders from the organizations represented in the Council, and the Lay Advisory Committee, consisting of individuals representing the public, functioned in a consultative capacity and provided counsel to the director (32).

Dr. Brown gathered data by making two extended field trips across the United States. She visited fifty geographically representative schools in all parts of the country, held three regional workshop conferences with nursing directors of 1250 schools which were held in Washington, DC, Chicago, and San Francisco,* and met with individual nurses, physicians, hospital administrators and trustees, and university personnel who contributed their best thinking about the present status and future prospects of nursing. This method provided an opportunity to see the conditions in nursing first hand and

---

* A detailed record of both the method and content of those conferences was contained in the document, *A Thousand Think Together*.

to hear a diversity of viewpoints at the grassroots level for participants nationwide. In total, approximately 2000 individuals took part in the study (43).

Dr. Brown's report, *Nursing for the Future,* was published by the Russell Sage Foundation in September of 1948. In it she recognized the nurse as a social necessity but observed that society did not assist nursing education as it did teacher training. Her findings revealed weaknesses that were well known to nurses but were persistently ignored (or frankly denied) by others. Ironically, the report dealt with many attendant problems similar to those that served as the focus of earlier studies.

The report pointed to the authoritarianism of hospitals with respect to controlling nursing education and practice. It stressed the need to define professional areas of responsibility in order to clear the confusion centered on the nurse's status and expectations of the graduates, especially in relation to practical nurses and auxiliary workers. It charged that the apprenticeship system of nursing education was still so pervasive that by no stretch of the imagination could the vast majority of the 1250 schools of nursing be conceived of as institutions for professional education. It pointed out that the inadequacies in nursing service were due primarily to an outmoded educational system that led to a shortage of competent nurses (25). It also emphasized that a number of improvements within the profession must be made before nursing could hope to attract enough recruits for present and future needs. On this subject it went so far as to remark: "Many thoughtful persons are beginning to wonder why young women in any large numbers would want to enter nursing as *practiced,* or schools of nursing as *operated,* today" (8).

The Brown Report, like previous studies, revealed that financial support for nursing education was shockingly inadequate. No remedy that Dr. Brown recommended had not been considered before, but her twenty-eight recommendations added up to nothing less than a call for thorough reorganization of nursing education and service (22). She recommended a number of far-reaching, forward-minded changes. Foremost, she suggested as the goal for the next decade the building of basic schools of nursing in universities and colleges, comparable to existing medical schools, that would be sound in structure and organization and well distributed to meet the needs of the country. Dr. Brown wanted to see nursing education as a whole brought into the mainstream of collegiate education.

Realizing that weak schools of nursing would continue to function unless faced with strong external pressures, Dr. Brown put forth three recommendations reflecting the desirability for national accreditation to be undertaken by the profession: that nursing make a long overdue official examination of every school and periodic re-examination thereafter; that lists of accredited schools be published and widely distributed at stated intervals; and that broad public support be sought for a program of accreditation (22).

She challenged nursing and the public to substitute an effective system of professional education for the presently ineffective apprenticeship training in hospitals. She also recommended that nursing ultimately be divided into two categories of personnel—professional and practical levels. She pleaded with society to recognize and accept its part of the responsibility for supporting the future development of nursing (43). Dr. Brown beseeched those interested in the study to treat it as a whole so that recommendations were seen in relationship to one another as intended. Its purpose was to serve as a guide to help nursing adjust to the needs of society with due regard for the welfare of nurses (11).

As excellent an historical and social document as the Brown report was, the responsibility for action rested heavily on nursing. The profession's first responsibility was to disseminate and interpret the report. The objectives were to stimulate awareness and to instill a positive attitude on the parts of nurses and public with respect to the urgent need for developing nursing education for technical as well as basic and advanced professional training (25). Over 18,000 copies of *Nursing for the Future* were sold during its first eight months of publication, and its influence reached other countries as well. Study guides were prepared and widely distributed to assist nurses in deciphering the report. This thought-provoking book encouraged a re-assessment of beliefs and attitudes about the entire system of nursing education and practice (56).

The boards of directors of the six national nursing organizations then in existence, all endorsed in principle the Brown Report. However, the study received mixed reviews from nurses, physicians, and hospital administrators, some of whom felt threatened by the findings and recommendations contained therein. Clearly, Dr. Brown called for a departure from the traditional hospital school training. Although she paid tribute to the accomplishments achieved by nurses in the past, her comprehensive report also strongly urged nursing to plan for ensuring a continuously increasing supply of highly qualified professionals in a more dynamic fashion (8).

With the timely publication of the Brown Report in 1948, the National Nursing Council achieved its final objective and dissolved that same year. However, in order for the study to be effectively used, the NLNE formed a committee to implement the recommendations of the Brown Report to analyze the problem areas in nursing, to propose solutions, and to initiate action at all levels. Steps in implementation centered on a master plan for types and distribution of schools of nursing, accreditation, financing, research, licensure, and definition of terms. That committee was later named the Committee for the Improvement of Nursing Services.

Even though Dr. Brown challenged nursing to study, experiment, and act without delay in order that the profession realize its full potential, some of the recommendations took years to implement and some still remain unfulfilled. However, large numbers of basic baccalaureate programs in numerous American colleges and universities can trace their own origins to the early 1950s, and their development as a response to this report's influence in encouraging nursing within the mainstream of higher education.

Nursing Schools at the Mid-Century (1950)

At mid-century the nursing profession paused to take stock of itself. Following the publication of the Brown Report in 1948, the Joint Committee on Implementing the Brown Report was organized under the aegis of the NLNE, with representation from all six national nursing organizations, the consumer public, and allied professional groups. Its objective was to develop programs to strengthen schools of nursing as a basis of meeting the new demands for more and better prepared nurses. In the spring of 1949, this Committee was renamed the National Committee for the Improvement of Nursing Services (NCINS), but its purpose remained the same as its predecessor.

The NCINS recognized that some method of study was essential in order to focus attention on the need for more rapid improvement in the training of nurses. Its early activities were concerned with collecting factual information on nursing education programs and with preparing an interim classification of schools as an initial step in developing a more comprehensive accreditation program. The NCINS adopted as its first task an examination of current practices in basic schools of nursing. Accordingly, the Subcommittee on School Data Analysis was appointed to carry out the study. Almost two years later, its findings were published in the report entitled *Nursing Schools at the Mid-Century* (72).

Shortly after its formation, the Subcommittee drew up a fifty-item questionnaire for the purpose of obtaining comprehensive and up-to-date information on nursing school facilities and practices throughout the country. Items on the questionnaire were selected after a series of conferences with experts in nursing and general education, who reviewed and tested the questions to make sure the tool would provide objective information about measurable aspects of nursing education (68).

In March 1949, these questionnaires were sent to all state-approved schools in the United States, Hawaii, and Puerto Rico. To encourage participation in the survey by the approximately 1195 existing schools, letters and announcements were sent to solicit the cooperation of nursing directors, hospital administrators, college and university presidents, and officers of local, state, and national nursing organizations. Other allied professional groups and the general public were also informed of the survey. Although participation was voluntary, an amazing 1150 schools, or 96 percent of the total number of schools, wholeheartedly responded.

The schools provided two sources of information: the data returned on the questionnaire and school bulletins and literature. In addition, supplementary materials included data on hospital facilities published by the American Hospital Association and data on educational facilities published by the U.S. Office of Education. Every effort was made to verify the validity of all data recorded. The data provided by each school pertained to their programs as of February 1949. The findings were considered to be as accurate as possible when employing this type of testing method (68).

Criteria were selected for use in evaluating the data submitted on the questionnaires. The criteria chosen represented those characteristics considered important as well as measurable and which also reflected current practices in the nursing schools. In order of importance for purposes of evaluation these were as follows: clinical facilities and experience; size and qualifications of teaching staff; curriculum; performance of students on state board examinations; student health programs; library facilities; organization and budget; number of students; salaries; selection of students; and use of achievement tests. Such items as school aims and policies were difficult to evaluate statistically and were, therefore, eliminated (57).

The U.S. Public Health Service provided the statistical services for analyzing the data tabulated on each item. Weight was given to the various criteria, which were then used as a basis for establishing a range between a minimum and maximum score for each item. Schools were ranked according to their total score on a 100-point scale based on long-accepted standards by the profession. Once the data were analyzed, the schools were classified against other participating schools. Degree-granting programs were evaluated separately from diploma programs, although identical criteria were used, with the exception of a few extra items asked of the university and college schools.

When ranked according to overall excellence, schools in the upper twenty-five percentile were classified as group I and those in the middle 50 percentile as group II. Not included in the classification were the remaining twenty-five percent of the schools, either because they ranked in the lowest quartile, they did not participate in the survey, or they preferred to be excluded from the final grouping (68). However, each school received, by mail, a confidential survey profile that showed where their program stood on each item in relation to the other schools in the study. All of the college degree-granting programs were classified in group I or group II (30).

In November of 1949, an "Interim Classification of Schools of Nursing Offering Basic Programs," based on information obtained from the School Data Analysis Study, was published in the *American Journal of Nursing*. The Interim Classification, which included the names of the top seventy-five percent of the schools offering basic programs, provided the nursing profession and vocational counselors with a statistically valid record to recruit students for schools having optimum rather than minimum educational standards. The survey also assisted schools to discover their strengths as well as their weaknesses and helped in their efforts to secure financial support. The modifier "interim" was used to indicate the temporary nature of this method of evaluating schools. Although the Subcommittee recognized the limitations of such a classification, it was an essential step for the nursing profession, which had seriously lagged behind all other professional groups in preparing a list of schools whose practices and standards the profession was willing to endorse (57). It was a courageous self-evaluation effort.

The reaction to the interim report was vigorous—both favorable and unfavorable. Some interpreted the purpose of the classification to be an attempt to eliminate some of the hospital schools. Instead, the intention was to give both diploma and collegiate schools an incentive to raise their standards to achieve educationally sound programs within their own patterns of organization (58). Following its publication, the NCINS spent several months assuring nurses, hospitals, and community groups of its intent.

So much interest had been aroused by the data survey and the entire classification of schools that the NCINS decided to publish the complete report of the Subcommittee project under the title *Nursing Schools at the Mid-Century* (72) in September 1950. The cost was underwritten by the six national nursing organizations, and within three months the sales had covered all expenses. Over 5000 copies of the report were sold (67).

This simplistic, graphic, factual publication provided a perfect yardstick for measuring individual schools of nursing and proved a useful tool for the schools to evaluate their programs and plan for further development to meet the needs and demands for nursing services (47).

When the interim classification was released, schools of nursing were promised a second study within two years. However, further developments prompted the NCINS to reconsider. It was decided that a program of accreditation would be more helpful than a second classification. Early in 1949, the National Nursing Accrediting Service was organized under the auspices of the six national nursing organizations, and it accepted responsibility for the accrediting program. The NCINS was dissolved in 1953, after five years of contributing significant leadership to the profession (24).

The American Nurses' Association Position Paper on Education for Nursing (1965)

This publication (2) in and of itself should more accurately be referred to as a landmark statement rather than as an actual study per se. However, it is included here because, in reality, it involved a number of years of study before the American Nurses' Association took a stand on the issue of what should be the initial educational preparation for professional nursing.

The tremendous significance of this paper by the ANA can be most appreciated when examined from an historical perspective. To understand what prompted the ANA to take such decisive action, one must look at the major changes in society and the trends in nursing that were occurring at this particular period of time. First, it cannot be forgotten that the overall purpose of the ANA since its founding in 1896 was to ensure quality nursing care to the public by fostering high standards of nursing practice, promoting the professional and educational advancement of nurses, and protecting the welfare of nurses. To this end, the Association made clear its responsibility for determining the scope of nursing practice and guaranteeing the competence of those who nurse (5).

During the 1950s and early 1960s, the explosion of knowledge affecting health practices, the increasing level of education in the United States, the accelerating scientific advancements in the medical field, and the greater public demand for more and better health care made it mandatory for the Association to once again examine its position on the nature and scope of nursing practice and the type and quality of education needed by nurses to assume exceedingly complex roles (2).

In addition, the Association redirected its focus on nursing education when the ANA's Committee on Current and Long-Term Goals proposed in 1960 that baccalaureate education be the basic level of preparation for professional nursing practice. This proposal was adopted for study by the ANA, and at the 1964 biennial convention, its House of Delegates voted that the Association continue to work toward this goal (5). Meanwhile, the need for a statement on educational preparation for practitioners of nursing became apparent when the ANA's Committee on Education was formed in 1962, its primary function being to formulate basic education principles essential for effective nursing practice. Further, the need for a statement gained national recognition as a result of the Surgeon General's Report on Nursing in 1963, which recommended to the profession that a comprehensive investigation of the system of nursing education be undertaken nationwide. With the federal enactment of the 1964 Nurse Training Act, it was more imperative than ever that the ANA provide the necessary leadership. Requests from governmental agencies for the profession's opinion on the definition, responsibilities, and training of different types of workers in nursing added urgency to the need for an official position statement on education from the ANA (16).

Thus, within this framework, the ANA during the early 1960s embarked on a study and examination of nursing education, of the nature and characteristics of nursing practice, and of the scope of preparation and responsibilities of nurses. The Association's Committee on Education was delegated the task of acting ". . .with all deliberate speed to enunciate a precise definition of preparation for nursing at all levels" (16). The Committee, after approximately two years of effort, issued in 1965 the Association's first position paper on education for nursing (2). Adopted by the ANA Board of Directors that September, released in December of the same year, and approved by the Association's membership at its biennial meeting in San Francisco in 1966, this publication reinforced the professional association's interest in and responsibility for raising the standards of nursing, with the ultimate aim of improving the quality of nursing service.

The basic position taken by the ANA was that preparation for those employed in nursing should take place in institutions of learning within the general system of education. More specifically, the Association concluded in a series of statements that:

> *The education for all those who are licensed to practice nursing should take place in institutions of higher education; minimum preparation for beginning professional nursing practice at the present time should be baccalaureate degree education*

*in nursing; minimum preparation for beginning technical
nursing practice at the present time should be associate degree
education in nursing; education for assistants in the health
service occupations should be short, intensive preservice programs in vocational education institutions rather than on-
the-job training programs [2].*

The assumptions or premises on which this position was developed were:

- Nursing is a helping profession and, as such, provides services
  that contribute to the health and well-being of people.

- Nursing is of vital consequence to the individual receiving services; it fills needs that cannot be met by the person, by the family, or by other persons in the community.

- The demand for services of nurses will continue to increase.

- The professional practitioner is responsible for the nature and
  quality of all nursing care that patients receive.

- The services of professional practitioners of nursing will continue to be supplemented and complemented by the services of
  nurse practitioners who will be licensed.

- Education for those in the health professions must increase in
  depth and breadth as scientific knowledge expands.

- The health care of the public, in the amount and to the extent
  needed and demanded, requires the services of large numbers of
  health occupation workers, in addition to those licensed as
  nurses, to function as assistants to nurses. These workers are
  presently designated nurses' aides, orderlies, assistants, and attendants.

- The professional association must concern itself with the nature of nursing practice, the means for improving nursing practice, the education necessary for such practice, and the standards for membership in the professional association (2).

The rationale for taking such a definite stand on the future direction of nursing education was based on the recognition by the profession of its heritage, its immediate problems, the emerging social
issues and trends, the nature of nursing practice, and the extent to
which nurses could realistically enact changes for continued professional progress. In particular, the ANA pointed to Florence Nightingale's vision of nursing and nursing education, stressing the inherent worth of the principles that the profession had yet to achieve

(especially with respect to the importance of nursing schools functioning as independent educational institutions, separate and distinct from the service agencies) (2).

The ANA also recognized the increasing complexity of society, which not only was forcing nursing to become more specialized but also was necessitating a greater interdependence of nursing with other groups in society. In addition, the changing patterns in education and the increased role of government toward providing more federal aid for nursing were leading to expanded educational facilities, greater opportunities for professional advancement, an increased supply of potential nurse recruits, and more diversity in the types of programs available to prepare various levels of workers. Innovations in science and technology were altering the traditional role of nurses by extending and expanding their scope of practice. Demographic changes, advances in medical therapies, and greater consumer awareness and expectations were placing varied and increased demands on nursing (2).

The ANA believed that since nurses were required to master an exceedingly complex and constantly enlarging body of knowledge as well as to make critical, independent judgments about patient care, the primary aim of nursing education must be to provide an environment in which the nursing student can acquire the skills and knowledge necessary for expert practice.

The implications of the Association's official position were numerous, pervasive, and profound, even though the ideas behind it were far from novel. Although this long-awaited paper recognized the realities of the day, set directions for the future, and supposedly provided the foundation for effecting change in an orderly, constructive way, it nevertheless aroused intense controversy within and outside of the profession. Its implications and possible effects reached far beyond nursing—to colleges and universities, to hospitals, to physicians and other health care practitioners, and to all those involved in providing nursing service to the public (2).

The statement had significance for hospitals, which historically were responsible for preparing nurses. Despite the fact that approximately three-fourths of nurses in practice at the time were graduates of hospital-based diploma schools, the economic pressures in the hospital as well as other societal developments were encouraging the move of nursing education into collegiate institutions. The trend toward growth in baccalaureate and associate degree programs and away from diploma schools was most evident in the ten-year period from the mid-1950s to the mid-1960s (30). In light of this tendency, colleges and universities were called on to establish undergraduate and graduate curricula in nursing, expand existing programs, distinguish between professional and technical education, and provide facilities and faculty for continuing education, advanced study, and research in nursing. Furthermore, the ANA's statement proposed that the profession recognize the need for more practical nurses, who could be educated to assume greater responsibilities. This would provide a means for alleviating the shortage of registered nurses and improving the delivery of nursing care to the public. The Association recommended that preparation for practical nursing be upgraded to beginning level technical education in junior and community college programs (2).

Such implications proved to be a threat to many camps. This publication produced serious conflicts of opinion between individual nurses as well as a source of professional confrontation with other health disciplines and service agencies. Instead of leading to collaboration and cooperative planning for change to ultimately improve nursing care as hoped, it marked the beginning of an ever-widening schism in nursing education (30). It became an issue that, to this day, has caused a polarization between nurse educators and nursing service administrators and a divisive force in the profession as a whole.

The consequences of this position paper cannot be underestimated. The Association remains firmly committed to its stand that all nursing education should be housed in institutions of higher education, thus phasing out hospital diploma schools according to a definite plan. But almost twenty years after this epochal statement was made, the profession is still struggling to unify itself and reach a consensus on the issue of basic educational preparation for entry into nursing practice. To this day, a number of nurses and many more physicians and hospital administrators believe in diploma school education, rather than a combined liberal and professional education which takes place in colleges and universities.

The future of the entire profession is at stake, for a divided body cannot function as a powerful or influential force. A profession must be strong if it is to protect its rights, remain viable and independent, and progress. Continuing discussion and efforts to work together are essential in bringing about understanding, collaborative planning, and action in order that the ANA's position may become a reality for the profession in the relatively near future (6). Until the issue of education is settled and nurses, like other professions, are products of the higher education system, other problems will also remain unsolved. Advancement of clinical practice, preparation for advanced roles, and the development of nursing research and theory all depend on the establishment of entry in professional nursing practice at the baccalaureate level, and a commitment to educating nurses in junior and senior colleges—not hospitals.

An Abstract for Action (1970)

The impetus for undertaking this study was a direct outgrowth of a recommendation issued by the Surgeon General's Consultant Group on Nursing in its 1963 report entitled *Toward Quality in Nursing* (71). In their document, this body of experts advised that a separate national investigation of nursing education be conducted with the objective of determining, in particular, the responsibilities and skills required by nurses to render high-quality patient care.

Within a short time after this report appeared in print, the American Nurses' Association and the National League for Nursing joined forces to initiate action toward establishing an entirely independent commission to carry out a comprehensive inquiry of nursing nationwide. These two major nursing organizations appointed a joint commission to decide how such a study could be financed and operated. After much brainstorming, the committee agreed that the scope of the proposed study should be enlarged to include an examination of not only the present-day changing nursing practices and educational patterns but also the probable future requirements in the profession (34).

Despite the fact that the President's National Advisory Commission on Health Manpower was preparing to investigate the manpower needs of all the health professions, the Board of Directors of the American Nurses' Foundation—confident that the problems in nursing extended beyond the manpower issue—in the fall of 1966 appropriated $50,000 as seed money to launch a national study of nursing. Recognizing the profession's willingness to fund such a study prompted the Avalon Foundation (currently known as Mellon) and the W. K. Kellogg Foundation to each donate $100,000 in support of this investigation. A coincidental contribution of $300,000 by an anonymous benefactor raised the total amount to $550,000, which ensured the study's undertaking (34).

A few months before, in April 1966, W. Allen Wallis, president of the University of Rochester, had been approached by the ANA and NLN's joint committee to chair the study if adequate financing could be obtained. Once monies were secured, Mr. Wallis agreed to accept the presidential appointment, and in January 1967, he met with the committee to discuss the organization, membership, and directorship of the proposed study group. Exactly one year later, in

January 1968, the National Commission for the Study of Nursing and Nursing Education (NCSNNE) became formally operational (34).

For all intents and purposes, it was set up as an independent agency to function in an autonomous, self-directing manner. Even though the idea to conceive the Commission had arisen from a vested concern on the part of the ANA and the NLN, the Commission was given full power and total authority to plan and conduct an investigation under its own terms, without interference from any self-interest group. Such freedom to act demanded that responsible participants be selected for their broad knowledge of nursing, their skills in the related disciplines of medicine and health administration, or their competence in relevant fields of economics, education, management, and social research. In all, twelve commissioners were chosen (including three nurses, one of whom was Eleanor C. Lambertsen, who also served as secretary of the NCSNNE). In addition, a project director (Jerome P. Lysaught), an associate director (Charles H. Russell), and a small organizational staff were appointed to carry out the actual operations of the investigation. Dr. Lysaught, a professor of education and research associate in medical education at the University of Rochester as well as a known contributor to professional literature, had already conducted research in both nursing and medical education and was considered highly qualified for the post (37).

A full three-year timetable was established for the study: from January 1968, when the project became truly operational, with the release of the final report planned for January 1970, to January 1971, which provided an extra twelve months to disseminate and initiate implementation of the Commission's recommendations.

Identifying the magnitude of troubles facing the nursing profession, the Commission decided to delineate its assignment by focusing on the dimensions of four key problems: the supply and demand for nurses, nursing roles and functions, nursing education, and nursing careers. After summarizing the emerging trends affecting the entire health care system, such as social and cultural changes, advances in the medical sciences, and the economics of supply and demand, the Commission specified as its primary question: "How can we improve the delivery of care to the American people, particularly through the analysis and improvement of nursing and nursing education" (34).

The Commission was determined, though, not to study nursing in isolation but rather to examine the primary concerns and the underlying issues relating to the social system in which the student nurse learned and the graduate nurse practiced. The goal of the final report, therefore, was to represent a platform for action that would ensure mechanisms for interdisciplinary colleagueship and multidisciplinary efforts to solve problems stemming from the essential fabric of health care in the United States (33). The single criterion—better patient care for all people—served as the basis for the findings and recommendations of the Commission. To this end, two general approaches were necessary: the analysis of current practices and patterns and the assessment of future needs.

The methods of investigation used consisted of direct observation, descriptive tasks, and the collection and analysis of findings from previous studies. The Commission's conclusions, recommendations, and future projections were then scrutinized by individuals and groups associated with the health care delivery system. This approach was similar to the basic methods employed by Abraham Flexner in his inquiry into American medicine in the first decade of the twentieth century and also refined, in particular, by the work of Esther Lucile Brown in her 1948 study of nursing (see previous section). In addition, two advisory panels were appointed to serve as valuable resources for input and feedback regarding methods, findings, and recommendations of the investigation. A nursing advisory panel of ten advised the Commission on plans for the study, suggested locations for site visits, and offered constructive reviews and criticisms of each stage of the work. A health advisory panel of ten with broad backgrounds and experience in related health and social service fields provided a diversity of viewpoints and a balanced perspective of the approach and analysis of data (34).

In the course of investigation, the Commission made an extensive search of the literature for all articles and research reports on nursing education and practice, developed specific surveys to obtain additional information, and designed questionnaires that were distributed to thousands of randomly selected nursing faculty and students. Supplemental to this, the staff initiated more than 100 site visits to nursing educational institutions and service agencies widely recognized as outstanding and innovative, interviewed thousands of individuals across the country, and held a series of three invitational regional conferences attended by leaders representing nursing education, nursing service, medicine, health administration, consumer groups, and third-party payers (34). Thus, the final recommendations of the study evolved from a widespread and in-depth examination of many sources of information.

A summary report and recommendations of the Commission were published in the *American Journal of Nursing* in February of 1970 (42), followed by the release in June 1970 of the final report, *An Abstract for Action*, often referred to as the Lysaught Report (34). In

December of that same year, a second volume (*Appendices*) appeared, which provided more detailed information on the conduct, preliminary findings, and evolving outcomes of the investigations (35).

In all, the Commission formulated major recommendations, each accompanied by a detailed discussion of findings. These recommendations for change in nursing were seen in terms of four basic priorities:

1. Increased research into the practice of nursing and the education of nurses

2. Improved educational systems and curricula based on the results of that research

3. Clarification of roles and practice conjointly with other health professions to ensure the delivery of optimum care

4. Increased financial support for nurses and for nursing to ensure adequate career opportunities that will attract and retain the number of individuals required for quality health care in the coming years (34)

In summarizing the results of the report, the Commission issued four central recommendations (34):

1. The federal Division of Nursing, the National Center for Health Services Research and Development, other government agencies, and private foundations appropriate grant funds or research contracts to investigate the impact of nursing practice on the quality, effectiveness and economy of health care.

2. Each state have, or create, a master planning commission that will take nursing education under its purview, such committees to include representatives of nursing, education, other health professions, and the public, to recommend specific guidelines, means for implementation, and deadlines to ensure that nursing education is positioned in the mainstream of American educational patterns.

3. A National Joint Practice Commission, with state counterpart committees, be established between medicine and nursing to discuss and make recommendations concerning the congruent roles of the physician and the nurse in providing quality health care, with particular attention to the rise of the nurse clinician; the introduction of the physician's assistant; the increased activity of other professions and skills in areas long assumed to be the concern solely of the physician and/or nurse.

4. Federal, regional, state, and local governments adopt

measures for the increased support of nursing research and education. Priority should be given to construction grants, institutional grants, advanced traineeships, and research grants and contracts. Further, we recommend that private funds and foundations support nursing research and educational innovations where such activities are not publicly aided. We believe that a useful guide for the beginning of such a financial aid program would be in the amounts and distribution of funds authorized by Congress for fiscal 1970, with proportional increases from the public and private agencies.

Inherent in the final report were important implications for both nursing educators and nursing service directors in all types of institutions and agencies. They were seen as major change agents in implementing the recommendations put forth by the Commission. The fundamental objective of the Commission was to present a series of proposals for nursing practice and education that would contribute to more and better quality health care for all Americans. Of principle concern to educators was the need for improved educational approaches and achievements, expanded educational opportunities for professional advancement, and adequate funding for preparatory, graduate, continuing, and inservice education programs (36). Of specific interest to nursing service administrators were four major areas of need: to strengthen career advancement opportunities for nurses, to develop personnel policies and standards to support clinical nursing practice, to create a system of joint appointments for nursing educators and practitioners, and to secure appointment of nursing leaders to health care planning and policy-making groups (55).

The Commission recognized that drastic changes could not be implemented by the creative and courageous leaders in nursing alone, but required involvement of many nurses at the grassroots level as well as a multidisciplinary approach to dealing with the problems in the overall educational and organizational system of health care delivery (33).

Reactions to the report were generally favorable, if not enthusiastic. Many of the recommendations pertained to the long-desired goals of the profession's leaders, and, therefore, support for these findings was understandable. However, the support tended to discourage any questions, to ignore controversial viewpoints, and to suppress the criticisms that were raised. Certain shortcomings of the report were recognized with respect to the authenticity of the historical base so extensively referred to in the report, the validity and reliability of the research methodology, and the consistency of some of the recommendations with relation to accepted definitions and concepts of health and to the specific data from which the recommendations were drawn (15).

Eventually, though, all of the major nursing organizations along with the American Medical Association, the American Hospital Association, and other allied health groups either supported the report or endorsed some or all of it in principle. In 1971, the Board of Directors of the NLN appointed a task force to evaluate each of the recommendations in depth, to determine the impact of the implementation of them on the present and future nursing needs of the people, and to advise the NLN Board accordingly. Any revisions by the Task Force were accompanied by a rationale for each suggested change. The greatest concerns were with the two career patterns (episodic and distributive) proposed for nursing practice in recommendation 7 and the specific proposals on nursing education and their implications referred to in recommendations 1, 2, and 3 (54).

This three-year study on nursing and nursing education was followed by another three-year period of effort during which the Commission attempted to initiate implementation of the recommendations advocated in its final report. Thus, the Commission formally switched its emphasis from investigation to implementation. The ANA and NLN without hesitation endorsed the continuation of the Commission, whereupon the Kellogg Foundation made a new grant of $270,000 to support the follow-up activities for two years and an additional sum to share with nursing (ANA and NLN each pledged $25,000) the support for a third year (38).

A recollection of history served as a constant reminder that nursing studies alone never induced change in our health care system. Change had to be engineered with widespread participation by all involved in the delivery or consumption of nursing service so that desired progress could be achieved. Change was absolutely essential if the potential contributions of nurses were ever to be realized in solving the country's many health problems. The Commission's objectives, which shaped its activities and interim goals during the beginning months of the implementation effort, were:

1. The development and expansion of nursing practice together with a re-examination of role relationships among the health professions

2. The repatterning of education systems in nursing to meet current exigencies and provide a foundation for innovation

3. The emergence of an unambiguous profession that would, in fact, be a full partner in shaping health policy and in serving the needs of our people (38)

In moving from the phase of research to one of action, adjustments had to be made in the organization of the Commission. Half of the original twelve commissioners who had to restrict their involvement because of other committees agreed to continue as members of the National Advisory Council in order to underscore the solidarity, unanimity, and continuity of the Commission. A reconstitution of the Commission resulted in enlarging and diversifying the body to twelve members in order to deal with the variety of concerns confronting it. Chancellor Wallis, who requested to be relieved from his position as president of the Commission, was replaced by Dr. Leroy C. Burney, president of the Milbank Memorial Fund and former Surgeon General of the United States Public Health Service. The expanded Commission was represented by leaders from nursing, medicine, health management, general education, and national health policy agencies. To supplement their talents, advisory committees were established to provide for additional input and evaluation. Jerome P. Lysaught, director of the three-year study, remained in his staff position.

Nine states were designated as targets for initial, intensive implementation efforts. These states represented a microcosm of economic, geographic, and social patterns that mirrored the problems besetting the health care system across the country. They served as laboratories and demonstration centers for changing methods in providing nursing services, in revising nurse practice roles, and in restructuring nursing education. Also, a handful of select individuals were appointed as regional associates to function as consultants and advisors to various local, state, and regional groups (38).

Three key areas of focus involved: (1) the development of joint practice between nursing and medicine; (2) statewide participation in planning for nursing needs and resources in education and practice; and (3) efforts to disseminate information to the public. The first goal was achieved with the creation of the National Joint Practice Commission (NJPC) in September of 1971 by the AMA and the ANA. The purpose of this autonomous, interprofessional organization of nursing and medicine was to expand communications and increase collaboration between the two professions in the interest of better health care (44). Sixteen members, eight physicians appointed by the AMA and eight nurses appointed by the ANA, put forth specific guidelines, objectives, and recommendations concerning the congruent roles of the physician and nurse in providing quality health care to the public. NJPC's aims were to study the roles of both professions, to recommend changes in professional education for the preparation of practitioners for expanded roles, to eliminate sources of professional differences, and to assist in the development and growth of state joint practice counterparts. The initial work of the NJPC was joint practice counterparts. The initial work of the NJPC was jointly funded by the ANA and the AMA; later a series of grants from the W. K. Kellog Foundation made possible the implementation of important new programs. The NJPC remained active until January 1981 (31).

The second activity was accomplished by establishing statewide master planning committees in each of the nine target states. These committees were to compare state findings with national findings and recommendations and then prepare a long-range plan of action for the state in order to position nursing education in the mainstream of general education. The third area of emphasis included informing the concerned public about the problems in nursing, marshalling public opinion in sympathy with nursing, and securing support, understanding, and cooperation for changes in patterns of nursing education and practice. A series of pamphlets were developed and disseminated to present information on the Committee's concerns, recommendations, activities, and objectives.

This three-year implementation period culminated with the publication of a second report entitled *From Abstract Into Action* (37). The Commission recognized that after three years of intense effort, the real work of change was just getting underway and further accomplishments of implementing the Commission's recommendations depended on widespread involvement by nurses themselves. To measure further progress, the Commission in 1973 devised a set of benchmarks to serve as future determinations of the degree to which change occurred.

The extent to which the three-year study and the succeeding implementation efforts of the Commission directly affected nursing and health care delivery is not easy to estimate. Lysaught and co-workers did conduct a national survey of nursing service directors in 1977 to assess the current state of affairs within their institutions in relation to the recommendations put forth by the Commission's final report. The results showed that after seven years, the pace of change was slow and that minimum progress had been made at the grassroots level with respect to joint practice, institutional reward systems based on competence in practice, enhancement of careers in nursing service through recognition of clinical expertise, and increased articulation between nurse educators and practitioners (39).

Lysaught concluded that, unmistakably, nursing remains the "ambiguous" profession. Even though he saw nursing moving in positive directions, it was evident that the rate of progress was tortuously sluggish. He recommended that nursing take stock and re-examine the goals and priorities advanced by the NCSNNE in 1970 and subsequently endorsed by almost every nursing organization in the country. He concluded by stressing that the next seven years be ". . .characterized not by further search but by accomplishment and fulfillment" (39). How much more the profession will be able to claim has been achieved toward those recommendations by the end of 1983 is yet to be determined.

The Study of Credentialing in Nursing: A New Approach (1979)

The impetus for undertaking an investigation of credentialing, the latest of the historical landmark studies in nursing, was essentially twofold: (1) concern within the profession about the fragmentation, inconsistency, proliferation, and confusion of credentialing mechanisms for nurses, and (2) increased threat of further state and federal government involvement in the credentialing of health manpower if appropriate self-regulatory measures were not taken by the professions to assure the consumer public of the competence, accountability, and availability of various health care practitioners. In addition, a credentialing study in nursing was long awaited because many of the professions's major issues (scope of practice, entry into practice, educational mobility, standard setting were and still are intimately related to the subject of credentialing (64).

The term "credentialing" was coined around the 1950s to include the various processes used to evaluate an individual's qualifications or an institution's ability to meet predetermined standards in order to be awarded status by a profession for the ultimate benefit of safeguarding the public. There are numerous forms or types of credentialing mechanisms, the most common ones being licensure, registration, accreditation, certification, educational degrees, charter, and approval with respect to professional personnel and professional organizations (see Chapter 3).

Overall dissatisfaction with the current credentialing system in nursing prompted the ANA House of Delegates in 1974 to pass a resolution directing the ANA Board of Directors ". . .to examine the feasibility of accreditation of basic and graduate education programs" (4). Following the 1974 convention, the ANA Commission on Nursing Education sponsored two national invitational conferences, one in the fall of 1974 and the other in the winter of 1975, for the purpose of identifying how to implement the resolution. They were attended by representatives from the ANA, the American Association of Colleges of Nursing (AACN), the National League for Nursing (NLN), other nursing organizations and health professions, and the U.S. Office of Education.

It became apparent during the first conference that the issue of program accreditation was intricately interrelated with other credentialing mechanisms, such as licensure and certification of individuals and agencies. At the second conference, a basic outline was developed for a comprehensive examination of all forms of credentialing. After considerable deliberation, the conferees recommended to the ANA Commission on Nursing Education that the scope of the proposed feasibility study be broadened to include an assessment of the entire credentialing system in nursing. It was also recommended that the NLN be invited by the ANA's Board of Directors to co-sponsor the study. Initially the NLN accepted the offer but later withdrew its support of the study because the League claimed alleged deficiencies in the study design. Pursuant to this decision, the ANA alone sponsored as well as financed the study (3).

Accordingly, in August 1976, the ANA appointed the Committee for the Study of Credentialing in Nursing. Chaired by Dr. Margretta Styles, professor and dean of the School of Nursing at the University of California at San Francisco, the Committee consisted of an additional fifteen members, ten of whom were nurses. Dr. Inez G. Hinsvark, professor in the School of Nursing at the University of Wisconsin-Milwaukee, was selected as project director, and a contract was signed by ANA with that school to conduct the credentialing study. The contract provided staff and services for the project, with the Committee accepting responsibility for the actual study program while the administrative responsibility was assumed by the University of Wisconsin-Milwaukee. The project became fully operational on April 1, 1977 (17).

The purposes of the study were:

1. To assess current credentialing mechanisms in nursing including accreditation, certification and licensure

2. To suggest ways for increasing the effectiveness of credentialing

3. To recommend future directions for credentialing in nursing

Given all of the different forms of credentialing mechanisms then operating, the study Committee chose to examine those that it believed were of high priority in a system of nurse credentialing and redefined them according to their applicability to the profession. Although modified from the universally accepted definitions originally set forth by the Public Health Service in a 1971 Department of Health, Education and Welfare report (70), the following related but distinct categories of health manpower credentialing were the most commonly referred-to mechanisms that the profession considered essential for the protection of the public and of nursing personnel:

> Licensure—*a process by which an agency of state government grants permission to individuals accountable for the practice of a profession to engage in the practice of that profession and prohibits all others from legally doing so. It permits use of a particular title. Its purpose is to protect the public by ensuring a minimum level of professional competence. Established standards and methods of evaluation are used to determine eligibility for initial licensure and for periodic renewal. Effective means are employed for taking action against licenses for acts of professional misconduct, incompetence, and/or negligence.*
>
> Accreditation—*the process by which a voluntary, non-governmental agency or organization appraises and grants accredited status to institutions and/or programs or services which meet predetermined structure, process and outcome criteria. Its purposes are to evaluate the performance of a service or educational program and to provide to various publics information upon which to base decisions about the utilization of the institutions, programs, services, and/or graduates. Periodic assessment is an integral part of the accreditation process in order to ensure continual acceptable performance. Accreditation is conducted by agencies which have been recognized or approved by an organized peer group of agencies as having integrity and consistency in their practices.*
>
> Certification—*a process by which a non-governmental agency or association certifies that an individual licensed to practice a profession has met certain predetermined standards specified by that profession for specialty practice. Its purpose is to assure various publics that an individual has mastered a body of knowledge and acquired skills in a particular specialty [17].*

A variety of techniques were used by the Committee to accomplish its complex task. The study began with an exhaustive review of the literature and an analysis of position papers, documents, and state laws relevant to credentialing. Other approaches involved individual and group interviews, seminars and conferences, survey questionnaires, a modified Delphi appraisal, and telephone surveys. In addition, representatives of forty-six cooperating groups of nursing and related health organizations participated in providing feedback and useful resource information throughout the course of the Committee's work (17).

Three concurrent activities developed and carried out by the Committee permitted the study to be completed within a reasonable two-year time frame. The first activity was construction of a model composed of three separate areas of focus for analysis: governance, policy, and control of credentialing within nursing; credentialing in the job market; and credentialing in nursing education. The second activity was the development of a basic set of fourteen principles to be used as tools to evaluate current credentialing systems. The principles were derived from the underlying premise adopted by the Committee that "credentialing exists primarily to benefit and protect the public" (17). The third activity was the identification of the following seven critical issues (17), each accompanied by broad position statements and a rationale for their adoption, which were agreed on by the Committee as crucial to the process of credentialing in nursing:

1. Definitions of nursing

2. Entry into practice

3. Educational mobility

4. Control of credentialing

5. Cost of credentialing

6. Accountability

7. Competence

Released in January 1979, the final 98-page report officially entitled *The Study of Credentialing in Nursing: A New Approach* was the result of two years of intensive work by the Committee of the ANA. While the report reflects the opinions of the Committee members, it must not be forgotten that the project staff and representatives from the cooperating groups provided invaluable assistance, feedback, and perspective throughout the entire investigative process. The first three chapters of the report explained, respectively, the history of the study, its purpose and the methods of operation, and general observations about credentialing as it affects nursing. The next four chapters identified the basic premise, principles, and definitions of credentialing as well as outlined the Committee's decisions about how the credentialing process should be applied to nursing. Chapter VIII reviewed the findings, conclusions, and recommendations of the Committee.

In essence, the findings of the study were that the current system of licensure and certification of nurses and accreditation of nursing services and education—all those credentialing processes intended for protection of the public and safeguarding the welfare of nursing personnel—was uncoordinated, fragmented, duplicative, costly, confusing to the public and nurses alike, and debilitating to the profession (65). The importance of credentialing as a social process arose as the public's expectations for health care and education of health practitioners increased. The scope of credentialing as a method for monitoring quality in education and practice dramatically expanded with the revolution in health care delivery following World War II. But the institutional frameworks through which credentialing operated became increasingly inadequate and fragmentary during the past three decades. From the Committee's viewpoint, the question that clearly presented itself was not whether reform in nursing credentialing was necessary, but rather what kind of reform should be undertaken and how it could be achieved (17).

As a result of its years of study and deliberation, the Committee concluded that it was imperative that reform in credentialing for nursing be instituted in a timely and systematic fashion. It resolved that maintaining high-quality nursing care for the public benefit was the basis of any mechanism used in credentialing nurses, nursing education, and nursing services. To this end, the Committee proposed far-reaching, radical changes in the credentialing system and issued specific, but what proved to be controversial, recommendations for the profession (17).

In summary, the recommendations called for a restructuring of credentialing into a coherent, articulated, comprehensive system. As credentialing relates directly to individuals, the Committee recommended the following: national registration for persons prepared at the associate degree or diploma level for limited scope of practice; state licensure for baccalaureate-prepared professional nurses responsible for the entire scope of nursing practice; and certification for professional nurses who demonstrate expertise in a specialty area of nursing practice. Furthermore, in keeping with its beliefs that responsibility for defining nursing, for determining the educational level for entry into practice, and for assuring accountability for the scope of nursing resides with the profession, the Committee recommended that the ANA be given control for overall governance of the profession.

To accomplish these proposed goals, the Committee advocated that a free-standing national nursing credentialing center be established for coordinating licensure (acknowledged to be a prerogative of each state), conducting the registration and certification of nurses, and carrying out the accreditation of nursing services and education for basic and advanced practice (65). In addition, this center would monitor all credentialing activities, act as a focus for research and development, and serve as a national resource for data on credentialing. Run by a federation of organizations, the purpose of such a facility would be ". . . to study, develop, coordinate, provide service for, and conduct credentialing in nursing" (17).

This thorough twenty-four-month study succeeded in putting

into historical context and proper perspective the issues, concepts, and interrelationships of credentialing of nurses and of service and educational programs in nursing. An addendum to the report included a follow-up plan that called directly on the sponsor, the ANA, to appoint a task force to make an in-depth study of the Committee's recommendations and promote their implementation, especially with respect to its major recommendation of creating an independent national center to act as an umbrella for all credentialing mechanisms in nursing.

In late March of 1979, the ANA Board of Directors acted to establish the task force as an autonomous transitional body to educate nurses and the public about credentialing as well as to build consensus and support for a national agency to centralize activities carried out by many private and governmental groups. The following fall, a thirteen-member task force of nurses and public representatives was officially appointed by the ANA. Dr. Rheba DeTorynay, dean of the School of Nursing at the University of Washington, Seattle, was chosen to serve as chairperson. Invited to act as resource groups for the task force were 140 organizations interested in or involved with some aspect of credentialing. Funded by the American Nurses' Foundation, Inc., its priority goal was to eventually implement the recommendations of the study committee. The key issue was and has been the interrelationships among organizations that currently conduct credentialing of nurses and of nursing education and service programs.

Its initial attention focused on facilitating articulation and coordination of present credentialing mechanisms, establishing a centralized information and data collection system, providing technical services, monitoring trends and developments impacting on credentialing, and stimulating as well as conducting research on the entire subject of credentialing. A tentative two and one-half year timetable set by the Task Force for the operation of a credentialing center targeted the start-up data for July 1982 (48). As of April 1982, the Task Force issued a report calling for a coalition of fifteen national voluntary nursing organizations that perform credentialing. It recognized that progress toward establishing a center will not occur until these groups ". . . are willing to address credentialing issues in a cohesive and systematic fashion" (52). Also, sources that might be willing to initially finance the project will not commit funds unless these organizations demonstrate cooperative participation in the center's development.

The proposed design for the center suggests it be directed by a board of governors. The time is ripe for nursing to restructure its system of credentialing for the benefit of the profession and the ultimate protection of the public. Nursing has an unprecedented opportunity for achieving this historic goal because of the momentum that presently exists (52). It is in the interest of all concerned, the community of nurses and consumers alike, to closely monitor the Task Force's activities in the coming months, provide additional input, and offer support for its efforts. Whether a National Credentialing Center will eventually be established, whether finances and cooperation among vested interest groups in nursing will encourage it, and where the control of the proposed center will be vested are questions that only history will answer. The ANA, NLN, and National Council of State Boards of Nursing will undoubtedly be principal actors in any on-going activity.

Summary

Many other studies have been conducted for and about nursing. Historically, those discussed are the most significant. However, the preliminary and final reports of the Commission on Nursing (1981, 1983), the nursing study undertaken by the National Institute of Medicine, the Magnet Hospital study undertaken by the American Academy of Nursing, and the 1982 NLN statement *Nursing Roles—Scope and Preparation* will most certainly have great significance for nursing in the future. These may prove to be the epochal reports of the 1980s, but until their impact is felt and can be measured, their historical significance cannot be judged.

As history has shown, the nursing profession has had difficulty implementing recommendations on the education and practice of nursing put forth by various committees, task forces, and/or organizations. Tradition has been a deterrent, but so has the social, economic, and political climate of the times. Cost is a powerful factor as is the strength of public opinion and the influence of other self-interest groups in the health care field.

The profession has never become discouraged by the obstacles it encountered but rather continued to pursue the steps necessary to reach a greater appreciation of itself, a better understanding of its problems, and a means to facilitate action. It has always remained open to constructive criticism from within and from without in order to pave the way to progress and positive change. Certainly the landmark studies, position statements, and reports have been stimuli for this change and nursing's movement to professional status.

References

1. America's Nursing Care, Editorial, Am J Nurs, 48:413–414, July, 1948.

2. American Nurses' Association: Educational Preparation for Nurse Practitioners and Assistants to Nurses: A Position Paper. New York, The Association, 1965

3. American Nurses' Association: House of Delegates Reports 1974–1976, 50th Convention. New York, The Association, 1976

4. American Nurses' Association: Summary Proceedings: ANA House of Delegates, 49th Convention. New York, The Association, 1974

5. American Nurses' Association's first position on education for nursing. Am J Nurs 65:106–111, 1965

6. ANA's first position on education for nursing. Am J Nurs 66:515–517, 1966

7. Beard RO: The report of the Rockefeller Foundation on nursing education: A review and critique. Am J Nurs, 23: 358–365; 460–466; 550–554, 1923

8. Brown EL: Nursing for the Future, A Report Prepared for the National Nursing Council. New York, Russell Sage Foundation, 1948

9. Burgess MA: Nurses, Patients and Pocketbooks, Report of a Study on the Economics of Nursing. New York, Committee on the Grading of Nursing Schools, 1928

10. Burgess MA: Problems involved in the grading program. Am J Nurs 26:919–927, 1926

11. Burgess MA: Six questions and answers on grading. Am J Nurs 28:25–26, 1928

12. Burgess MA: The first grading. Am J Nurs 29:429–432, 1929

13. Burgess MA: The official Grading Committee program. Am J Nurs 27:19–24, 1927

14. Capan SP: A member of the Grading Committee speaks. Am J Nurs 32:307–311, 1923

15. Christy TE, et al: An appraisal for an abstract for action. Am J Nurs 71:1574–1581, 1971

16. Coming soon: ANA statement of position on education. Am J Nurs 65:11, 28, 30, 1965

17. Committee for the Study of Credentialing in Nursing: The Study of Credentialing in Nursing: A New Approach, Vol. 1. Kansas City, Missouri, American Nurses' Association, 1979

18. Committee on Curriculum: A Curriculum Guide for Schools of Nursing. New York, National League for Nursing Education, 1937

19. Committee on Education: A Curriculum for Schools of Nursing. New York, National League for Nursing Education, 1927

20. Committee on Education: Standard Curriculum for Schools of Nursing. New York, National League of Nursing Education, 1917

21. Committee on the Grading of Nursing Schools: Nursing Schools Today and Tomorrow, Final Report. New York, The Committee, 1934

22. Dr. Brown's Report, editorial. Am J Nurs 48:609–610, 1948

23. Fitzpatrick EA: Grading schools of nursing. Am J Nurs 26:627–630, 1926

24. Five years with the NCINS. Nurs Outlook 2:81–83, 1954

25. Gelinas A: Our basic educational programs. Am J Nurs 49:47–50, 1949

26. Goldmark J: Nursing and Nursing Education in the United States, Report of the Committee for the Study of Nursing Education. New York, Macmillan, 1923

27. Grading schools of nursing. Am J Nurs 26:401–402, 1926

28. Gray CE: The Standard Curriculum for Schools of Nursing. Am J Nurs 18:790–794, 1918

29. Johns E, Pfefferkorn B: An Activity Analysis of Nursing. New York, Committee on the Grading of Nursing Schools, 1934

30. Kalisch PA, Kalisch BJ: The Advance of American Nursing. Boston, Little, Brown, 1978

31. Kelly LY: Dimensions of Professional Nursing, Fourth Ed. New York, Macmillan, 1981

32. Koos EL: The School Study: What does it mean? Am J Nurs 48:177–179, 1948

33. Lambertsen EC: A platform for action. Am J Nurs 70:267, 1970

34. Lysaught JP: An Abstract for Action, Report of the National Commission for the Study of Nursing and Nursing Education. New York, McGraw-Hill, 1970

35. Lysaught JP: An Abstract for Action: Volume Two (Appendices), Report of the National Commission for the Study of Nursing and Nursing Education. New York, McGraw-Hill, 1970

36. Lysaught JP: Continuing education: Necessity and opportunity. J Contin Educ Nurs 1:5–10, 1970

37. Lysaught JP: From Abstract Into Action. New York, McGraw-Hill, 1973

38. Lysaught JP: From abstract into action. Nurs Outlook 20:173–179, 1972

39. Lysaught JP, Christ MA, Hagopian G: Progress in professional service: Nurse leaders queried. Hospitals 52:93–98; 120, 1978

40. McKee CV: A book review of a curriculum for schools of nursing. Am J Nurs 27:325, 1927

41. McKee CV: Value of the curriculum from the standpoint of the nurse examining committee. Am J Nurs 26:957–960, 1926

42. National Commission for the Study of Nursing and Nursing Education: Summary report and recommendations. Am J Nurs 70:279–294, 1970

43. Nelson SC: Tasks accomplished. Am J Nurs 48:756–757, 1948

44. Nurse and medical practice acts must permit flexibility, NJPC says. Am J Nurs 74:602, 1974

45. Nurse, patients, and pocketbooks. Am J Nurs 28:674–676, 1928

46. Nursing for the future, editorial. Am J Nurs 48:549, 1948

47. Nursing schools at the mid-century. Am J Nurs 51:50, 1951

48. Piemonte RV: Task force on credentialing in nursing. Imprint 27:26, 29, 1980

49. Progress in nursing education, editorial. Am J Nurs 20:220–222, 1919

50. Progress in plans for grading nursing schools, editorial. Am J Nurs 25:117–119, 1925

51. Rawnsley MM: The Goldmark Report: Midpoint in nursing history. Nurs Outlook 21:380–383, 1973

52. Report calls for credentialing coalition. Am Nurse 14:3, 32, 1982

53. Report of the Committee on Nursing Education, editorial. Am J Nurs 22:878–880, 1922

54. Report of the Task Force. Nurs Outlook 21:111–118, 1973

55. Russell CH: The nursing service administrator and the report of the NCSNNE. J Nurs Admin 1:12–16, 1971

56. School study report a best seller. Am J Nurs 49:474, 1949

57. Sheahan MW: School data survey methods. Am J Nurs 49:719–721, 1949

58. Sheahan MW: The NCINS reports. Am J Nurs 50:350–351, 1950

59. Stewart IM: Curriculum revision: An essential step in the reconstruction of nursing education. Am J Nurs 35:58–66, 1935

60. Stewart IM: Progress report of the Curriculum Committee. Am J Nurs 36:925–931, 1936

61. Stewart IM: Revision of the standard curriculum. Am J Nurs 25:213–217, 1925

62. Stewart IM: What standards shall we accept for the new curriculum? Am J Nurs 35:359–366, 1935

63. Stewart IM, Clayton LS, Jamme AC: Department of Nursing Education. Am J Nurs 16:419–420, 1916

64. Study recommends new credentialing center. AORN J 29:974, 979, 1979

65. Styles MN: Credentialing study: What does it mean for you? AORN J 31:599–604, 1980

66. Taylor EA: Hopeful Changes in Three Years, Am J Nurs, 33:667–669, July 1933

67. The National Committee for the Improvement of Nursing Service. Am J Nurs 54:322–325, 1954

68. The school data survey. Am J Nurs 49:636–637, 1949

69. The "School Study" report. Am J Nurs 48:461, 1948

70. U.S. Department of Health, Education and Welfare: Report on Licensure and Related Health Personnel Credentialing, DHEW, Pub No (HSM) 72–11. Washington, DC, U.S. Government Printing Office, June 1971

71. U.S. Public Health Service: Toward Quality in Nursing: Needs and Goals, Report of the Surgeon General's Consultant Group on Nursing. Washington, DC, U.S. Government Printing Office, 1963

72. West M, Hawkins C: Nursing Schools at the Mid-Century. New York, National Committee for the Improvement of Nursing Services, 1950

73. Wolf AD: Putting the new curriculum into effect. Am J Nurs 37:1256–1261, 1937

INDEX

early training schools for, 67–68

see also National Association of Colored Graduate Nurses

Blackwell, Elizabeth (Dr.), 61

Blackwell, Emily (Dr.), 61

Bolton, Francis Payne, 73, 74, 150, 163, 223

Bolton Act, 74

"Born nurse," 7

Boston University, School of Nursing, 206–207

Brewster, Mary, 15, 193

Bridgman, Margaret (Dr.), 79

Brown, Esther Lucille, 75, 80, 120, 169, 236, 249

Brown Report (*Nursing for the Future*), 75–76, 77, 80, 93, 133, 235–239

Joint Committee on Implementing, 239

Bruckner, Sophia A., 115

B.S.N., 97

Bunge, Helen Lathrop, 86, 167

development of nursing research and, 209–212

Bureau of Registration of Nurses (Cal.), 130

Burgess, Elizabeth, 107

Burgess, May Ayres (Dr.), 150, 206, 223

Burney, Leroy C. (Dr.), 253

Cabaniss, Sadie Heath, 116

Cadet Nurse Corps, 29, 74, 86, 93, 169, 200

Candian Nurse Corps, 44

Canadian Nurses' Association, 168

Carnegie Foundation, 72, 75, 83, 216, 236

Catholic Hospital Association, Council on Nursing Education, 132

Century of Nursing with Hints Toward Organization of A Training School, A (Bacon), 66

Certification, certificates, 105, 106, 126–129, 255, 256

definition and function, 257

Charaka-Samhita, 3

Children, welfare of, 16

Christianity

early, visiting nursing during, 10–11

medieval, public health under, 11–12

Civil War

influence on nursing education, 62–63

nursing during, 38

see also Colonial period to Civil War

Clayton, S. Lillian, 217

Cleland, Virginia (Dr.), 84

Cleveland Visiting Nurse Association, 159, 161

Client, see Nurse-Client relationship

Coalition for Health Funding, 178

Colleges and Universities

baccalaureate programs in, 70–71, 78–79

education, attitudes toward, 120

nursing programs in, 75, 79, 245–246

early, 71–73

Colonial period to Civil War, home nursing during, 6–7

Commission on Nursing, 261

Committee on the Grading of Nursing Schools, 71, 131, 163, 206, 222

reports, 226–229

Committee on Structure of the National Nursing Organizations, 158

Committee for the Study of Credentialing in Nursing, 139

Committee for the Study of Nursing Education, 217–218

Committee on the Training of Nurses, 62

Commonwealth Fund, 72, 82

Community colleges, nursing education in, 94–95

Community Health Activities, of NSNA, 178

Drugs, use, during antiquity, 4
Drugs and Solutions (Goostray), 207

Ebers Papyrus, 4
Economic background of American Nursing, 57
Education, *see* Nursing education
Education of Nurses, The (Stewart), 200
Education of Nursing Technicians, The (Montag), 93
Educational programs, accreditation of, 133–136
Educational Standards for Nurses (Robb), 192
Educational Status of Nursing, The (Nutting Report), 216–217
Eldredge, Adda, 148
Ethical Culture Society of New York City, 15
External degree programs, 77

Facts About Nursing (Nursing Information Bureau), 203
Fallon, Irene T., 115
Federal government, funding for nursing education, 199–200
for research, 86, 87
Federation of Specialty Nursing Organizations, 176
Fenwick, Ethel Bedford, 108, 111, 146, 191
Fifty Years of the School of Nursing, The Children's Hospital, Boston (Goostray), 207
Fillmore, Anna K., 175
Financial support
lack of, 229
NSNA and, 178–179
for nursing education, 237
Finding Themselves (Stimson), 47
Finney (Col.), 45
First National Congress in Nursing, 180
Flexner, Abraham, 249
Flexner Report, 216–222

Fliedner, Theodor (Pastor), 14
Focus, 181
Formal education, documentation of, 105
Fox, Elizabeth, 173
Franklin, Martha, 155
From Abstract into Action, 254
Fry, Elizabeth Gurney, 14
Fulmer, Harriet, 116
Functional Specialists, phase of doctoral education development, 84

Gardner, Mary S., 159, 160
Gelinas, Agnes, 167
G.I. Bill of Rights, 75
Ginzberg Committee, 93
Godey's Lady Book, 65
Goldmark, Josephine, 163
Goldmark Report (*Nursing and Nursing Education in the United States*), 70, 77, 120, 131, 150, 203, 216–222, 227, 231, 235
Goodrich, Anne W., 43, 45, 48, 72, 165, 167, 197, 217
Goostray, Stella, 199
nursing administration and, 204–207
Gowan, Olivia (Sr.), 167
Grace, Helen (Dr.), 84
Grading
mechanisms, study on, 223–227
of nursing education, 227–229
Grading Study, 235
Graduate education in nursing, 78–84
"Graduate Nurse," 115
Graduate nurse(s)
before establishment of organization, 144–145
overproduction, 225
Grant, Amelia, 170, 171
Gross, Samuel D. (Dr.), 62

Hall, Lydia Williams, 36
development of a conceptual model for nursing practice, 207–209

Long-Term Care Committee,
178
reorganization, 134
Subcommittee on Baccalaureate
Education and Research,
76
Subcommittee on Graduate
Education in Nursing, 81
support of baccalaureate
education, 77–78
National League for Nursing
Education, (NLNE), 44,
45, 75, 77, 80, 123, 131,
145–151, 153, 156, 161,
167, 168, 170, 171, 197,
199, 200, 206, 222, 223,
238, 239
accreditation of schools, 132–
133
Central Curriculum
Committee, 233
Committee on Early Nursing
Source Materials, 206
Committee on Grading or
Nursing Schools, 232
*Curriculum Guide for Schools
of Nursing, A*, 229–235
Education Committee, 131,
164, 206, 229, 230, 232,
233
Pre-Nursing and Guidance Test
Service, 151
reorganization, 134, 169
see also American Society of
Superintendents of
Training Schools
National Mental Heealth Act, 76
National News Bulletin, 156
National Nurse Accrediting
Service (NNAS), 76, 80,
133, 134, 169
National Nursing Council, 169–
170, 236, 238
National Nursing Council for
War Services, 74–75, 200
National Organization of Public
Health Nurses (NOPHN),
45, 123, 126, 127, 132,
150, 153, 156, 167, 168,
170, 171, 172, 173, 175,
176, 177, 223
formation and activities, 159–
164

reorganization, 134, 169, 170
National Recovery Act (NRA), 28
National Student Nurses'
Association, formation
and activities, 176–179
Navy Nurse Corps, 48
emergence of, 43
NCLEX, 122, 125
NCSNNE, 248, 254
New York State Nurses'
Association, 113, 115,
116
Committee on Legislation, 115
Nightingale, Florence, 7, 13, 14,
91, 121, 244
model of nursing education,
63–64
schools based on, 65–68
Nightingale Fund Training School
for Nurses, 63
Nightingale School of Nursing, 64
aims, 64
"Nightingale schools," 7
theories, 7–8
Nightingale system and
development of hospital
schools in America, 61–
68, 108
1980s, nursing care in hospital
during, 37–38
Nineteenth century
care of sick, 57–61
nursing care in hospital, 18–23
North Central Association, 135
Notes on Hospitals (Nightingale),
64
Notes on Nursing (Nightingale),
64
*Notes on Nursing: What it is and
What it is Not*
(Nightingale), 91
Nurse
credentialing of, 107–111
defined, 2
employment, during depression
years, 28
qualities
during antiquity, 3
mid-nineteenth century, 58–
59
role of
during colonial period to
Civil War, 7

275